£9.95

KEY IDEAS
in
MEDIA

D0544546

Mike Edwards

Published in 2003 by:
Nelson Thornes Ltd
Delta Place
27 Bath Road
CHELTENHAM
GL53 7TH
United Kingdom

03 04 05 06 07 / 10 9 8 7 6 5 4 3 2 1

A catalogue record for this book is available from the British Library

ISBN 0 7487 7319 3

Page make-up by Florence Production Ltd

Printed and bound in Spain by GraphyCems

Contents

Introduction   v
Acknowledgements   vii

Media Texts and Representations   1

Codes and Conventions   2
Intertextuality   5
Narrative   7
Genre   16
Semiotics   27
Poetics   34
Semiotic Analysis   37
Psychoanalytic Approaches   43
Postmodernism   48
Representations   52
Ideology   64
Identity   67
Discourse   71

Media Organisations   79

Branding   82
Marketing and Promotion   84
Target Audience   89
Demographics   93
Share, Ratings and Scheduling   96
Stars and Celebrities   100
Alternative Media   106
Cultural Imperialism   118
Globalisation   123

Regulation   128
Hypermedia   140

Media Audiences   155

Passive Audiences and the Effects Tradition   157
Active Audiences and Reception Theories   164

References   176
Index   181

Introduction

The last 150 years has witnessed a huge growth in media technology with a whole range of different delivery systems that provide the media reader/viewer/listener/user (at least in the developed world) with a massive range of options. There has been a corresponding growth of students interested in the systematic study of these modern media and the implications of what is sometimes termed the phenomenon of 'media saturation'. It is suggested by cultural commentators that 'we' not only live in our situated culture but also in a *'culture of mediation'* (O'Sullivan et al. 1994). Media Studies has developed a framework of ideas, theories, concepts and approaches to enable the study of the culture of mediation. The aim of this book is to introduce the student of the media to this framework and to discuss some issues that arise in our increasingly mediated world.

Media Studies has evolved out of a whole range of specialist discourses – art, design, technology, moving image, linguistics, gender, sociology, psychology, business – to create its own distinctive field of study and much of its attraction is due to its open and interdisciplinary nature. As media technology has developed it has invaded more and more of our social world (from the amazement and fascination of early audiences for the movies to the rich interactive spectacles of the multimedia world) and an interdisciplinary approach in today's globalised and interconnected world would seem to be a prerequisite of the creation of richer understandings of both our historical and modern experience of such developments.

The term 'media' applies to the information and/or entertainment based texts produced and circulated which are increasingly distributed through electronic means. The various approaches to media study put an emphasis on understanding media producers and businesses, on the construction of media texts and on the reception, influence and effects they have on media audiences. The framework for media study consists of three distinct but inter-related areas: texts and representations, organisations and audiences (see Figure 1). For each idea, theory, concept and approach I have aimed to present a clear introductory overview. Each has been broken down into small, manageable chunks with clear definitions of the terms that the student will need. These are often supported by case studies and examples of how the student might develop their understanding further through an exploration of main media forms. It is important to stress the dynamic and evolving nature of Media Studies and the interaction of the study areas. The subject evolves dynamically under a variety of pressures, many of which are concerned with evolving technology and how organisations change and develop in response to this and the ways in which audiences can react and behave. This would characterise what some media commentators (e.g. Gauntlett 2000) describe as 'old' and 'new' Media Studies. The distinction rests on the possibility that 'new' Media Studies will be characterised by an emphasis on the 'making' of media and with new kinds of issues and conflicts for the audience. New ideas and approaches will be developed to deal with this and no one is sure of the direction that will be taken.

This creates a dynamic situation for students. However, 'newness' as a value in Media Studies is based on the exploration of the ideas and concepts that have been developed, mostly in the twentieth century. 'Newness' always has a history. A thorough understanding of these ideas, theories and concepts is needed to test out the evolving media forms of the millennium. This is done through active application in textual analysis and research on organisational and audience issues. The three study areas represent for the media student sites of exploration in which they can use the descriptive and analytic tools of Media Studies to develop and enrich their understandings of the intricacies and challenges of media production in the past, present and future.

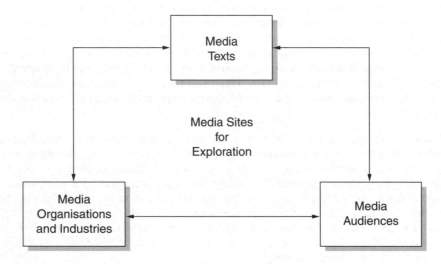

Figure 1 The three study areas

Acknowledgements

An area of study as diverse as Media Studies means that no one is an expert on all the possible areas of interest to media students. I owe an enormous debt of gratitude to students in schools and colleges, to former students on the MA (Media education) course at the University of Wales Institute, Cardiff (UWIC), many of whom have become exceptionally capable, gifted and expert presenters on Media Studies topics, and especially to Cathy Grove at UWIC Press and Tom Barrance at Media Education, Wales for their trust, ideas and support. Successive officers at the Welsh Joint Education Committee (WJEC) have tolerated my approaches with Media Studies candidates in the effort to reward candidates at all levels in the 14–18-year-old education system. Perhaps most of all I owe a huge debt of gratitude to the presenters at the annual Media Education Conference in Cardiff, in particular Jude Brigley, Barbara Connell, Jill Poppy and Mandy Esseen for their energy, experience, expertise and willingness to share their considerable knowledge of classroom practice. Finally, I am grateful to Barbara Connell (cultural imperialism, globalisation), Simon Drakefield (hypermedia), Paul O'Connor and Helen Iles of under*currents* (alternative media) for their advice and expertise. They are in no way responsible for the use I have made of their work.

The author and publishers would like to thank the following for permission to reproduce material:

- Paul O'Connor and Helen Iles of under*currents*
- © Photosphere Images Ltd (p. 29)

Dedication

For my children, Clare and Luke, over whom now I only have bragging rights.

Media Texts and Representations

A TEXT IS A COMBINATION OF SIGNS. A SIGN IS MADE UP OF A SIGNIFIER AND THAT which is signified. The signs in the text have *connotations* that can be decoded by different groups. The process of decoding will depend on time, place, class, gender, ethnicity, age and experience of the decoder. The *denotations* of the sign are those connotations of the sign that appear to be the most stable and obvious both to the encoder and decoder of the text. They feel like 'common sense'. One of the key things such analysis can 'lay bare' is how and why encoders (or producers of media) construct their products. They are produced in social contexts for particular kinds of audiences by particular technologies. Media production carries traces of the activities of the range of people involved in it. They have a diversity of backgrounds and training: art and design, publishing, business etc. Because of the way media texts come about as the result of the labours of a number of people, they are penetrated by their memories, values, histories, training and attitudes. This is equally true of decoders (or media audiences).

The main consequences are:

- The values in a text are never ultimately fixed and can be a source of conflict.
- The effect of the text is not always predictable.
- The meaning of the text is not contained in the text but emerges in the reader's dialogue with it.
- The meaning of texts is never fixed but is negotiated through sets of shared or opposing values which can change.

Media Codes and Conventions

The Idea

THE IDEA THAT A POP STAR CAN BE A 'TEXT' AND THAT SUCH A POP STAR CAN BE 'read' in the same way that text can be read is potentially confusing. Equally confusing might be the idea of becoming media literate through the acquiring of knowledge and understanding of the rules which are in some way related to your ability to read and write. Clearly these terms 'text', 'read', 'literate' are metaphors which suggest that you need to experience how media productions are organised, how they communicate to their audiences and how audiences receive those messages. What you 'read' when you analyse media texts are the presentational codes and conventions of a particular media form. For instance, the presentational codes of comics are signs that indicate such things as dress, setting, sexuality, colour and the rules that govern their use – such as frames, panels, speech panels and bubbles. For the student, it is useful to think of these codes and conventions as those things that have become established through their use in a particular media form. To be media 'literate' is to have a knowledge and understanding of these codes and conventions and how they work in any media text.

The mediated world is all around us in the forms of films, radio and television programmes, pop music, newspapers, magazines, comics, websites, interactive games, and the texts or productions that organisations produce in these forms – all of which have patterns of similarity and difference in the way they organise their codes and conventions. It is through the organisation of media texts that we experience the mediated world. In Media Studies this is commonly referred to as the text's *construction* and the activity of analysis is described as *deconstruction*. Media texts offer us information, entertainment and diversion. They can be a source of intense pleasure, extreme irritation, comfort and reassurance, or controversy. Increasingly, though, we are invited not only to participate as a spectator of these texts but also to create (or author) such media texts in, for instance, websites where we can tell our own digital stories, and in media messaging on phones in which we can communicate with others using multimedia to construct our social worlds. A recent advertisement, for instance, extols the virtues of picture messaging using the icon of a coffee cup to symbolise an invitation to another person to join the sender of the image. As media communication is developing, so we move more easily between the roles of spectator (consuming, watching, reading, listening, analysing, deconstructing, responding, reacting) and participant (creating, authoring, making, constructing, researching, using).

Media analysis of such texts has emphasised the importance of 'reading' them with a concentration on *how* the text worked from the point of view of how they offered meanings to the 'reader'. The reader was free to make their own interpretations of texts but within 'meaning systems', which were generally accessible within a culture. This freedom was limited by the experience of the reader of these meaning systems and much of the activity of textual production was to tap into the cultural experience of the group at which a text was aimed. Texts needed to appeal primarily to this group. These were not an innocent target group: readers have a range of experience and knowledge of other media texts. So they come to the text with all sorts of prior knowledge and expectations. However, in the prior knowledge and experience of many media forms such as websites, computer games and CD interactive presentations, the metaphor of reading the text seems to break down to some extent. It seems more appropriate here to refer to the 'user' of the media form rather than the 'reader', who in order to operate the media text needs actively to do things with the signs rather than simply interpret them passively. In such media texts, the codes and conventions are more related to doing or playing rather than reading. Hence the phenomenon in such texts of talking to oneself about signs on the screen to identify with the character and the situation, explain and respond to on-screen events, encourage yourself, move on, go back or jump a level and so on. Clearly there are on-screen consequences of such actions. It becomes useful to start to think about *active* uses, which may empower the user with information or a skill, and *passive* uses of media texts, which can empower the reader in a different way. As a student of media you need to understand the dynamic nature of this relationship of the experience of the 'reader'/'user' of the text to the conditions of its production. The media text is the sum of the relationships between the textual representation (its use of typical codes and conventions), the audience interpretations of the text, and the industrial and organisational processes which created it.

Deconstructing the text

MEDIA students deconstruct media texts to understand how and why they make meaning. There is a basic procedural method for media students which allows them to begin to think about the codes and conventions, the audience interpretations and the organisational issues raised:

1. Locate the key signifiers in the text.

2. Suggest what might be the range of possible signifieds.

3. Identify the connotations and their possible meanings.

4. Identify the denotations of the text. In other words, the meanings that can be shared between the encoder and the decoder: the things that appear obvious. This stage can narrow down possible meanings.

5. Open out the assumptions of the common-sense relationship between the encoder and the decoder. Signs can disguise the assumptions which underlie their structuring, and analysis can lay these assumptions bare to reveal new ways of seeing the text.

Intertextuality

The Idea

TWO WORKING DEFINITIONS OF INTERTEXTUALITY ARE:

'in the space of a given text, several utterances, taken from other texts, intersect and neutralise one another' (Kristeva 1980).

'Any text is a new tissue of past citations. Bits of code, formulae, rhythmic models, fragments of social languages, etc, pass into the text and are redistributed within it, for there is always language before and after the text.' (Barthes 1981).

Intertextuality is the reading of the media text in the light of others of a similar nature. It can create extra layers of meaning and associations for the reader. Texts can inter-relate with one another in a variety of ways, from imitation, to parody, to confrontation. Computer programming has coined the metaphor of the parent–child relationship to link texts together (to save on coding time) and it is a useful way of thinking about the term. The child always bears traces of the parents and so can be said to be similar to them, but the child is not the same as the parent (however much the parent might wish it). They might want to reject or oppose or develop aspects of the parent and they will, even if they do not like it, be influenced by the parent. The relationship is clearly an elastic one which is determined by social circumstances. They are both similar and different.

In terms of textual relations the metaphor suggests some key features:

1. The relationship of one text to another is always reciprocal. They clearly affect each other.
2. There is an underlying structure in the child text linked to the choice and combination of signs in the parent text(s).
3. This relationship may be obvious to some readers and accepted, or rejected or modified by others, dependent on their recognition of these choices and combinations. They may detect patterns of similarity and difference or they may not.
4. The text can be read within the terms of this relationship or can be contrasted to other kinds of texts by the reader. New possibilities of interpretation can be

opened up by the reader. However, these new ways of looking (the child) still need to be related to the other text(s) (the parent).

5. Both the construction (encoding) and deconstruction (decoding) of media texts become active and participatory activities.

The Idea in Action

MEDIA TEXTS ARE OPEN TO A NUMBER OF POTENTIAL READINGS AND ARE THEREFORE said to be *polysemic*. However, within a cultural group, a text usually 'prefers' one meaning or occasionally more. It is usually the one which the maker of the text has created intentionally, for example to entertain, persuade, educate, startle, outrage, challenge etc (*preferred meaning*). The producer wants this to be the reading that the text prefers over other readings. This is often described as a *closed text*, that is, one which seeks to close down meanings for the reader. This characterises products of the mass media for some commentators especially those texts related to news, documentary and persuasion. By way of contrast *open texts* require a number of readings to be made simultaneously for their full texture to be appreciated. These, it is suggested, are more high culture texts such as films and are intrinsically more worthy of study. The distinction is one which most media analysts reject. They suggest that varied readings and interpretations of texts are always possible. Readers can read and use texts in a variety of ways.

Readers, it is suggested, have three types of encounter with media texts:

1. *Dominant or preferred reading.* The reader encounters the text taking the assumptions of the encoder at face value in a full and straight manner.

2. *A negotiated reading.* The reader accepts the dominant codes and conventions but may question their use in terms of their own social experience.

3. *An oppositional reading.* The reader opposes the dominant codes and conventions by challenging them, opposing or offering alternatives. The reader reads 'against the grain' of the text to uncover significant gaps and silences in the text and different ways of looking.

The Idea Today

THE SHIFT FROM THE TEXT TO THE READER HAS BEEN ONE OF THE MOST SIGNIFICANT shifts in the way in which texts are read in the late twentieth century. The emphasis now is upon what Roland Barthes described as the 'active, nimble' reader.

Narrative

M AN IS A STORY-TELLING ANIMAL. IT IS, THEREFORE, NOT SURPRISING THAT MOST media texts tell stories. At first sight this might seem to be a slightly curious concept. How can a single photograph tell a story? How can a front cover of a book or a poster for a film tell a story?

Essentially, a story contains the following features:

- *Who or what* did *what* to *who or what.* In other words there are protagonists who can be human or non-human who act upon others. Often these protagonists have typical roles in stories: the hero, the heroine, the villain, the victim. Stories are, therefore, made up of actions.

- *Closed stories.* There is a clear sense of the action being completed: a sequence of cause and effect has been played out. A single frame comic strip or cartoon demonstrates this.

- *Open stories.* We may see the start of the action, the end of which is inferred by the reader of the text who anticipates and speculates on the potential outcome(s). The reader infers closure. The cliché 'a picture is worth a thousand words' tends to affirm our sense of being told a story in which the audience infers an outcome. This is the way posters, trailers and front covers of magazines and newspapers work.

- *Where.* All stories take place somewhere even those inside our head.

- *Plot.* Essentially, this is the 'why' of the story. This function explains the causal links between the actions.

Narrative links story and plot together. It means the way in which stories are told and the way in which they construct their meanings to achieve audience understanding. Different media forms construct their meanings in different ways using the codes and conventions appropriate to the form.

Terminology

THERE are a number of useful terms for the understanding of narrative: script, frame, point of view and montage.

SCRIPT.   You may be more familiar with this term from work you have done in areas such as English, Drama and Film. In this context it refers to the way in which readers of media texts have a set of expectations about certain components occurring when they engage with a media text. So, for instance, when you read a magazine you usually start with the front cover and then flick through (or to, often based on selections made from the contents list) sections which interest you or catch your attention. Or when you visit a website you expect that when you click on an image with the mouse it will do something – take you to another image, play a sound, change colour, for instance. It is a good way to start thinking about our routine engagements with media narratives. We have the expectation that underlying our engagement there is a narrative structure. This is what is described as a script.

Clearly this draws attention to the underlying structure of the media text. If a text does not meet our expectations we may be turned off, or perhaps intrigued and want to question the use of a particular element of the construction. It clearly draws attention to the role of the reader/user of the media text. The use of the combination of old and new elements to attract the attention of the audience is a feature of genre. '*A script is a structure that describes appropriate sequences of events in a particular context. Scripts handle stylised everyday situations. Thus a script is a predetermined, stereotyped sequence of actions that defines a well known situation*' (Schank and Abelson 1977).

FRAME.   You may be more familiar with this term in relation to comics, films and television programmes, all of which have frames. In this context it is being used in a slightly different way. The makers of media texts have to make all sorts of judgements about how to present, organise or visualise their material to draw attention to the media text. They 'frame' or organise themselves in different ways. In moving image texts, time is always an important framing device to create effects such as tension, suspense, surprise and shock. The key is often to make the viewer expect, wait and then release the final resolution. The frame always seeks to draw attention to what the producer regards as meaningful. They select certain things and reject others in order to create their meanings. They seek to create relevance or saliency. The producer will seek to represent their meanings in ways which draw attention to features that are appropriate to the target group. Their choice will be influenced by their personal and professional belief systems, that is, their own frame and their knowledge of the belief systems of their target audience, that is, their frame. What this draws attention to is the complex relationship of the producer and the audience through the text. It leads to the issues related to representation, stereotyping, ideology and discourse.

POINT OF VIEW.   The story is always told from a particular perspective or framed in a particular way. In many media texts point of view is associated with the narrator of the story. For instance, the narrator of a documentary about animals on television tells the story in the form of a voice-over and may only appear on screen rarely, if at all. The job of the narrator is to offer a perspective on the events portrayed. In other media texts the story might be told from the point of view of one of the participants in the events being recounted. Yet other media texts, such as serial dramas, create a whole range of viewpoints for the audience on the unfolding dramas, with groups of characters that allow the viewer privileged access. In film, establishing shots and other types of technical devices such as steadycams help to position the viewer in the fictional space of the narrative through the creation of point-of-view shots. Even documentaries that aim to be objective actively present a case through their structuring and organisation of a point of view.

MONTAGE.   This has a wide variety of uses. Generally, montage refers to the combination of elements taken from different sources so as to produce a new whole in which the original elements can still be seen. In film, montage refers either to the general process of film editing or the specific type of editing which created meaning through the juxtaposition of individual shots that create a new meaning for the viewer. It can also refer to rapid cutting from shot to shot that is typical of many TV commercials and film trailers. It has been influential in photography, especially for experimental or political purposes. However, the assembling of visual images (postcards, photographs, magazine images, children's drawings) is a very common domestic activity. Such compilations often appear on family websites where they are increasingly supported by audio and music clips. It is interesting to note how such montages in the crime room have become a regular feature of the detective genre as detectives seek to piece together the evidence that will lead to the successful conviction of the guilty party. This seems to suggest that an important function of montage is in the piecing together of evidence that creates resolution for the reader. Most of the elements are there but they need bringing together in order to work out the meaning with the final piece of evidence. The detectives are seeking to put together the 'back story' in the same way that the audience is asked to participate in the story.

Montage works through the juxtaposition of elements and draws attention to the need for reader engagement. These elements are not simply visual images but can be medleys of voices and/or music and/or sound effects layered against each other. Modern technology has made the process of layering image and sound together much more accessible. And montage as a narrative technique has become increasingly important in the modern digitally based media.

The narrative film

MOST of the films we see at the cinema or on DVD are films that clearly tell a story. Even when films are factual they use story methods to get their viewpoint across. For example, a film documentary may tell the story of a yachtswoman captaining a team made up of males as they set out to break the speed record for around the world sailing. We are so familiar with the ways in which such stories are told that most of us have a 'script' and 'frame' to test them against.

Most of us expect:

- an opening sequence that gives us the who, what, where;
- a set of characters who interact;
- a series of connected incidents;

- problems and/or conflicts probably about gender roles;
- an ending which resolves the action (closure) or creates the possibility of another story (open-ended).

Hence we become engaged in the dynamic activity of spectatorship through picking up typical cues, testing against own experience and anticipating. The story may provoke curiosity, create suspense, engineer surprise and create empathetic moments. We will be constantly trying to guess what happens next and being proved right or wrong. By the time of the ending the spectator may see how all the elements fall into place or be able to review events in a new light.

Such a film does not yet exist though it might by the time this book is printed!

CONSTRUCTION. The director of the film needs to be able to control every element of the narrative. The knowledge acquired through professional training will ensure there will be an understanding and knowledge of the films that had similar adventures/quests at the basis of their narrative structure. However, the director will want to add something personal: a new take, slant or twist.

DECONSTRUCTION. As a media student you will not be simply watching such a film but deconstructing the separate elements which make up the narrative. You will need to break up the text into elements to see behind the work of the director. Most mainstream film directors want their productions to be seamless and deliberately disguise their production techniques. They use logical (this does not always mean sequential) ordering of events to reveal their viewpoint and to enhance the audience's enjoyment. Underlying the film will be a whole set of structural processes.

The narrator

AS we have seen, this function can be carried out in a number ways. In our example of a documentary journey text the narrator could be 'a voice of God' narrator, stitching together and making sense of a variety of incidents. This kind of narrator is in some ways above the events of the narrative offering an overview and often is literally behind the events in the sense that they are unseen on screen and represented by their voice. Alternatively, it could be the voice of the female protagonist telling the story from her viewpoint highlighting the trials and tribulations not only of the physical dangers but the psychological stresses of working with men. Yet again the voices of the crew members on the voyage could be edited and juxtaposed to create tension, suspense and resolution (uneasy maybe and to be continued!). In fictional film narratives, this position can be even more complicated as the narrator could be a 'personified' narrator who may be relatively anonymous to the audience. This narrator is a character in the story and exists in the time frame of the narrative but is clearly recounting from a character viewpoint. Often this narrator is looking back on events. Because of this the audience has to test the reliability of this voice – Does it have the full story? Do we believe what the character says? Do we suspect that either deceit or ignorance on his/her part requires us to see more than he or she does?

On-screen space

CLEARLY, our example is located somewhere – the ports, the oceans crossed and maybe domestic locations. In this case the locations would be real and obviously raise a whole series of questions about who films (extra crew members? Crew members? When? Who is in control?), with what equipment (weight and size? Storage?), where (on boat/off boat?) and costs (who pays? What is the deal with the crew, the captain, the sponsors of the boat, the shipbuilders etc.?).

Shots

GENERALLY directors tend to work with a limited range of techniques that they have developed during the course of their training and through their experience. These have developed into standard visual conventions with which the audience is familiar: for instance, the extreme close shot, especially of eyes, tends to suggest emotions such as shock or bewilderment. A shot has been defined as what has been recorded or filmed between the time the camera is turned on and turned off again. These shots, or takes, are reviewed at the end of a session of filming and whole or part sequences are selected as elements of scenes to be included in the final version of the text. Some shots may be shortened or edited out all together (they may become out-takes for DVD versions) in the post-production phase prior to the final release. In our example, some takes may follow these kinds of conventions: the port scenes, for instance. However, parts of the film may have been shot by inexperienced crew members not familiar with standard conventions and hence this might lead to several tricky editing situations. Much will depend on the documentary style of filming on which the director decides: this may be a video diary approach, or a voyeuristic surveillance approach using strategically placed cameras with interviews with the members of the crew (also known as *Big Brother*) using technologies such as the webcam or the presentation of a dramatised documentary of one woman's struggle against the odds. This will be linked to other decisions about the structure of the story.

Camera

THE positioning of the camera is the most important thing to be aware of when studying a film. The camera frames everything we see and we see only those things that are contained in the viewfinder. Apart from the common technique of zooming towards or away from the subject, we often see vertical or horizontal movement, made by panning the camera up, down or from side to side, or tilting shots created by tipping the camera. Amateur filmmakers should use such shots with care as a multitude of such shots can cause audience fatigue. In our example such shots may be used in storms and thus help to contribute to the reality of the scene. A common technique is shot/reverse shot, which is very useful in dialogue scenes.

In some films it is necessary to move the camera along the ground. Such shots are called tracking shots (originally named because tram lines or tracks were often laid to accommodate the planned movement of the camera), and aerial shots which track objects are also part of this. Many shots require the camera to be above ground level so the camera is fixed to a crane; hence they are known as crane shots. In these shots the camera is held steady. However, this is not always the case. Handheld cameras reflect the movement of the camera operator and can help create a more subjective viewpoint for the audience. Steadycam has been an important technical development. All such movements of the camera are collectively known as *mobile framing*. In the modern filmmaking environment these kinds of shots can be produced digitally to create special effects which are not possible in live filming. The famous scene on the boat in *The Titanic* is an example.

Sound

IT is important of be aware of what sounds are present (music, speech, noise) because sound anchors meaning for the visuals and helps to create audience emotional responses. Its loudness (or amplitude), its pitch and timbre are important ways of structuring the way the story is told. Sounds are regularly related to the images and may be *diagetic* or *non-diagetic*. Diagetic sounds have their source in the story space of the film and appear natural. Non-diagetic sound comes from a source outside the story space. The convention of movie music and the omniscient narrator who gives us information are typical examples. Often these types of sound are combined as in a typical shot of a stormy ocean in which the sound of the crashing waves may be diagetic (to create realism) and the accompanying music non-diagetic (to enhance the emotional effect).

Editing

FEW media texts are shot in order and the final version is constructed according to the original planning of the production. This is often done according to the plans made in 'outline treatments' of the story, storyboarding for sound, vision and action and a final shooting script which contains detailed directions about how each aspect of the production is to be created. Editing is the physical or digital process of joining the segments (sometimes the medical metaphor 'suturing' describes this process of stitching the film together) and is where the really interesting decisions get made. There is a whole set of terminology to describe editing such as cut, fade and dissolve, and numerous special effects transitions such as page curl, pixillate etc.

Narratology

THIS is the study of narrative texts as narrative structures. It proposes a science of narrative by creating a formal and scientific method for studying narratives. There are any number of theories about narrative available which have produced a vast literature. However, any theory needs to be tested in the field and this is one of the main activities of the media student. Theories need to be tested against examples. The testing may be in the form of analysis or may be in the attempt to produce models which can test the theories. In either case you will need to know a lot about the type of narrative you are studying or producing.

Here the work of only three important narrative theorists will be very briefly explored: Vladimir Propp (1968), Tzvetan Tordorov (1981), Roland Barthes (1972). Each has a different theory of how narrative works in texts and approaches it in different ways.

PROPP.   Propp studies folktales from the point of view of their structure. He attempts to classify their constituent elements to reveal how they are put together. In this sense, he is a *structuralist*. Rather than beginning with story, he begins with characters and classifies them according to their *function* in the story. These functions (he identifies 31) are the fundamental elements of the story; they include such elements as villainy, departure, struggle, return, pursuit, punishment, solution, difficult task, rescue. Certain characters (he points out that they may be animate or inanimate characters) are linked to certain elements in predictable ways in what he describes as *'spheres of action'*. Hence his focus is on what the characters do at any point in the story. Are they donor or helper? Are they the hero or the false hero or the villain? The princess or the father? Characters are not classified according to what they think, feel, think they are doing or intend to do, but what their function is in any of the spheres of action of the story. Modern theorists of narrative have used his classifications to analyse genres that have narratives other than fairytales: comics, cartoons, plays, films and television drama programmes etc. The story is a series of actions in Propp's theory. He offers an analysis based on the ways in which the spheres of action are linked by character in a chain. This sequential organisation means that the analysis is *syntagmatic*. One sphere of action follows another one. Clearly this causes difficulties in dealing with flashbacks in film, for instance, which are out of sequence.

Lévi-Strauss, the French anthropologist, developed Propp's theory a stage further by concentrating not on the syntagmatic structuring of narratives but on how meaning might be derived from them. He proposed that when we experience narratives we derive meaning from relationships between the elements. In particular if one element *is one thing the other is not that element*. Hence binary opposition is a fundamental way in which we understand stories. The analysis becomes *paradigmatic*, that is, examining the binary oppositions which exist in a text and that can be elicited from a text to give it meaning.

The structuralist method involves the following steps:

1. Find the binary oppositions with which the text is organised using typical codes and conventions, for example, male/female; old/young; rich/poor; dominant/oppressed; black/white etc.
2. Criticise or undo the invidious structure of these oppositions in that in any of these oppositions there is a preferred term. Reversing the terms is an excellent strategy.
3. Reconstruct a new meaning.

To be engaged in this structuralist activity is to be aware of ideology and the operations of power in society and out of 'false consciousness'. The activity can be unsettling by disturbing traditional common-sense modes of responding to create new ways of responding.

TORDOROV. Tordorov wrote about the structure of the 'fantastic', advancing the theory that narrative is a fictional environment which begins with a state of equilibrium (everything is normal) that is then disrupted (becomes out of order) before a new equilibrium is created. He begins with the idea that when we encounter a media text we try to connect events together and narrative is, therefore, a chain of events in cause–effect relationships that happen in time and space. Because this happens then that happens, just as tick follows tock. Because a character behaved this way then this was the consequence. Even when there is no obvious connection the audience still try to make one. In many ways this chimes in with our common-sense notions of narrative: what happens next? Stories always have beginnings, middles and ends. This is how we are in the real world. If we have a headache we attribute a cause to it. The narrative structure could be: a bad day (equilibrium), went to a club (disruption), met friends (cause/complication), got drunk (consequence) hence the headache hangover (new equilibrium). This can be described as a linear theory.

This has been further developed by Branigan (1992) who suggests the following narrative schema:

- introduction of setting and character
- explanation of a state of affairs

- initial disruption
- emotional response or statement of goal by protagonist
- complicating actions
- outcome
- reactions to outcome.

Such linear structures can be applied to both fictional and non-fictional forms. For example, they would be typical of the structure of a news report and a news programme on the television or radio, each of which have story modes. One of the important skills of the film director is creating mood and atmosphere by choosing certain shots in a particular order to build a picture in our minds. If the director shows a shot of a doll and then a shot of a child the audience is likely to expect the child to be involved with the doll. Montage as practised by Sergei Eisenstein, the Russian filmmaker of the 1920s, forced the audience to think and interact in less obvious ways with the shot as he juxtaposed it with other shots to create in the audience complex emotional and often political responses. As with Propp the emphasis remains on the sequence of events.

BARTHES.   In *S/Z: An Essay*, Roland Barthes identifies a number of codes (sets of rules) which are linked together in the production of all kinds of stories. These can be real stories, as in news stories, or fictional stories, as in comics or films. He proposes that all stories work using these five codes and that all the textual signifiers can be grouped under them to create narrative.

Barthes's narrative codes are:

- *Action code*. This depicts the events which take place in the story. It is what happens and is sequential. It is the where, when and who of the story.
- *Semantic code*. This refers to character and to characterisation. He describes this as the 'voice of the person'. The actions in the story are explained by the character's viewpoint on events. It is through character viewpoint that stories are explained and bring about revelation and possible closure to the events. Multiple character viewpoints are possible and in some stories essential.
- *Enigma code*. This code involves the setting up of mystery, its development and its resolution. Many types of media texts create enigmas: news, comics, magazine front covers, film and television trailers, home pages. In film texts there can be many red herring signs which deliberately mislead the character (and the viewer) to create intrigue, interest, suspense and excitement.
- *Referential code*. This has the function of informing or explaining. It tells us about context, setting, location, audio codes, dress codes, lighting codes, colour codes etc. The French term *mise en scène* is the equivalent of this code.
- *Symbolic code*. This code works on the connotations of signs which transform them into symbolic representations. Characters can symbolise, for example, bravery, treachery or foolhardiness. Incidents can symbolise moral issues and dilemmas, the triumph of good over evil, retribution and so on. Objects can symbolise character, such as the gun or the car. It can fill out our view of the character – for example, driving a certain kind of car indicates that you are a certain kind of person. It can propel the story forward to its inevitable resolution. It works, therefore, at every level of the story.

The Idea Today

T HE AMOUNT OF ATTENTION THAT NARRATIVE HAS RECEIVED FROM CULTURAL commentators means that it remains a challenging intellectual problem. We can ask why do we need stories – what are they for? It is useful to redefine this slightly into three key questions.

Why do we need stories at all?

HUMAN beings seem to surround themselves with stories and increasingly these are the staple component of such mediated forms as film, television, video, computer games etc. Part of being human seems to be our ability to engage in make believe or explore representations of our lives. Stories allow us to explore possibilities and to experiment with different versions of self. They are both a way of investigating and giving our selves pleasure. They are also a way of policing ourselves to ensure we are in line with our friends and neighbours. Such a view drives the American George Gerbner's assertion that whoever tells the stories of a culture has defined the terms, the agenda and the common issues human beings face. Stories are also places to experiment with alternative viewpoints; a place where reigning assumptions can be challenged and tested in 'what if' situations. Stories can do all of the things and often at the same time. They can affirm our sense of identity while at the same time extending and testing it. This tension informs many of the viewpoints in debates about the effects of the media.

Why do we need the 'same' story over and over again?

WE need narratives that affirm our sense of ourselves. They give sense to our world and the shape of that sense is a fundamental carrier of the sense. Children require stories to be told in exactly the same way often at the same time of day. It gives them reassurance and the repetition may in itself give pleasure. We also want repetition in the form of stories. The forms are repeatable and formulaic. This suggests the theme, characters, the setting, the message or moral are not in themselves sufficient. The plot is vital. This is the central message of the structuralist approach to narrative which emphasises the design of stories and the ways in which they affirm and reflect the basic assumptions. Their repeatability reinforces the basic ideology of a culture and therefore they remain the best place to question some of its assumptions.

Why do we always need more stories?

STORIES create a sense of closure and yet in closure there are still new possibilities. Media producers are well aware of the business imperative of using what is already familiar and accepted by audiences but varying the details to attract new audiences. It is the basis of the concept of genre. In one sense we need more stories because we need different twists and variations to satisfy our curiosity about life itself because in one simple sense we know that stories are only representations of life. We cannot 'read' life itself because it is 'unreadable'.

Genre

THIS KEY CONCEPT REFERS TO THE FACT THAT MOST MEDIA TEXTS FALL INTO categories or types. What is at stake in the study of genres is how these repetitive categories are made use of in society. The origin of the word is French and means 'type' or 'kind'. Media output can be grouped into categories, each with a set of typical codes and conventions. These categories are flexible and dynamic.

The characteristics of genre include:

- *The creation of a set of expectations in the audience.* It is a fundamental way in which media texts are understood. Genres are made up of codes and conventions recognised by audiences over time. In one sense they give advance notice of what to expect, which allows the consumer/audience the active choice of whether to be involved with it. Recognition by audiences is the main feature and in terms of choosing a film, television programme, website or magazine it can be an instant process. This suggests that the openings (or covers) of media texts are very important. The meeting of these expectations in a media text can equal pleasure and customer satisfaction.

- *The creation of characteristics and formulas by producers which audiences can recognise.* This can be at the level of textual organisation involving narrative, iconography, *mise en scène*, themes and representation. Genres function like a language, offering sets of rules and a way of talking about texts to organise meaning in them. Or at the level of what Neale (1990) describes as *'intertextual relay'*: that is, the systems and forms of publicity, marketing and reviewing that each media organisation possesses. He suggests that, because organisations name, label and brand their products, they help to reinforce generic categories through these processes.

- *A relationship between audiences and producers which minimises the risk of financial failure.* It is, therefore, implicated or constructed for commercial consumption. Formulas and repeats of ideas are commonplace in media production as they offer the promise of security for both parties involved in the transaction.

- *Dynamism and flexibility.* The dangers of staleness, even sterility, are ever present. Hence generic mutation is required to maintain a genre's vitality.

1. This can range from minor changes such as using the same hero (but played by a different actor) with a range of new gadgets and opposed by new types of villains – examples would be *Batman* films and *Bond* films – or the challenge to dominant systems of representation such as casting a women as the central hero, as in *Alien*.

2. Their boundaries are approximate and shifting to offer the audience more points of engagement with the text. Neale (1990) describes the process as follows: *'Individual genres not only form part of a generic regime, but also themselves change, develop and vary by borrowing from, and overlapping, with one another.'* Thus many genres can be mixed to create generic hybrids and offer a range of pleasures and recognition points for audiences.

- *At an ideological level genres can offer comforting reassurance and a sense of the closing down of the complexities of life.* When we settle down with a box of chocolates and a glass of wine with our favourite magazine, soap opera or film, and our favourite character is playing the lead, we rarely expect our assumptions about how we live to be challenged. Our ideas and values will often find reinforcement from the textual construction – the audience cues it offers and our ability to recognise how the text 'hails' us – and in addition, from the ways in which our sense of identification with the text has been created through a range of media. Hence, such typical features as continuity announcements, advance notice of stories through trailing in newspapers and star interviews, have an important role in establishing this reassurance.

Iconography

ICONOGRAPHY is a means whereby visual motifs and styles in films, magazines, posters and multimedia productions and websites can be categorised and analysed.

It can refer to the dress codes of the characters in the representation, or to the settings in which they find themselves. These connote not only time and place but they also reflect prevailing social values. Dress codes, for instance, tell us about oppositions and conflicts in filmic texts. In gangster films the flashy suits of the gangsters contrast and create an opposition to the detective in his sober suit. It can reveal much about the values of the film.

As societal values change so do the visual motifs and styles. It is always important in media texts to judge less from the appearance and to make more of the function of the motif or style.

Genres can change over time in terms of their visual look and these changes point to changes in attitudes and values. As such they can be markers of ideology. It is clear that the iconography of violence has changed in moving image texts. In television series such as *Casualty* we are spared nothing in terms of the representation of the consequences of illness and violence: blood, operations and cutting all form part of the *mise en scène*. Modern films such as *Gangs of New York* use graphic representations of shooting and fighting that create an 'aesthetics of violence' about which we are both horrified and fascinated.

Iconography draws attention to the way in which particular images are given specific meanings and the ways in which they are clustered together and the connotations which are set up. It focuses on the production of meaning.

Comics and popular culture

COMICS are part of the general low esteem in which much popular culture is held in the UK. In other countries with a positive attitude to the visual, such as France, Italy or Japan, there is evidence of a significant educational bonus and different audience types are attracted. Countries such as Vietnam and China have recognised the importance of comics for educational and propaganda purposes.

The influence of comics in advertising has been enormous. Can you think of examples of comic book representation in advertising, especially animated examples? Even traditionally based print media such as newspapers are increasingly visual in orientation and some, for example the *Guardian*, use comic book techniques to report complex issues, especially legal and educational ones.

Comics and film

THAT we 'read' comics is obvious in many ways. Every aspect of the comic can be read and the reader is required to exercise both visual and verbal interpretative skills to make sense of the comic.

The grammar of comics (linear representation, framing, sequencing, open and closed frames and panels) is very important to the study of film. Comics, while clearly different from films, share much in common with the film. While comics are not 'movies on paper' as Will Eisner once suggested, they are important in a cinematic story telling.

Filmmakers have studied the kind of shots found in the frames in comics to learn how to shoot films. There is also a strong cross over from comic book characters to film heroes and heroines. This is even more marked when we think about the 'stars' of computer games, such as 'Super Mario Brothers', 'Lara Croft' or 'Sonic the Hedgehog'.

Japanese Manga Comics

COMICS are generally regarded as appealing to a young audience in the UK and have often been accused of stereotyping, especially in relation to representations of gender. Manga comics have gained a reputation in this country for attracting young men, particularly through the violence and overt sexuality of the representations. These representations have been carried over into computer games.

Helen McCarthy provides a working definition of Manga:

'Manga is the Japanese word for comic though as is often the case in translation, there is no precise equivalent in English.

. . . the term was coined in 1815 by the great artist Hokusai and is usually translated as "irresponsible pictures". It stuck to products of the comic industry. Never used in Japan for moving pictures, although in the UK, the Manga Video label uses the term "Manga movies" extensively to describe anime released on their own label' (McCarthy 1993).

A brief overview

IN Japan, Manga magazines are considered one of the best ways to reach mass audiences and shape their opinions. Manga have nearly the same social status as novels and films. The total number of Manga magazines produced represents every man, woman and child having 15 or more. This does not include the fact that many of them, like newspapers and comics in this country, are passed on from reader to reader. A Manga story may start by being serialised in a weekly, bi-weekly, monthly, bi-monthly or quarterly magazine. It can be made into an animated film or an animated series for television. The stories also create synergy by being associated with a whole range of products from CDs to toys to stationery to nightwear to videos to table mats as souvenirs. Often they underwrite 'serious' literature and influence art and literature in much the same way that pop art did in the 1960s or punk in the 1980s in the UK. They have been exported and assimilated into American culture in particular, in cartoons, animation and computer games. One can argue that it is impossible to understand Japanese culture without studying the Manga's role and influence. Moreover, given the Japanese desire to export, it is impossible not to study their influence on the minds of young people influenced by these products in indigenous European cultures. The relationship between Japan and the USA is very profound and deep in cultural terms, as is the relationship of the USA to the rest of the globe in economic and cultural terms. They are an interesting example of cultural flow between countries. (Source: adapted from Schodt 1996).

What are Manga?

ORIGINALLY from the USA from the turn of the century, by a process of cultural hybridisation Manga became distinctively Japanese. Their key constituents were sequential panels with word balloons arranged on a page to tell a story. The distinctive Japanese hallmark was story-telling and character development by:

1. The decompression of storylines so that they expanded into Mangas that were hundreds of pages long.

2. Creation of different perspectives and visual aspects – often described as 'cinematic techniques'. Words are less important. The focus of attention moves from action to the minutiae of daily life. The importance of what McCloud (1993) calls 'aspect to aspect' framing is much more apparent. A single action might take pages to develop as successive frames reveal different aspects of the situation. Japanese Manga are very long, which creates space for startling cinematic story-telling.

3. The range of subjects is immense, despite their limited range in this country. Japanese comics and animation are proving to be as exportable as their cars and their technology.

4. Pages of artwork had to be 'flopped' to read left to right. The Japanese sound effect had to be replaced by English onomatopoeia. Some Japanese visual conventions, such as visualising sleep as a bubble coming from a character's nose, needed to be changed. To help reader identification the heroes were often drawn with very large Western-style eyes.

5. In the Western world the vogue for science fiction was important, especially among 'cyberpunks'. Japanese story-telling styles began to influence Western creators such as Frank Miller, the comic writer famous for his work on *Batman* comics.

6. The most well-known comic creation in the West is *Akira* (1988) by Katsuriho Otomo. Changes in the American cultural environment in the 1980s meant that many American comics fans and artists were looking for something different from the superhero genre. Marvel Comics (under its Epic Comics imprint) translated the comic. It was a dark sci-fi thriller drawn in a realistic style familiar to Americans. It had a dystopian theme about a delinquent biker with apocalyptic powers in neo-Tokyo and its drawing was dramatic and eye-catching. In addition, concessions were made to the American audience: the black and white images were colourised to fit in with prevailing conventions in the American comics industry. It was instantly successful and the animated feature version of the story was imported from Japan and dubbed to support its promotion.

Film genres

GENRE is a particularly important concept for the film industry because of the enormous amount of time, energy and money which film organisations put into the marketing and promotion of their products to mass audiences. One of the key selling points of a film is its genre. One much studied example is the western genre. To study it, analysts have broken down the genre by categorising its major codes and conventions. The following section is based on a conference presentation by Jill Poppy.

Major codes and conventions

- *Setting*. Mountains, deserts, plains of the American West, Mexico and Canada. Mining camps.
- *Location*. Cattle ranches, frontier towns.
- *Place and time*. 1865–1890s. End of the Civil War to the end of the Land Rush and the 'closing of the frontier'.
- *Characters*. Cowboys, homesteaders, sheriffs, marshals, outlaws, US cavalry, native Indian warriors, saloon girls, schoolteacher, temperance league, native American women, adolescent girls.
- *Style elements: visual and aural*.
  1. Landscape photography, long shots of riders and cattle on the plains.
  2. Technicolour, widescreen.
  3. Orchestral music, country and western music songs, harmonicas etc.
  4. Sound effects (sfx) of horses, cattles, wagons etc, the musical style of Ennio Morricone for the 'spaghetti western'.
- *Iconography*.
  1. Weapons of all sorts: Colt 45, Winchester rifle, Gatling Gun, bows and arrows, lances etc.
  2. Dress codes: Stetson, chaps, boots and saddles, spurs, cavalry uniform, contrasting dress for saloon girl and schoolteacher, beads, feathers, war bonnets.
  3. Significant objects: horses, cattle, mining gear, fences, railroads etc.
- *Typical plots*.
  1. Settlers confront native Indians who are defeated by the cavalry.
  2. Outlaws terrorise frontier town and are brought to book by a lawman.

3. Lone gunfighter saves town or farmers.

4. Ill-used hero seeks vengeance on villain.

• *Set pieces.* Chases, gun fights, bar-room brawls, bank-raids, train hold-ups, lynchings, attacks on native Indian villages etc.

• *Themes.*

1. The 'taming' of the wilderness.

2. The 'frontier' and the making of America.

3. Bringing 'civilisation' and 'law and order'.

4. The bringing of freedom and equal opportunity in the 'American dream'.

5. The growth of ownership and corporate values.

The western genre is important, it has been argued, because westerns have mythic qualities. Myths help to order everyday experience by giving people a sense of who they are and how they should live. Hence they are concerned with ideas and values.

Genre analysts not only categorise the elements of a genre they can also group genres together to explore these ideas and values. The typical binary oppositions found in westerns, for instance, can be found in other genres such as the gangster, science fiction, fantasy adventure, horror genres: inside/outside society, good/bad, weak/strong, civilisation/wilderness, civilised/wild etc.

Two basic categorisations of groups of film genres are useful: genres of order and genres of integration.

Genres of order can be categorised as follows:

• The *hero/heroine* (usually the male is dominant) will be an individual with a strongly marked persona (though sometimes this will be disguised).

• He/she will be in a *setting* which is a contested space in that what is at stake in the contest are sets of ideas and values as represented by people usually but can be nations or even the planet itself.

• The *conflict* will be externalised and expressed through violent action.

• The *resolution* will usually mean the elimination of the threat usually through death.

• *Thematics.* The hero/heroine takes upon him/herself the problems, contradictions inherent in society and acts as redeemer. There is often a macho code of behaviour, even with heroines. The character remains true to him/herself whatever the cost in personal terms: the loss of friends, loved ones. They have an isolated self-reliance and do not assimilate the values/lifestyle of the community they save. They maintain their individuality.

Genres of integration such as musicals, comedies, melodramas can be categorised as follows:

• The *heroes* are couples or collectives (e.g. family, friends). The genres tend to be female dominated/focused.

• They will be in a *setting* which is civilised space; this will often be a domestic space. It will be ideologically stable in that members strive for the same values and ideas.

• The *conflict* will be internalised and expressed through emotion.

- The *resolution* is the embrace representing love. There is a sense of completion through the settling of emotional differences.
- *Thematics*. The couple or family are integrated into the wider community and their personal antagonisms resolved. The maternal and familial codes are re-established and reinforced. There is community cooperation and a sense that all will be well.

Personal home pages

EACH website has a home page. This page is like a table of contents. Usually it is the first page of a site, but more and more sites are including an entry page (also called a splash page or front door). This is rather like the title page in a book and leads to the home page.

Home pages are constructed from a variety of sources (text, image, sound) rather than simply written. Claude Lévi-Strauss spoke of a *'dialogue with the materials and means of execution'* (Lévi-Strauss 1973). His notion of the *bricoleur* who appropriates the materials that are ready to hand is widely employed in relation to cultural practices in youth subcultures. The appropriation of popular cultural imagery for personal purposes has been described by various commentators (Hebdige 1979, Jenkins 1992).

The home page is interesting as it can be a point of intersection between professional web developers trained in design and the novice or 'newbie'. Very sophisticated software (e.g. 'Dreamweaver' from Macromedia) appears to make the production of websites easy, and in many senses it is. However, there is a huge discourse about what constitutes a good or a bad home page (or website), which is often conducted through software user groups or through training manuals/style guides. Hence its codes and conventions can be the subject of some interesting and occasionally offensive comment. The home page (and the website) is a genre where it is possible to see the codes and conventions being actively argued over and constructed by a wide range of groups – some with professional training and others without.

Most work on personal home pages has concentrated on young people and the representations of personal identity (see Chandler and Roberts-Young 1998). Essentially such research is concerned with content and its organisation. In the media first impressions count and if developers want like-minded people to visit their site they need to offer both design and content. Appearance matters in media presentation.

Generic features of personal home pages

KEY features of the genre of the personal home page are categorised by Chandler and Roberts-Young (1998):

- Themes: Who
  - Personal statistics
  - Biographical details
  - Roles
  - Personal qualities
  - Interests, likes and dislikes (including hobbies)
  - Ideas, values, beliefs and causes (religious, political, philosophical)
  - Friends, acquaintances and personal 'icons'

- Formulaic structures: Forms of content (related genres)
  - Personal ('lonely hearts') advertisement, matchmaking form
  - Curriculum vitae
  - Visiting card
  - Commercial advertisement
  - Staff handbook entry
  - Diary, personal journal, autobiography
  - Photograph album
  - Pinboard, scrapbook
  - Fanzine
  - FAQ (frequently asked questions)
  - Structural organisation
  - Contents page, index
  - Rooms
- Technical features
  - Links
  - Access ('hit') counter
  - Frames
  - Forms (guestbook, feedback forms)
  - E-mail
  - Chat system
  - Code (HTML, JavaScript etc)
- Iconography
  - Background
  - Colour
  - Wallpaper
  - Typography (font, size, colour)
  - Page layout
  - Graphics (icons, photographs, other artwork)
  - Moving images (video-clips, animations)
  - Sounds (voice, music, effects)
  - Written style.
- Modes of address
  - Posited audience
  - Self
  - Intimates
  - Friends, workmates
  - Acquaintances (including virtual friends)
  - Peers in general (epistemic, age, class, gender, sexual orientation, ethnicity, nationality)
  - Employers
  - Formality and directness: language and 'gaze'.

The design debate

IN *The Non-Designer's Web Book* (Williams and Tollet 2000), the authors make the point that, *'No one makes bad-looking web pages on purpose'* and they go on to offer advice on good and bad design approaches. They contrast the professional with amateur in ways which allow the amateur to become more proficient; in doing so they illustrate design conventions of which they disapprove/approve. These they suggest can help the creative decisions made by the 'newbie' developer. They are clearly aiming to develop the look and usability of websites by offering design standards in a relatively new medium. Good and bad design approaches are summarised below.

BAD DESIGN

- Text in all capitals especially on a black background with a line length which covers the page.
- Artificially breaking lines of text because the user can set different text defaults.
- Links which do not work.
- Asking the user to adjust their browser.
- Buttons which are not actually buttons but look like buttons.
- Text which is too small, in a font which is difficult to read (serif) using a colour which does not contrast effectively with it.
- Mixing different types of font.
- Making users scroll sideways.
- Having 'jaggies' (anti-aliasing effects).
- Using animated gifs which do not stop.
- Headings not appropriately lined up with their subheadings.
- Poorly scanned images.
- Putting scroll bars in the middle of pages.
- Poor guidance about how to navigate (forward, back, links).
- Anything that blinks, especially text.

GOOD DESIGN

- Clarity of communication with good feedback for the user.
- Visual (repetition of elements, colours, alignment), conceptual (metaphors, iconography, styles, information hierarchy) and mechanical (location, action states, sounds associated with navigation elements) consistency.
- Using contrast effectively.
- Striving to make it uncluttered and simple.

Clearly, as the Web is developing it offers production possibilities to non-specialists. It is one of the central features of 'new media'. There is a sense that these non-specialists are being inducted into a professional discourse which itself is evolving through contact with audiences, word of mouth (in specialist user groups) and critical discussion. Rules are being negotiated and conventions established. Genres are being established both through content and design.

The Idea Today

F OR *AUDIENCES*, GENRE IS A POPULARLY UNDERSTOOD STARTING POINT TO READ media texts. Audiences know the difference between dance and rap music; they understand the difference between soaps and documentaries; they distinguish between romantic and action films. Hence genre is an important means of communicating information about the text and helps to frame audience expectations, not only in relation to its inscription in publicity but also in relation to previous experience and cultural knowledge

For *media students*, genre is a way in which they can manage the diversity of cultural forms such as pop music, television, film, computer games, websites etc. To understand the characteristics, conventions and pleasures of a particular genre is to understand a great deal about the cultural form to which it belongs. From genre it is possible to learn a great deal about the historical dimension of media production. One difficulty for students that has been identified is that genre theory is circular. A writer will define genre in a particular way using categories and then dismiss any texts that do not fall within the categories proposed. A second difficulty is that genre criticism tends to deal with ideal versions of a genre and then a new version is criticised for not conforming. It is interesting to relate this to the 'fan' response to genre in which highly informed criticism based on a long engagement with the genre becomes a cause for concern to the fans who tend to prefer 'original' versions. This is particularly evident in forms such as television, which need to refresh their formats more than most other media forms. An excellent example would be the way in which television has broken down the distinctions between series/serials/soaps in programmes like *The Bill* in order to sustain a long-running brand. This is further stretched when characters from the programme cross over into advertising. They become the central protagonists in a series of advertisements which aim to sell the ITV brand to advertisers. In a further development in May 2003 a new Saturday night series has been developed from the mid-week episodes using the familiar characters but allowing the organisation to bring in new characters familiar from other television dramas. It also allows them to drive down production costs. The drive to involve the audience in such programmes through phone calls, emails and websites, means that such programmes are more susceptible to audience taste. Hence genres are tweaked by the intervention of the audience in a direct manner. An interesting example in 2003 is the long-running community/police drama series *Heartbeat* (ITV) which, using some of the same characters, has developed a new version in the medical/hospital genre called *The Royal*, with which it switches in the same primetime slot on a Sunday evening. The new show draws on favourite characters, a variation in settings and the new (but familiar) genre of the medical drama.

Genre (and the related terms 'iconography' and 'intertextuality') is a key concept for postmodernism. By allowing patterns of recognition to take place, media texts can relate to the audience's prior understanding of the text. Films will often refer to other films and so Martin Scorsese makes use of the western in general and in particular *The Searchers* (dir. John Ford, 1956) for his film *Taxi Driver* (1976). Steven Speilberg's film *Saving Private Ryan* starring Tom Hanks also refers visually to the work of the

British photographer Don McCullin for intertextual references. The opening scene in particular is heavily reliant on the dark documentary style of McCullin. (See Postmodernism, p. 48).

For *media producers*, genre can help to define a project by relating to other, similar texts. By marking out the difference(s), it is possible for media producers to develop a new take or angle on an existing text. It has become important in niche marketing in which audience preferences for particular genres is a key feature. Whole television channels have been marketed on the basis of genre, for instance sport, music, video, lifestyle etc. For example, in 2003 BSkyB introduced three new music channels for their customers to subscribe to, each targeted at a different kind of audience. The increasing competition for audiences in the media has meant that media producers have to change and adapt. Good examples of this are the television news and documentary genres, which have been increasingly influenced not only by the need to educate and inform but by the need to entertain and amuse.

The Infotainment Debate is an argument about the relationship between television and public life. It became an increasingly important debate during the 1980s and early 1990s in European countries with a strong tradition of public service broadcasting (PSB). In PSB television channels are financed from the public purse with a specific mission of educating and informing the population. In this period two buzzwords dominated: *deregulation* and *privatisation* (see Regulation, p. 128). Deregulation referred to the dissolution of the rules and regulations that restricted but also protected the status of the public services. In the UK the Broadcasting Act of 1990 created the Independent Television Commission (ITC) which controlled the commercial sector but which required it to exercise a 'lighter touch' over ITV, Channel 4, satellite and cable services. Companies who bid for broadcasting licences needed to satisfy a 'quality threshold'. This had three components: regional programmes, high quality news programmes at peak times and a diverse range of programmes for a diversity of audiences. The need to compete forced the BBC particularly into a competitive strategy to attract audiences to their programmes especially as there was increased competition for the audience from a range of sources other than ITV.

Genre was a particularly significant area for competition especially in terms of drama, news and new styles of documentary. This led to a phenomenon popularly referred to as *dumbing down* or more technically *infotainment*. Privatisation refers to the process by which previously state-owned television channels were taken into the private sector, especially in France and Italy. This led to increasing calls for the BBC, as a public body funded through the licence fee, to justify its privileged position in the broadcasting world and to make it more accountable to the audience. The debate remains a very intense one. On the one hand, there are those commentators who suggested that infotainment is about identity and celebrity rather than the education of the modern citizen. For these commentators the media intrudes upon private life and exploits personal emotions for the gratification of prying and fascinated audiences. For other commentators, commercial communication creates new opportunities to democratise media audiences and break down the high culture minority representations of the world.

Semiotics

The Idea

M AN IS A SIGN MAKER AND HAS ALWAYS BEEN FASCINATED BY SIGNS AND THEIR interpretation. There is no escape from signs in any world in which man exists. However, the systematic scientific study of signs and sign systems has been a twentieth-century phenomenon. The desire to cross boundaries between different forms of expression has driven the semiotic project, and semiotic thinkers have all striven to develop a theoretical framework applicable to all semiotic modes. They have sought to demonstrate how within any expressive form similar meanings can be expressed in the different semiotic modes such as moving image (film and television) and print based (newspapers, magazines, comics) and increasingly the combination of these in multimedia. It has in the process created controversies about the status of certain expressive modes.

One of the central aims of the investigation has been to reveal how *ideology* is at the basis of our ways of interpreting signs and has provided a method in the form of a powerful set of analytic tools for the task. This scientific approach aims to lay bare how our knowledge of the world as revealed in signs is constructed to legitimate unequal power relations. The primary focus of systematic investigation has been the text and its meaning.

During the twentieth century the idea of 'text' has been expanded from linguistic forms, such as books and newspapers, to one which embraces a diversity of forms, such as still and moving image (photographs, posters, films, television, computer games, comics, websites, interactive presentations and radio programmes). The metaphor of media language has been used to express how each of these forms can be 'read' through a knowledge and understanding of their presentational *codes* and *conventions* and an awareness of their typical patterns of similarity and difference. What semiotics does is to foreground and problematise the process of representation.

Some of the conceptual tools used in semiotics are: signifier, signified, referent, icon, index, symbol, paradigmatic, syntagmatic, denotive, diegesis, connotative, metonymic, metaphor, synecdochal, code, mythology, polysemy, preferred reading, appellation, anchorage, relay-function, structuralism, deconstruction, binary opposites. (See Chandler 2001 for a full list of terms used).

There are two different versions of semiotics:

1. *Structuralist semiotics.* This seeks to look behind or beneath the surface of the text to discover its underlying organisation. It explores the connotative meanings of signs as realised in the codes and conventions. It is primarily concerned with textual organisation.

2. *Social semiotics.* This reflects an increasing concern with the reader/user of the text. It alerts us to how the same text can generate divergent meanings with different readers/users.

M ANY PEOPLE HAVE CONTRIBUTED TO THE UNDERSTANDING OF THE DISCIPLINE AND among them are four influential thinkers who contribute many of the terms and tools for the analysis and understanding of expressive texts.

Ferdinand de Saussure

FERDINAND de Saussure (b. 1857), a Swiss academic, studied linguistics and sought to develop a systematic understanding of how language works. He argued that the sign was the basic unit of language and that it was composed of two components: the *signifier* and the *signified*. The signifier is the sound or image that is attached to the signified. The signified is the idea or concept attached to the signifier. Pierce calls the signifier the 'object' and others call it the 'referent'. The two are bound together in the sign. *'A sign is always thing-plus-meaning'* (Williamson 1978) and the meaning is *arbitrary* and conventional. By arbitrary, Saussure meant that it always occurred in a context, and by conventional that society had typical ways of interpreting signs within that context. It made human communication possible. So the word 'baby' depends for its meaning or significance on where it occurs. In American culture (and sometimes in British culture), for instance, it can refer to young women rather than the very young. Saussure proposed that a new science which *'studies the life of signs within society is conceivable; it would be part of social psychology and consequently of general psychology; I shall call it semiology'* (1966).

The first step was taken. It is worth asking why the significance of what Saussure proposed was so crucial to semiology.

- It meant that the relationship between the signifier and the signified was problematic and subject to questioning.

- It was a way of exploring signs and their meanings; the first stage of which was semiotic analysis (see p. 39). This sought to identify and categorise the signs and then to explore their meaning in the context of their use.

- It meant that all kinds of signs, not just linguistic signs, were open to scrutiny.

Use the examples below to identify the signifier (the object or concept) and the signified (what it means or refers to):

Try to explain what kind of knowledge and understanding you need to carry out the task. You will be a proto-semiotician. You will be starting to explore the *denotation* of the image. This is its obvious link to the world and is fairly easy to identify usually. What is more ambiguous is the significance we attach to the representation: its *connotations*. What happens between the signifier and the signified is a process of understanding that can be influenced by a whole range of factors: age, ethnicity, nationality, gender etc.

Charles Sanders Pierce

CHARLES Sanders Pierce was an American philosopher (b. 1834) who extended from the study of linguistic signs to visual signs. The discussion of the meaning of visual signs was much more 'motivated' by their use than linguistic signs generally were and therefore potentially more ambiguous and capable of multiple meanings. He proposed that there were three kinds of signs.

ICON.   The sign resembles what it describes.

Photographs are usually thought of as iconic, even though Barthes suggested they were without a code. Icons are a central feature of comics, cartoons, animated representation and the computer environment (screens and games).

INDEX.   The sign works by association with another sign that it indicates or points to.

SYMBOL.

A sign can be simultaneously any of these depending on time and circumstance and this means that their significance can change over time. This is a basic premise of work with signs created by the media and signs have become very powerful in the process of *symbolic exchange*.

Roland Barthes

ROLAND Barthes (b. 1915) was a French writer who profoundly influenced semiotics. He stressed imagistic as well as linguistic signs. He particularly drew attention to advertising, photography and audiovisual material and the ways in which they were related to ideology. His discussions remain provocative and interesting today; *Mythologies* (1957, translated into English in 1972) is still an important read for media students. Barthes was concerned with 'myth' which he argued was created through the interaction of denotative signifier and connotations of the sign. This produced ideology in the form of a myth. The task of the cultural analyst was to strip away the 'natural appearance' of the sign to 'expose' or 'lay bare' or 'make strange' its codes. In doing so it challenged common-sense readings of signs. He noted how the image remained *polysemic* (having an open range of meanings) until closed down by a process which he called *anchorage*. This was the way in which the image could be closed down by surrounding text. For example, an image of a baby which could have multiple meanings (a new arrival, an advert, a cute card) can be closed down. This original sense has been developed in the modern media to audio commentary which can act as anchorage and so close down the potential meanings of a represented event. Sports commentary would be an excellent example of the way in which the commentator draws attention to the significant action. Barthes further exemplifies this in what he describes as the *relay function* in the interaction of signs within the text. Individual signs in the text do not act independently but come together to close off potential meanings. Williamson (1978) in her study of advertisements argues that adverts worked by transferring (or attempting to transfer) meanings from one signifier to another signifier. Hence signs connoting strenuous activity could be linked by transference to signs concerning attractiveness. This kind of research was typical of work drawn from a semiological basis which used as its basic premise that in any represented text a number of *codes* are interacting to produce meaning. By 'code' semioticians mean the set of conventionalised ways of meaning that are specific to particular groups of people which could be decoded by them.

The basic approach is:

- Decide what the signs are in the text under study.
- Decide what they signify in themselves.
- Think about how they relate to other signs within the text and within other images.
- Explore the connections (and the connections of the connections) to wider systems of meaning to uncover the 'mythologies'.

M.A.K. Halliday

M.A.K. HALLIDAY (b. 1925) was a British linguistic theoretician whose work on language has been widely adopted in cultural studies. Later cultural theorists have developed his understandings of language into the approach called social semiotics. This model is based on the linguistic theories of Halliday on functional grammar. His view was that grammar was not a prescribed set of rules but that it does things in the 'real' world. Grammar helps us to perform functions (i.e. transact with the social world). It also helps us to 'transform' the world. Therefore, grammar is centrally involved with who controls the 'language' system. What social semioticians do is apply this not just to language but to a whole range of semiotic systems which can be said to have a 'grammar'. So it becomes possible to talk of the 'language' of film, comics, television, music, mime and so on. We can use such terms as 'media literacy' or 'cineliteracy'. We can also distinguish between different media 'languages'.

There are three key functions of a language:

1. *Ideational (representations)*. In this function the speaker/writer/producer embodies in their work the experience of the external world and makes it available. Different semiotic systems have different (and sometimes similar) ways of representing/mediating objects and their relationships. The implication of this is that media students need to have access to and experience of a variety of different ways of representing meaning to be regarded as being 'media literate'.

2. *Interpersonal (audience and organisation)*. In this function the speaker/reader/ listener/viewer/operator transacts with the social world. Different semiotic systems have different ways of relating the producer of texts and the receiver of texts. One way of describing these relationships is that they have different *modalities* depending on the audience targetted. The implication of this is that students need to have a wide experience of these relationships because it widens the range of their transactions with the mediated world.

3. *Textual.* This function links the other two because the speaker or writer or producer of the media text can produce a text and the listener, reader or viewer can recognise one. Semiotic systems create different kinds of texts by the different arrangements of the elements of the semiotic system. These arrangements are the 'grammar' or 'rhetoric' of the text. The implication of this is that to understand these conventional elements better, students need experience of the making of a variety of media texts. The making and studying of texts are constantly intertwined in media studies approaches.

Towards a definition of modality

'IN a social semiotics, modality is the term which describes the stance of the participants in the semiosic towards the state and the status of the system of classification of the mimetic plane' (Hodge and Kress 1988).

This kind of language (which can be typical of semioticians!) needs some unpacking.

• Children's books (or animated cartoons if you prefer) can be a very useful example in that they propose a clear orientation to the child audience. (In the quote this is carried by the word 'stance').

• You can test how 'real' a text is – adventure, fantasy, information – for the proposed audience. (This links to the 'system of classification').

• You can test the 'reality' of the text – e.g. cartoon or photorealistic. (This links to the 'mimetic plane'). Are some drawings of objects and people more 'real' than other drawings? (Mimesis).

• You can test in a purely visual text what visual audience cues the text provides. (Audience orientation in the 'semiosic').

- You can categorise the text by the degree to which it is anchored (if at all) by a verbal text (speech bubbles, captions, text panels, voice-overs). You can ask how the reading of written text or the voice-over is affected in terms of such issues as informality, accent and vocabulary, especially if the reader is an adult.

Some issues which emerge are:

- *The organisation of the text is always social and subject to controls.* Even apparently realistic texts have degrees of 'realism'. And when they seem to be 'natural' and the 'prescribed' way of doing things they are in fact closed off to other readings. This would be the case even with children's books that are made up of pictures. As these are meant to be read at the parent's knee primarily, they are enclosed by parental discourse. It might help explain why cartoons are felt to be more of a problem for parents than books, in that parents are not controlling the discourse and are worried about what their children are getting up to and the effects on them when they watch cartoons or 'Teletubbies'.
- *The visual text is always coded.* The codes include us to exclude us. One consequence of this is that we have to share our 'readings' with children and they have to share *theirs*. The children have 'codes' of which they have knowledge and we do not have as adults, and we have 'codes' they do not have access to. This might explain the phenomenon of 'pester power', for example, when young children badger their parents into buying the most fashionable trainers, clothes or toys at Christmas.

Towards a definition of transitivity

THIS is an essential tool in the analysis of representation. It is concerned with the way in which the same event or situation can be represented or 'framed' in different ways.

'Since transitivity makes options available, we are always suppressing some possibilities, so the choice we make – better the choice made by the discourse – indicates our point of view, (and) is ideologically significant' (Fowler 1991).

The following questions need to be asked in media analysis of transitivity:

- Who was the *agent* or doer of the action?
- Is this agent male or female, animal or human, natural or manufactured?
- How significant is this in your chosen material?
- How was this agent behaving?
- Who or what is the *acted upon* (the goal of the action)?
- How are they behaving?

As the process of making is social then it can be intervened in and transformed. Agents can become acted upon and vice versa. This draws attention to the importance of what readers bring to the media text as a result of their gender, race, class and ethnic group. The key concepts that this approach explores are drawn from work on ideology and discourse, particularly associated with Barthes and Foucault. It can be extended by use of the work of the Russian theorist Bahktin and his work on speech genres. In Britain, the work of Basil Bernstein on children's language is also important. He talked of the significance of 'extended' and 'restricted' linguistic codes (see Discourse, p. 71).

Poetics

The Idea

THE CENTRAL CONCERN WITH THIS APPROACH IS WITH THE AESTHETICS OF THE medium under study. The approach often interacts with approaches drawn from semiotic approaches to media texts. There are two important ideas in the approach: *mise en scène* and the trope.

Mise en scène

MISE en scène was originally the term derived from the theatre and implied 'staging'. In the first instance it connotes setting, costume and lighting. Second, it concerns the movement *inside* the frame.

It clearly has a place in the analysis of a wide variety of visually based media forms in advertising (print and film based), situation comedy, television drama, documentary, quiz/game shows, web pages. It can also be useful in terms of discussing sport on television. Old Trafford, the home of Manchester United, is commonly talked of as 'the theatre of dreams', for instance. It has been regarded as important in multimedia presentations in which a diversity of images have been constructed within a frame to attract the user (text, colour, perspective, depth, lighting, animation, sound etc.) and offer them clear advice on how to navigate the rest of the presentation.

Mise en scène has enormous importance in film and is the source of a range of debates about the *auteur* of the film text. It is primarily associated with the 'style' of particular filmmakers. It differs from the technical codes of composition such as camera angle, lighting and so on, though it is obviously related to them.

Mise en scène concentrates on: setting, props, codes of non-verbal communication, dress codes, movement in the frame (panning, zooming, shot, reverse shot, etc. in film and television), and eye movements (direction of gaze) in print-based environment.

Technical codes of composition (paradigms) are: shot size, camera angle, lens type, composition, focus, lighting codes, colour and film stock codes.

In essence, it is concerned with the *interaction of images within the frame*.

The trope

THE visual image has to attract attention to itself. To do so it uses a whole range of textual embellishments. The term which describes all the decorative and rhetorical effects of the text is 'trope'. The image, then, becomes defamiliarised (Russian formalism) or made strange (Brecht) or foregrounded (Jakobsen).

The following are examples of typical tropes.

THE VISUAL SIMILE.   Advertisements regularly visualise something as being like something else. You may know the famous photograph 'Le Violin d'Ingres' (1924) in which the photographer, Man Ray, plays with a rear view of the female form to produce a representation of a violin. Or his equally famous 'Glass Tears' (c. 1930). Both are very common as postcards in craft shops.

THE VISUAL METAPHOR.   This works by condensing two visual images into a new image. Morphing is an excellent example and is a common feature of sci-fi films, modern horror films and many film advertisements. It works by violating the physical reality of one image by the imposition of another image through a process of blending to create a response. These responses can vary: surprise (how clever) or shock (how appalling) or funny (how *risqué*) depending on the function of the media product.

Surrealism has been an important feature of advertising imagery through eye grabbing visual paradoxes. The sexual metaphor has been much used to attract attention to products especially in relation to cars, food and drink products. The Barthesian concept of 'relay function' is very important to the metaphor in that the visual images are nearly always supported by audio or text to draw attention to the preferred reading.

Software multimedia design programs such as Macromedia's Director are clearly based on the cluster of metaphors based traditionally on the stage (cast, stage, behaviour etc.). In multimedia presentation generally the designer will often use a controlling metaphor to attract the audience and create coherence in the production. A much-used example is the television screen as a metaphor for the user who can switch or change channels by clicking various icons such as the channel changer (often supported by audio clicks).

The most arresting effects are often created from small distortions to the existing image.

THE VISUAL PUN.   This 'plays' on the different meanings of the symbol in which the alternatives are equally possible. So in many advertisements objects such as flames, doughnuts or fried eggs, not only represent themselves but also represent the brand. S4C's (the Welsh television channel) flaming dragon, for instance, is an example of metaphor and a pun which also substitutes for both Wales and the television station.

METONYMY AND SYNECDOCHE.   Both are forms of visual substitution: the fog in black and white films as a substitute for London as 'the smoke'; the use of the bowler hat and brolly to substitute for the English gentleman in *The Avengers*; the use by Ripley in the *Alien* series of films of a huge weapon to substitute for her revenge; or the regular use of parts of women's bodies to substitute for sexual availability.

A metonym, then, is a figure of speech in which the thing really meant is represented by something which can substitute for it. Words can be metonyms, for example, the press (for all newspapers) and the stage (for all aspects of theatre). Photographs can be metonyms: starving African children substituting for the general African situation. These kinds of substitution are, like stereotyping, a kind of shorthand and therefore can be associated with the politics of representation.

HYPERBOLE AND LITOTES.   The use of exaggerated size (hyperbole) is very common, especially in advertisements but also in children's films, for instance. Its opposite is miniaturisation (litotes). The *Lord of the Rings* trilogy (2002–2004) uses this extensively.

The growth of animation techniques encourages this, as does the ability of computer-generated imagery (CGI) to manipulate 'reality'. Changing the size of the central character (or part of the character, especially the face) so that it seems to come towards us is a common feature of magazine covers.

PERSONIFICATION AND SYNAESTHESIA.   Abstract ideas are presented in terms of people (personification) or animals (anthropomorphism). It is a key component of animation in the sense that the aim of animation is 'breathing life' into the material or inanimate world to create an impression of reality.

Synaesthesia goes further in seeking to mix one kind of sense impression in terms more appropriate to a different sense. It is a key component of the television and film environment which, as yet anyway, cannot smell things, so smelliness is represented metaphorically in a variety of visual ways. Much the same applies to comic representations where a whole variety of senses have to be represented visually through drawn lines (hence snoring bubbles, thought bubbles, dreaming bubbles, use of fonts, motion lines etc).

REPETITION AND PARALLELISM.   In the print-based environment patterns of colours, forms and shapes can create the visual equivalent of verbal rhyme.

Film has its own term for this: *mise en abime*. This refers to texts in which there is reduplication of images. The signifiers in a text or subtext mirror each other. The film within a film is a common presentational device: *The Truman Show* – life and the media; *The French Lieutenant's Woman* – narrative within narrative.

Repetition in a number of forms is a constant feature of advertising.

ANTITHESIS.   This refers to visual ideas which contrast with each other, often associated with binary opposites as a structural or narrative device:

- the use of black and white with colour is often related to the past/present;
- the contrast of clothes/material possessions and nakedness is used in media texts of all kinds;
- contrast of male and female in terms of muscularity or the contrast of a man using women's dress codes and vice versa.

CHIASMUS.   This is the cross-over of visual ideas. For example:

- in *Absolutely Fabulous*, the television programme, the mother and daughter usually exchange roles;
- in the film *ET*, the child-like alien is shown to have adult/human wisdom.

Semiotic Analysis

C HANDLER (2001) OFFERS THE FOLLOWING ADVICE TO HIS STUDENTS WHEN embarking upon the semiotic analysis of media texts:

'I strongly recommend detailed comparison and contrast of paired texts dealing with a similar topic: this is a lot easier than trying to analyse a single text. It may also help to use an example of semiotic analysis by an experienced practitioner as a model for your own analysis'.

Identifying the text

WHEREVER possible, include a copy of the text with your analysis of it, noting any significant shortcomings of the copy. Where including a copy is not practicable, offer a clear description that would allow someone to recognise the text easily if they encountered it themselves.

Briefly describe the medium used, the genre to which the text belongs and the context in which it was found. Consider your *purposes* in analysing the text. This will affect which questions seem important to you among those offered below.

- Why did you choose this text? Your purposes may reflect your values: how does the text relate to your own values?
- How does the sign vehicle you are examining relate to the type of text? Is it one among many copies (e.g. a poster) or virtually unique (e.g. an actual painting)? How does this influence your interpretation?
- What are the important signifiers and what do they signify?
- What is the system within which these signs make sense?

MODALITY:

- What reality claims are made by the text?
- Does it allude to being fact or fiction?

- What references are made to an everyday experiential world?
- What modality markers are present?
- How do you make use of such markers to make judgements about the relationship between the text and the world?
- Does the text operate within a realist representational code?
- To *whom* might it appear realistic?
- 'What does transparency keep obscure?'

PARADIGMATIC ANALYSIS:

- To which class of paradigms (medium, genre, theme) does the whole text belong?
- How might a change of medium affect the meanings generated?
- What might the text have been like if it had formed part of a different genre?
- What paradigm sets do each of the signifiers used belong to? For example, in photographic, televisual and filmic media, one paradigm might be shot size.
- Why do you think each signifier was chosen from the possible alternatives within the same paradigm set? What values does the choice of each particular signifier connote?
- What signifiers from the same paradigm set are noticeably absent?
- What contrasted pairs seem to be involved (e.g. male/female, active/passive)?
- Which of those in each pairing seems to be the 'marked' category?
- Is there a central opposition in the text?
- Apply the commutation test (reversing the terms) in order to identify distinctive signifiers and to define their significance. This involves an imagined substitution of one signifier for another of your own, and assessing the effect.

SYNTAGMATIC ANALYSIS:

- What is the syntagmatic structure of the text?
- Identify and describe syntagmatic structures in the text which take forms such as narrative, argument or montage.
- How does one signifier relate to the others used (do some carry more weight than others)?
- How does the sequential or spatial arrangement of the elements influence meaning?
- Are there formulaic features that have shaped the text?
- If you are comparing several texts within a genre look for a shared syntagm.
- How far does identifying the paradigms and syntagmatic structures help you?

RHETORICAL TROPES:

- What tropes (e.g. metaphors and metonyms) are involved?
- How are they used to influence the preferred reading?

INTERTEXTUALITY:

- Does it allude to other genres?
- Does it allude to or compare with other *texts* within the genre?

- How does it compare with treatments of similar *themes* within other genres?
- Does one code within the text (such as a linguistic caption to an advertisement or news photograph) serve to 'anchor' another (such as an image)? If so, how?

SEMIOTIC CODES:

- Do the codes have double, single or no articulation?
- Are the codes *analogue* or *digital*?
- Which conventions of its genre are most obvious in the text?
- Which codes are *specific* to the medium?
- Which codes are *shared* with other media?
- How do the codes involved relate to each other (e.g. words and images)?
- Are the codes *broadcast* or *narrowcast*?
- Which codes are notable by their *absence*?
- What relationships does the text seek to establish with its readers?
- How direct is the mode of address and what is the significance of this?
- How else would you describe the mode of address?
- What cultural assumptions are called upon?
- To whom would these codes be most familiar?
- What seems to be the *preferred reading*?

The Idea in Action

IN *TRIGGER HAPPY* STEVEN POOLE (2000) MAKES THE POINT THAT '*VIDEOGAMES TALK to us with signs*' and that '*they constitute a kaleidoscopic,* prestissimo *exercise in semiotics, which is the everchanging interaction of signs*'. To argue his point he uses the playing screen of Pac-Man which he suggests is a symbolic system of signs waiting to be used. He categorises the screen as follows:

1. The little disc is Pac-Man the character. He is a *symbol* in that the circle can be said to represent him.
2. He is animated and moves about the screen. Part of him opens and shuts like a mouth. So part of him is an *icon* in that it resembles (or looks like) a mouth.
3. He is situated in what appears to be a maze, which is an *indexical sign* pointing to a route to be taken or not taken.
4. The dots on the screen are also *symbolic* in that they represent the food which Pac-Man munches with his mouth.
5. The jellies with eyes are both *symbols* and *icons* (as the eyes are well defined). The eyeballs have mobile pupils. Where the eyes point is where the jellies with eyes will go next so they are an *indexical* sign. The jellies are to be avoided if Pac-Man's search for food is not to end in death.
6. The smaller versions of Pac-Man below the screen are the lives which the character has left so they function symbolically and indexically (in that they point to the number of lives left).

7. Near the corner of the maze there are large dots (blobs). Their increased size tells you that they function indexically to earn a bonus for Pac-Man.

8. The blobs also function as 'power ups' which enable Pac-Man to chase jellies with eyes. So they are a second order sign – a sign about a sign. It allows a temporary enhancement of the character.

9. The cherries below the screen also act as a power up. They are iconic in that they look like what they are: food to be munched for more energy. They are also indexical in that they point to the future appearance of a symbol about other symbols.

Poole uses this example to argue that:

1. Videogames are complex sign systems.

2. For the user to play the game they must experience these signs and the complex ways in which they interact.

3. Users learn to interact by playing.

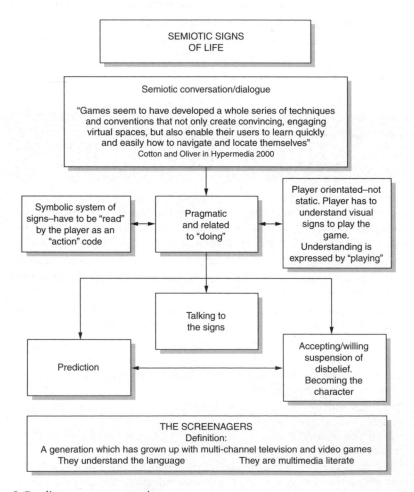

Figure 2 Reading computer game signs

4. The user takes on the point of view of Pac-Man to play the game, has to understand the 'rules' and makes predictions about possible consequences.

5. This identification of the user with the character is typical of videogames.

6. Timing is an essential feature.

   a. Pressing a button at the right time and good reactions are essential user qualities.

   b. Users need to develop a sense of strategic timing to deploy skills over time.

   c. Part of the pleasure of gaming comes from alternate periods of anxiety and satisfaction. Gaming sessions need to be broken up into periods of suspense and periods of shock.

7. Characters are an important feature because of the subjective viewpoint.

The Idea Today

SEMIOTICS HAS A CENTRAL CONCERN WITH MEANING MAKING PRACTICES ACROSS A variety of academic disciplines though it has unsettled many academics by the breadth of its claims. Traditional semiotics concerned itself with textual analysis in a formal manner, which crushes the aesthetic response to a text under a welter of terminology. It tends to assume that meaning is explicable only through textual structures that the reader interprets as nimbly and ably as she/he can. More recent versions of semiotics have attempted to address the social position of the reader.

Chandler (2001) lists the strengths of the semiotic approach as follows:

1. It foregrounds and problematises the process of representation.

2. That 'obvious', 'natural', 'universal', 'common-sense' assertions about our world are concerned with representational systems which are socially constructed.

3. As such they are subject to the processes of mediation. Whenever we are in the presence of a sign we are in the presence of sets of values and ideas which helped motivate its construction.

4. Signs then become sites of struggle over meanings. They are the places in which meaning is actively constructed.

5. They have the potential to be read in different ways but those readings are constrained by sets of codes and conventions.

6. Our sense of identity can be established through signs. It can help focus on how we make sense of ourselves.

7. It was an important way in which dominant signs could be challenged especially for women in early developments in the challenge to patriarchy.

8. It helped undo the invidious distinction between high and popular culture to help us avoid the privileging of one type of discourse over another one.

9. It can help develop more ways of communicating through a variety of media (spoken, video, image) rather than privileging the written mode.

Chandler (2001) also discusses some of the criticisms. Most of these are concerned with structuralist semiotics.

1. It is the subjective and assertive criticism of texts from a formalist viewpoint.

2. It creates significance for texts which are not worth the bother and in some way threatens the existence of those that are.

3. Semiotics needs support from other approaches to shed light on how people in particular social contexts actually interpret texts.

4. The idea that we 'read' all signs has become a cliché. Hence we become 'health literate' or 'computer literate'. Some also have argued in relation to photography and audiovisual material that most of the conventions make a good deal of sense to the first time viewer (Messaris 1997).

5. Analysis pretends to be objective when in fact it is subjective. It also creates its own jargon, which is impenetrable to the outsider.

6. There is a tendency to use semiotic analysis as a simple exercise in elaborating the codes at play in the text to reveal the 'real' world.

Psychoanalytic Approaches

The Idea

SEMIOLOGY HAS SOME CONNECTION TO PSYCHOANALYSIS. WHAT IT DOES IS TO offer a way of interpreting signs of an image in relation, not to particular referent systems, dominant codes or mythologies, but rather in relation to the unconscious and its dynamics. It is a huge field of endeavour for cultural theorists. Most of the key ideas are derived from Freud, in particular scopophilia, subjectivity, the unconscious mind, dreams, sexuality. These ideas were further developed and added to by the French writer Jacques Lacan (1977). He included the ideas of phallocentrism, the mirror stage, the imaginary, the gaze and the symbolic. Each of these ideas will be briefly introduced.

Scopophilia

FREUD suggested that pleasure in looking was one of the basic drives with which young children who were sighted were born. It is one of the key components of modern culture, addicted as it is to the visual. It is not surprising, then, that film in particular has been a focus for many commentators. Films manipulate the visual, the spatial and the temporal world of the viewers by structuring their way of looking and structuring the ways the film looks at the spectator. It follows that film can on the one hand very powerfully address the sense of ourselves while at the same time have the potential to distance and objectify what is looked at. This process is described as *voyeurism*. There has been much analysis on gendered spectatorship in film (Mulvey 1975).

Subjectivity

THIS refers to the fact that we make sense of the world in a whole range of complex and often non-rational ways of understandings. We fantasise, feel, dream, wish, hope, take pleasure and can feel rejection, dejection, repulsion. We can be ambivalent, contradictory, fractious, panic-stricken and in love. Sometimes we feel things that appear to be beyond words. Psychoanalytic approaches to media texts focus on such subjective and emotional states of mind.

The unconscious mind

FREUD distinguished between the conscious mind, which consists of all the mental processes of which we aware, the preconscious mind, which contains memories that can be called into consciousness under certain circumstances and the unconscious mind, which contains our biologically based instincts or drives. Among these drives were the drive for sex, the drive for aggression, the drive towards death. While we are aware of what is going on in our conscious mind, our feelings, motivations and decisions can be powerfully affected by our preconscious and unconscious minds. The influence of the latter categories could be seen, Freud argued, in areas such as dreams, apparent accidents (synchronicity), myths and stories and parapraxis (slips of the tongue or 'Freudian slips').

Dreams

THE major function of dreams was the fulfilment of wishes. There were two aspects to the content of dreams: the *manifest* content (what the dreamer remembered) and the *latent* content (what the manifest content represented or wished for). There was a set of transference processes from the latent to the manifest called the *dream-work*:

1. *Displacement.* A process which altered whatever we were really bothered about into something or someone else.
2. *Condensation.* A process which combines different factors into one aspect of the manifest content. In essence, it is a metaphorical process. It is particularly evident that the surrealists (such as Salvador Dali) were interested in the visual aspects of this.
3. *Symbolisation.* A process by which one object comes to represent another.
4. *Secondary elaboration.* A process by which the elements of the latent content are drawn into a logical story.

Defence mechanisms

ACCORDING to Freud, these are the mechanisms which we use to protect ourselves from painful, frightening or guilty feelings.

1. *Denial.* The refusal to admit or face up to an unpleasant fact or event.
2. *Repression.* The inability to remember such events.
3. *Displacement.* Redirecting a strong emotion such as jealousy from one person to another.
4. *Reaction formation.* The adoption of a position which is exactly the opposite of what we really feel.
5. *Sublimation.* The channelling of strong emotion into creative activity.
6. *Regression.* The use of child-like behaviours to comfort ourselves.

Sexuality

FREUD proposed that psychological development takes place in fixed stages. Sexuality, as understood by Freud, refers to a child's libido and the pleasure which the child takes in his/her organs.

1. *The oral stage* (Year 1). The focus is the mouth, especially in breast-feeding. This provides comfort and reassurance. Such characteristics can be carried through into adulthood and manifested in activities such as comforters, thumb sucking, smoking and oral sex.

2. *The anal stage* (Years 2–3). The awareness of the child has developed enough to recognise that their wishes can bring them into conflict with the demands of the outside world. It tends to come to a head around the issue of potty training. It is suggested that aspects of character can be developed in this stage, such as obsessive tidiness, punctuality, respect for authority (anal-retentive) or messy, disorganised and rebellious (anal-expulsive).

3. *The phallic stage* (Years 3–6). The focus shifts to the genitals as gender awareness develops. The child recognises the growing separation from the gendered parents. Freud developed the *Oedipus complex* to explain this: essentially this stated that at an *unconscious* level the child has sexual feelings for his mother and desires to kill his father. Freud felt it was the most important stage in that it was the stage in which boys began to repress their feelings for the mother and sought to imitate the father. He proposed that girls had what he described as 'penis envy' (when they saw that boys had one) which is sublimated into the wish to have a baby.

Phallocentrism

THE concept of the phallus as opposed to the object itself represents a subject position which suggests that the masculine position is to look and the feminine to be looked at. It suggests an 'active' role for the male and a 'passive' role for the female. In this opposition the preferred term is the male subject position and this idea proposes that the world of media representations is structured around this difference.

Mirror stage

ACCORDING to Lacan, babies go through a mirror stage when they recognise an image in a mirror as their self. When they do, Lacan argues that they *mis*-recognise in that the baby knows it is not themselves but an image of themselves. The mirror is and is not themselves; it is recognition and misrecognition. This is the founding point of the *imaginary*: the way in which we relate to represented objects. This idea was further developed by Louis Althusser and used in Judith Williamson's account of advertising and the powers it had in producing a sense of the spectator's self (Williamson 1978).

The gaze

LACAN'S version of the gaze is culturally constituted. It is the visuality into which we are born and is adopted by us as a way of seeing the world. It reminds us that all things pass: that life is fleeting and only a series of glimpses. These glimpses (signs) are substitutes for the real thing. Signs are a mark of absence. In this sense they are *symbolic*. They are different to the things to which they refer. Such a view means that we are never in control of the sign. Men and women can look but neither is in control of the look. This can break down the simple binary distinction that men look and women appear, as suggested by phallocentrism. The meaning of the sign can be contested. Three areas which have become sites of contestation are fantasy, gay and queer identity, and masquerade.

FANTASY AND DESIRE. Fantasy is located between the conscious and unconscious. Fantasy is where the transactions between these zones take place. It explores what has been unsaid, silenced, made invisible and covered over. Its central concerns are with inverting elements of this world and recombining them in the stories we tell to give ourselves pleasure or to understand our worlds. It is often described as a kind of staging of wishes and desires. The implications in terms of cinematic/media concepts such as *mise en scène* should be clear. The fantasising about what has been lost or neglected is called *desire*. In many media representations, such as Hollywood cinema, there are traces of non-dominant ways of seeing both in the film and in its audience.

QUEER IDENTITY. *'Faced with a media world where heterosexuality reigns virtually unchallenged, queer audiences have rapidly learned the survival skills of refashioning heterosexual images to suit our own purposes, reworking them with an adroit subversiveness until they speak to our needs and desires'* (Medhurst 1998).

Medhurst advises that you should put yourself into the film in some way. In doing so you will be attending to its *compositional modality* by engaging with its form, organisation and composition from a viewpoint of your own choosing. It allows the spectator to fantasise on the range of subject positions within a film so that as a spectator you do not take up one dominant viewpoint but can be positioned in ways which suit individual needs and wishes.

In this way fantasy can become powerfully subversive.

MASQUERADE. The idea of masquerade is that womanliness could be assumed and worn as a mask. It is not natural but constructed. It can be taken on and off in the same way as a mask. In this sense it is very similar to the idea of the persona which is also a constructed identity. It could therefore be played with through mimicry and parody. The idea has a longer history than the media and can be related to theatre, poetry and dramatic presentation generally. The interplay of the 'real' person and the assumed 'persona' of a soap opera character is of particular interest in debates about television: the character can be like the 'real' person or different to them in a range of contexts (announcing career changes or doing a magazine interview as the character for instance).

It could be marked by such strategies as:

1. *Excess.* The exaggeration of womanliness so that the audience becomes aware of the representation of the woman's body as significant. In the film *Erin Brockovitch* Julia Roberts constantly draws attention to her body in a way which parodies other previous appearances in the context of a film based on a real life story of a woman's struggle to right a wrong in her society.

2. *Construction of identity.* A good example would be the work of the American photographer Cindy Sherman who dresses in a variety of ways (props, make up, hairstyle, dress, comportment, filmic and photographic styles) to explore her sense of who she is.

3. *Repetition.* Especially through intertextual reference building on previous representations to copy and mimic. Parody in this sense always points to what is not present in the representation.

Post-structuralism

THIS is a theory which gained much ground in the 1970s and which reacted against the systematic, theoretically rigid close analysis of signs as offered by the structuralist analysis of texts. It can be closely linked to psychoanalytic theory, especially through the idea of subjectivity. It is most commonly associated with the work of Jacques Derrida and the idea of deconstruction. This philosophical idea should not be confused with the activity of deconstructing media texts into their presentational codes and conventions. The principal result has been to shift attention away from the text towards the interaction of the text with the media audience.

Deconstruction

THIS is a method of reading and theory of language that seeks to subvert, dismantle and destroy any notion that a text or signifying system has any boundaries, margins, coherence, unity, determinate meaning, truth or identity. Associated with the writings of Jacques Derrida, deconstruction is the way in which signifiers in a text constantly battle for supremacy. Because every term can be read referentially or rhetorically, the reader is unable to arrive at any ultimate decision and is left in the double bind of trying to master a text that has no boundaries and cannot be totalised. Not only is *aporia* or *undecidability* endemic to texts, it is thematised in them.

The Idea Today

IN CONTEMPORARY PSYCHOLOGY FREUD'S IDEAS HAVE NOT BEEN WELL RECEIVED. THE emphasis on sexuality has proved an embarrassment and feminists have objected to ideas of penis envy, for example. His ideas have proved difficult to substantiate. However, his ideas about subjectivity have provided cultural theorists with a framework for analysis of texts and artists, designers, advertisers and filmmakers with a rich fund of inspiration. Not too surprising in that his theories are drawn from the stories that his patients have constructed for him in therapy sessions. Story-telling is the crucial element of the approach.

Psychoanalytic criticism draws attention to:

1. The way in which the conscious mind constantly seeks to discipline subjectivity through what Freud describes as its 'executive' function.
2. The instabilities of the unconscious, which always threaten to break or leak out, rebel and cross boundaries.
3. The process of subjectivity. It is never fully formed but always in a process in our symbolic encounters with the world.
4. The way the audience is centrally implicated in the construction of a text. *'Visual discourses already have possible positions of interpretation (from which they "make sense") embedded in them, and the subjects bring their own subjective desires and capacities to the "text" which enable them to take up positions of identification in relation to its meaning'* (Hall 1999).
5. The ways in which sexual difference is established and (often precariously) maintained.

Postmodernism

THE USUAL STARTING POINT IS TO DESCRIBE POSTMODERNISM AS A TERM BY CON-trasting it with modernism. In one sense, it is the idea that modernism, as a cultural movement, is now in the past.

What is modernism?

MODERNISM is a preoccupation with *modernity* (modern-ness) characterised by novelty, technical progress, focus on form, and individual experience of time and space. Historically, modernism developed out of the Victorian industrial period, as a cultural response to technological innovation and social change. In the 1930s it was associated with movements such as futurism where there was an emphasis on mechanical repro-duction and the machine. Technology would be harnessed to relieve human beings of the dangerous and repetitive tasks of industrialisation. Modernism was associated with progressive political positions and the pursuit of a better world capable of yielding better living conditions for all. The 'master narrative' was progress from one state to another better state.

The pursuit of 'truth' and the ability of human beings to seek it in a variety of rational ways can be seen in the arts – for instance, T.S. Eliot, Samuel Beckett, James Joyce, Virginia Woolf and Picasso's cubist paintings. It can be closely linked to the avant-garde in that it ignores the possibility of popular culture being read in the same way as texts produced by 'significant' artists. Such artists concentrated on form and reflexivity to foreground the processes of artistic construction. They attacked traditional realism and traditional modes of representation in order to reveal the 'truth' of the human condi-tion through the production of 'high art'. Modernist film, for instance, is profoundly anti-illusionist through the foregrounding of editing techniques (e.g. Eisenstein and montage). Modernist filmmakers emphasised rather than hid the 'collisions' produced by editing. They aimed to 'make strange' and 'distance' or 'alienate' the audience from the representation. They emphasised the reactionary nature of conventional realistic forms and sought to make the audience question what they saw. Crucially they questioned surface appearance to create a critical and questioning stance in their audiences.

What constitutes the shift from modern to postmodern?

THE answer to this question lies in the loss of faith in the idea of progress dating from about the 1960s associated with the intellectual and aesthetic debates and practices that have dominated the 1980s and 1990s. If modernism stems from a fundamental belief in progress and the pursuit of truth through representational practice then postmodernism is about the absence of such an overarching concept. It challenges the assumptions of such an *essentialist* view and rejects 'grand narratives'.

'Grand narratives have become barely credible . . . Neither liberalism, economic or political, nor the various Marxisms emerge from [the last] two centuries untainted by accusations of crimes against humanity. We can make a list of names, names of places, persons, dates, capable of illustrating and substantiating our suspicion. Following Theodor Adorno I have used the name "Auschwitz" to signify the extent to which recent Western philosophy seems inconsistent as regards the "modern" project of the emancipation of humanity' (Lyotard 1988).

- The anti-nuclear and environmental movements bears witness to the loss of faith in technology as a liberating force.
- There has been a loss of faith in a single authoritative worldview. There is no religious consensus and the world may even be more divided than ever on the basis of religion. Marxist sociological questioning of scientific practice had not created a more ethical or more moral or more just society.
- There has been an equivalent loss of individual identity and any striving for new means of expression that can encompass it. Hence the key components of a postmodernist approach to representational practice: pastiche, parody, allusion, intertextual references (see Intertextuality, p. 5), bricolage, carnivalesque in all art forms.

PASTICHE.   Pastiche borrows narrative and stylistic conventions and iconography from other works, usually of the same genre. Such works emphasise recombination at the expense of generating meaningful themes themselves. The diner scene in Quentin Tarantino's *Pulp Fiction* (1994) is a pastiche of 1950s American popular culture representations. Pastiche is a very important element of advertising which regularly adopts the stylistic conventions of other works, for example in representations of the classical myths in modern contexts. The Icarus myth has been used in this way to advertise deodorant.

PARODY AND ALLUSION.   A humorous imitation of another (often serious) work of art, genre or style. Parody always draws attention to the original representation. The modern world seems fascinated by our ability to refer back to ourselves in an unending mirroring process. It is in this sense that media texts are said to be self-reflexive. Advertisements which aim to present goods or services to us are ripe for parody, because the characters, their modes of speaking, and the typefaces and fonts used are already excessive in terms of their visual design. Parodies can mock in order to make us think but they can be affectionate in their reference to previous ad campaigns: nostalgia for the 1960s is very prevalent in lots of modern advertising for cleaning materials. The use of parody suggests that audiences have a wide repertoire of styles and allusions that they can recognise. The fact that consumers recognise a lot about advertisements has become something of a cliché in the term 'advertising literate'. Certainly once audiences are familiar with a film genre then it becomes a target for parody. Mel Brooks's *Spaceballs* (1987) sends up George Lucas's *Star Wars* (1977). Parody always draws attention to the audience's role in the construction of meaning.

BRICOLAGE. Lévi-Strauss's term for the appropriation of pre-existing materials which are ready-to-hand is widely used to refer to the intertextual authorial practice of adopting and adapting signs from other texts. It is most visible in contemporary advertising which frequently makes use of sounds and images from 'high art' and links them to goods and services. It is a feature of web pages where 'cut 'n' paste' is regarded as a necessary (and licensed practice in some cases as many designers allow the use of their images for free) method of construction. It can be found in borrowings from classic cinema which glance at or even draw heavily on recycled meanings. *Wild at Heart* (1990) by David Lynch uses borrowed images from Hitchcock and *The Wizard of Oz* (dir. Victor Fleming).

CARNIVALESQUE. The term is derived from the work of Mikhail Bahktin (1968) who sought in his writings to explore the significance of carnival in the Renaissance and Middle Ages as a form of popular culture. In it he found that people were able to challenge and oppose aspects of the dominant culture. The key feature of the carnivalesque is laughter, in which traditional authority patterns can be turned upside down. It emphasises the grotesque, distortion and the powerful pleasures of the 'vulgar'. If high culture emphasised the mouth then 'low' or 'popular' culture emphasised the anus as source of pleasure. It has proved to be particularly popular to some media theorists such as John Fiske (1989a, b) in celebrating the resistance of audiences to dominant media messages.

In such approaches there is an emphasis on transgression and boundary crossing which has been useful in the debates about gender representation (see Active Audiences and Reception Theories, p. 164).

The Idea in Action

IN A HIGH STATUS ELITE CULTURE THE VALUE OF NEWS TEXTS DOMINATES OVER LOW status popular culture. The early BBC radio broadcasts assumed an educated audience and used RP (received pronunciation) and were part of the way in which the audience were provided with authoritative information about the world. It would not have been acceptable to use slang or show emotion.

In the modern mass media there is a greater diversity of accents among news presenters (still not enough some would argue) which reflect regional accents in regional news programmes. This can be argued to reflect a breakdown of high culture in that a diversity of accents can now be heard in broadcast media. This can be related to consumerism, in that the audience is more clearly reflected through the representations, and can lead to a sense that standards of news presentation have slipped. Modern media developments assumes a mass audience defined by marketing categories who need to feel at home with the ways in which they are addressed. However, this can create controversies about what is acceptable and what is not in terms of language and presentation. There have been many attempts to make news programmes attractive to 16–24-year-olds.

Cultural practices such as news presentations have had clear conventions until recently; only a few organisations attempted innovation. Until the 1990s television news presentation clearly worked within typical conventions (studio, presenters, outside links, range of topical stories etc.). They were very 'samey'. However, cultural practices play around with form and image under the increasing pressure of competition from other sources of news. Their audience is culturally proficient, has more access to a range of information sources and demands more of them (interactivity, informal and dramatic presentational styles, infotainment, changes of setting). Television news needs to 'hail' new audiences and the consensus of what constitutes news has broken down, become fragmented and susceptible to audience pressure.

Consequently, it is possible to trace a sense of what one critic (Langer 1998) calls 'tabloid television' in which news about celebrity, the lives of ordinary people and personal tragedy is more important than national news etc. He lists a series of propositions:

- Television news is primarily a commodity enterprise run by market-orientated managers who place outflanking the 'competition' above journalistic responsibility and integrity.
- Television news is in the business of entertainment, like any other television product, attempting to pull audiences for commercial not journalistic reasons.
- Television news has set aside the values of professional journalism in order to indulge in the presentation of gratuitous spectacles.
- Television is overly dependent on filmed images that create superficiality and lack information content.
- Television news traffics in trivialities and deals in dubious emotionalism.
- Television news is exploitative.

To this list it would be possible to add:

- Television news now concentrates on the 'drama' of the event (tears, laughter, surprise, suspense) routinely using 'ordinary' members of the public caught in unusual situations.
- Television news engages in excessive personalisations of issue by proposing a relationship between the story, the news presenters (as one of us) and the audience especially in relation to the audience participating in the construction of the news. People are regularly invited to phone, text or email their opinions which in themselves become part of the presentation of the story.
- Television news is increasingly tied up with promotional activity of all kinds (by, e.g., stars, celebrities, good causes).

Representations

REPRESENTATION IS A KEY CONCEPT IN THE STUDY OF MEDIA BECAUSE IT IS THE POINT at which audiences engage with the products of the media producers. Aspects of 'reality' such as people, places, objects, events, cultural identities and other abstract concepts are constructed by media producers. Such constructions of reality may be monomodal (e.g. speech or writing or still pictures) or multimodal (i.e. words and still pictures or moving images which combine sound and pictures in time or multi-media combining spoken or printed word, music, sound effects, visual images in still or animated form).

The term refers to the *processes* involved as well as to its *products*. Representation involves:

1. how identities are constructed within the text;
2. how they are constructed by the processes of production to attract the attention of the audience;
3. the reception of such representations by people.

A key concern in the study of representation is with the way in which systems of representation are made to seem 'natural'. *Systems of representation* are the means by which the concerns of *ideologies* are framed to create ways of looking at texts. Such value systems 'position' their subjects.

The main methods of exploring textual representations are semiotics and content analysis.

Semiotic analysis (see p. 39) foregrounds the process of representation by 'unmasking' or 'laying bare' or 'deconstructing' the underlying codes of construction. Our media experience of the 'real' is always represented in that it is encoded. Representation always involves 'the construction of reality' from a particular point of view. They become familiar through constant reuse and come to feel 'natural' and unmediated. Barthes describes these as 'myths'. Representations require the audience to actively decode them or interpret them. We make modality (how realistic? how typical? how shocking? etc.) judgements about them.

Content analysis (see p. 160) – because representation is unavoidably selective and foregrounds some things, backgrounds others and leaves some things out altogether, it is possible to count the number of instances of a person, object, idea, event etc., to analyse patterns of representations in texts. Realists focus on the 'correspondence' of such representations to 'objective' reality (in terms of 'truth', 'accuracy' and 'distortion'), whereas constructivists focus on whose realities are being represented and whose are being denied.

Hermeneutic suspicion is the process of asking questions about the meaning of appearances. The questions posed by Richard Dyer (1993) are a useful starting point:

1. What sense of the world is it (the media text) making?
2. What does it imply is typical of the world and what is deviant?
3. Who is speaking? For whom? To whom?
4. What does it represent to us and why – how do we respond to this representation of the world?

These allow the consideration of:

1. Whether more than one person/agent is speaking in any text and whether they are addressing or appealing to more than one audience. This raises issues about the layering of address or appeal.
2. The categories of representations (e.g. young people). It raises issues of their typicality (or representativeness) and recognises that such categories are only selections from the world chosen for their saliency (or relevance).
3. It raises the issue that some human agency has made these choices for motivated reasons. Alternative choices could have been made. Representations, in such a view, are not right or wrong but sites of conflict over meaning.

The Idea in Action

THE STUDY OF REPRESENTATIONS CAN BE UNDERTAKEN IN THREE MAIN WAYS: THRO genre; through the study of a specific media form; and through the st theme.

Genre – Documentary film

CENTRAL to documentary film is the notion that it focuses o
people and events, often in a social context, thus offering
engaging with the way in which these have been represe
persuade or inform but many recent styles of documenta
and have been described as *infotainment*. Generally, they
mation about the world and will often make a case, pres

a solution. As such they seek to present the facts and seek to organise the evidence in compelling ways. They are based on the concept of *realism*.

No account of realism progresses very far before it recognises that realism, like all other approaches to art, relies on a system of conventions of representation. It is a representational practice composed of different strands. In news and documentary there is what John Corner calls *'straight imaging of the real'* (1991) and in fictional film what he calls *'imaginatively convincing'*. In film, a Bazin film critic writing in the 1960s pointed out that the drive behind successful technical developments such as synchronised sound and deep-focus cinematography was to give the viewer as perfect an illusion of reality as possible.

What we see on television or film documentary is a succession of images organised as a story using a range of techniques. We expect some of them (news and outside broadcasts, current affairs reports and factual documentaries) to be an accurate reflection of the real world. We expect them to present truthful information about the world, to be objective and accurate historically. As such they raise the question of mediation. We can ask to what extent a documentary or news report is truthful. Have the events described been manipulated in any way? In an age which offers media producers the ability to digitalise, manipulate and present images in an even greater variety of ways these become urgent questions.

However, the prime aim of documentary reportage is to present an aspect of the complex reality with which they deal not as a truth there to be observed, but as a social and historical reality which can only be understood in context. It lays no claim to objectivity, but seeks to actively present a case through the structure and organisation of *point of view* (see Narrative, p. 9). It offers an interpretation of the world. A documentary's relation to the real is not that of mirroring. It is a more subtle relation of making contact with the living world through a process of narrative construction. In this sense it can be said to have the dramatic values of tension, conflict, suspense, emotion, surprise. The power that the drama of actuality has is one of using the concentration of the film form to create an experience of the world, its people and its values.

Documentary production techniques include:

1. The use of a narrator/commentator/voice behind the camera to anchor and link the presentation together. They are often the guarantors of authority and have been chosen on the basis of personal voice qualities that appeal to the target audience.

2. The producers use real locations, real people and real events. 'On the spot' and 'being in close proximity' are important production values. Sometimes staging of events is necessary if it enhances the value of the report and conveys more useful information to the audience. Authentic depiction of events beyond the capability technology (as the representation of catastrophic events in the universe) or potential harm to people (as in the case of air raids or nuclear attack) and is generally accepted as a true representation of an event.

    of argument in order to convince. Andrew Tolson (1996) offers such arguments can be constructed in documentary texts:

    This can be factual, definitive, evaluative or advocative.

    is can be in the form of: experts, eye witnesses, voice-over s, maps, diagrams, graphics, written, audio, still pictures,

Stage 3. Justifications.

- Motivational – what is desirable or undesirable, achievable or not, positive or negative.
- Authoritative – they appeal to the authority of the presenter who clearly establishes credentials for the approach. Educates and informs by revealing the 'truth' and brings the unknown into clearer focus.
- Substantive – identification of causality and the presentation of deductions based on the evidence (deductive). Generalisation and classification based on inductive reasoning. Comparative based on analogy or comparisons.

4. They also seek to make the known appear strange and interesting through artistic approaches to add variety.
5. They use fictional devices such as music and credits, montage, seamless editing, reconstructions, open and closed narratives, interwoven storylines.
6. They use the camera to follow/endorse a point of view – increase the reality of the presentation through camera shake, zoom, pan etc.; increase audience sympathy/identification through close-ups and extreme close-ups especially of faces; increase objectivity through the use of hidden cameras and/or using fly-on-the-wall techniques.
7. Modern television documentaries, in particular, seek to entertain and some critics argue that they have lost the central drive of a documentary. Documentary filmmaker Molly Dineen comments, *'I don't know where documentary is going but at the moment it is fast becoming a soap opera in order to keep its place in the schedules'*.

A number of sub-genres have emerged which have proved very popular with audiences:

- Institutional documentaries (e.g. *Children's Hospital*). Key features: setting, celebrity presenter, everyday routine, practices, characters.
- Surveillance footage has been used to construct entertaining programmes (e.g. ITV's *Police, Camera, Action)*. Key features: actuality footage, anchoring commentary, voyeurism.
- Docusoaps (e.g. *Driving School, Airport, The Cruise*). A generic hybrid mixing social realism with drama. Key features: everyday setting, typical problems and challenges, main character, narrative structure using drama values of suspense, laughter and tears. Many of the people (characters) featured have gone on to be celebrities and have forged out a media career.
- Reality television (e.g. *Big Brother, Castaway*). A generic hybrid that adds the game show and talk show elements: a set of contestants (often specially selected), a closed setting, creation of tension, conflict, relationships and drama, tears and confessional talk.
- Drama documentaries (e.g. *Death of a Princess*, ITV). Aims to create as accurately as possible history as it happened. Characters cannot be invented, names have to be real and have to be based on real events. They have often been enormously controversial.
- Video diaries (e.g. BBC *Video Diaries*). These are short intensely personal essays made by amateur filmmakers (members of the public) who tell their own stories. Editing is done professionally with a right of veto by the filmmaker.

A specific media form – animation

ANIMATION draws attention to its represented nature through design, voice, sound effects and music. The animated film has become very important through:

- the continuing global dominance of the Disney Studios;
- the proliferation of cartoons on mainstream television for a variety of audiences;
- the significance of cartoon elements in advertising where it is particularly appropriate. The 'look' of various kinds of animation is distinctive through the creation of colourful characters and impossible yet authentic scenarios/settings. In a short way (typically 30 seconds) the promise of the product can be dramatised to create memorable and enduring product identity;
- the popularity of films influenced by the Japanese Manga tradition;
- its place as a central feature of multimedia approaches. Here, although it still can have cartoon elements, it has other functions for the user of multimedia materials. Animation is used to provide feedback to the user through cursors, rollovers and image effects such as zooming, wiping, dissolving and pixellating. Such animated effects are often (increasingly) supported by music, voice and sound effects. It is a central element in the design of such materials.

The predominant form of animation is drawn and painted. This is described as *cel animation*. An outline is inked onto a sheet of acetate (cel) which is then painted. These cels are photographed one by one in succession to create the impression of motion. It is a slow, laborious process which can be quickened up through the use of computer software such as Adobe's ImageReady.

Clay animation constructs models (they can be clay or plastic) which are gradually moved in a succession of frames to create 'persistence of vision', that is, the impression of motion. The early pioneers of animation discovered the golden formula for the illusion of smooth, natural motion: 24 frames per second.

Computer-generated imagery (CGI) has become a central feature of modern film production. This allows for situations to be filmed which would be impossible in real life. An example would be the shot of the bow of the *Titanic* or the powerful battle scenes in the *Lord of the Rings* trilogy. There are dedicated software programs such as Macromedia's Maya, which provides a wide variety of methods for creating characters, backgrounds and effects at an industry standard, or Flash MX, which allows the non-professional more access.

Some issues in representation

THE cartoon simplifies and exaggerates as a design strategy (Wells 1998). Through the study of the representations the cartoon produces, it is possible to see what lies at the heart of animation: its transformative possibilities. What is at issue in representations is the use to which such transformations are put.

THE BODY.   For example:

- It can be squashed and stretched to fit into all sorts of spaces. It can grow or be miniaturised.
- It can be broken into pieces and reassembled in a different way or linked to other objects.

- Parts of the body can be replaced by other objects as in eggs for eyes or a sausage for a smile or grimace.
- Bodies can be represented as machines and vice versa (personification and anthropomorphism).
- Bodies can have impossible abilities: eyes that stretch on coils, recoiling arms, extending lips. These parts of the face can have a life of their own. They can fly, make impossible movements, experience violence without pain.
- Faces can express extremes of emotion: maniacal grins, slavering chops, grotesque smiles, contortions.
- Parts of bodies can be exaggerated or enlarged producing great contrasts between different physical features.
- The distinction between male, female and animal can be blurred. Age can be manipulated or racial identities changed through image manipulation.

THE FEMINISTIC AESTHETIC.   Women animators developed over a number of years a specific approach to animation. Gillian Lacey of the Leeds Animation Workshop says of the work here that there is *'the use of style that is accessible to a wide audience combined with the creation of cartoon women who do not have huge tits and eyelashes'* (Lacey 1992).

This kind of approach:

- moves the woman from object to subject – in doing so it resists the typical representation of men as doers and women as reactors, or women as objects of the gaze;
- offers a safe place for the exploration of concerns of women in creative contexts which could, if required, exclude men. It could aim to be subversive and challenge patriarchal norms by being in control;
- allows the creation of radical texts which offer the audience greater participation and pleasures;
- allows the exploration of a woman's relationship to her own body; her social interactions; her sense of her place and role; her social and political identity; her own sense of her sexuality, desires, gratifications and creativity.

RACE.   It is very clear that there is self-evident racism in the early history of cartoon caricaturing and such racial stereotyping in the USA was familiar and reassuring to white audiences. Since then, under intensive lobbying, more positive images of black people have emerged: the modern black person, the academic, the policeman/woman etc. In many senses the question of 'good' or 'bad' representations is not the main question; it is the ways in which the debate is about *mis*representation.

One of the preoccupations of cartoon animation has been the Arabian or oriental stereotype. Said (1985) suggests that orientalism is a discourse through which the West has colonised and reinvented the Orient as a mode of 'otherness'. In such a relationship the West is perceived as ideologically superior to the strange alien culture of eastern countries. In films such as *Aladdin*, made by Disney, it is still possible to see these mythic connotations of strangeness, mystery and exoticism which characterise oriental representation. This disguises the complexities of such cultures and allows the view that the West is more enlightened, more technologically advanced and more desperate to stay that way. It has enormous resonances at the time of writing (2003). It clearly raises issues of national and religious identity which in many countries have been part of the agenda of creating a distinctive animation culture which resists Disneyfication to tell their own stories in their own way.

Through the study of a theme – the female body in women's magazines

REPRESENTATIONS of the female body are one of the most densely packed with meaning of all signs in modern society (or perhaps in any society). Although representations of the male body in magazines have begun to appear, it is at the level of the image that the violence of sexism has been experienced. It is at this level that women construct much of their personal identity, and magazines offer role models, heroines and heroes, idols and icons for people's dreams and fantasies and mirror the world back to them. It raises innumerable issues for the reader in terms of control, unattainable ideals, stereotyping, eating disorders, anorexia etc.

Some of the typical codes and conventions of female representation in magazines are as follows:

- Head and body tilting. The tendency is to push forward the head or lean the body towards the camera. This is often emphasised by the lighting.
- The lowering of the head and eyes lowered slightly can be conventionally read as submissive and passive, and an eyelid wink read as a 'come on' sign.
- Child-like, playful, kittenish poses, wide expansive smiles and open eyes can be read as 'cuteness', innocent sexuality, trust. Often when combined with other elements, such as fur, cuddly toys, animals in the *mise en scène*, they can be read as betraying a lack of seriousness.
- Images of bashfulness, casual and trusting gestures, open body postures with the arms behind the body can be read as openness and trust into which a reliance of the goodwill of the onlooker can be read.
- Where hands cover the eyes, lips, parts of the face it can be read as 'licensed withdrawal'. Shadows and veils can perform the same function. All these signs can be read as suggesting obedience, mystery, secrets, intrigue, enigma.
- Where eyes are averted it can suggest shame or secrets.
- An unfocused gaze can suggest sexuality, inner secrets, dreaming.
- Where eyes meet the gaze of the viewer it can be read as a challenge (in much the same way as hands on hips) or as a come on.
- Images of exaggerated emotional display such as tears, laughter, arms in the air can be read as typically female signs in that traditional representations tend to foreground such emotional display by women.

In his study of women's magazine advertisements, Trevor Millum (1975) distinguished between these forms of attention as expressed in the gaze:

- attention directed towards *other people*;
- attention directed to an *object*;
- attention directed to *oneself*;
- attention directed to the *reader/camera*;
- attention directed into *middle distance*, as in a state of reverie;
- direction or object of attention *not discernible*.

He also categorised relationships between those depicted thus:

- *reciprocal attention*: the attention of those depicted is directed at each other;
- *divergent attention*: the attention of those is directed towards different things;

- *object-oriented attention*: those depicted are looking at the same object;
- *semi-reciprocal attention*: the attention of one person is on the other, whose attention is elsewhere.

In his study, Millum found that actors by themselves are likely to look at the reader. Women accompanied by women tend to look into middle distance, while women in mixed groups are more likely to look at people (though *less* so than men are). Women alone tend to regard themselves or to look into middle-distance (Millum 1975). Millum, then, draws attention to the important idea of eyes and the face in media communication and the idea of 'the gaze'.

The gaze

THIS section develops and extends Daniel Chandler's 'Notes on the Gaze' to be found at http://www.aber.ac.uk/media. 'The gaze' (sometimes called 'the look') was originally used in film theory in the 1970s. Media theorists use the term to refer both to the ways in which viewers look at images of people in any visual medium and to the gaze of those depicted in visual texts. In media texts, a genuine exchange of gazes through the textual frame is not possible. The viewer looks at those depicted in the text but cannot be seen by them. Hence the viewing of media texts has a *voyeuristic* aspect. It points to the importance that the viewer attaches to the act of looking and so raises complex issues to do with pleasure, gratification, needs, attraction, modelling etc. It implicates the viewer in the act of looking. A key feature of the gaze is that the object of the gaze is not aware of the current viewer. They may originally have been aware of being filmed or photographed and may be aware that sometimes strangers could subsequently gaze at their image. Only in a general sense do the objects of the gaze grasp the conditions in which their images are used, circulated and consumed. Stars, celebrities and individuals caught in the media spotlight will often contest the use and circulation of their images complaining of intrusion and misrepresentation. Often, as with pictures of people in the developing world, the represented have no idea to what use their representations are put. Such examples raise complex issues about ethics, ownership, intrusion and privacy.

One important area of study seeks to list the different types of 'looker'. A number of aspects of this have been identified.

- *The spectator's gaze*. The viewer engages with the representation – a place, person, animal, or object – in the text.
- *In the space (or frame) of the representation the gaze of one of the participants can be directed at another object, person or place in the representation*. This is often in film and television texts described as the subjective 'point-of-view' shot. It has the function of creating empathy and identification.
- *The gaze of a person* (who could be presented as an object in the frame as in the case of camera pointing at the imagined, or addressed, audience) looking 'out of the frame' as if at the viewer. This is a direct mode of address that is often associated with suitable gestures and postures. There has been controversy in new programmes about such issues in that modern news presenters are said to be too dramatic and prone to extravagant hand gestures rather than presenting their story in accurate, balanced and unemotional ways.

- *The look of the camera*. This is what the camera points at, selects and focuses on. It emphasises the camera as an intermediary between the 'looker' and the 'looked at'. Theorists who have studied photography suggest that photographs are: 'traces of reality' (Sontag), 'quote from reality' (Berger), are 'without a code' (Barthes). However, in the age of digitalisation the 'manufacture' of images has become an important issue.

- *People looking at other people looking at media texts*. Outside the world of the text, the gaze of another individual in the viewer's social world catching the latter in the act of viewing. This raises issues about where people choose to view and whether they should view them. It raises issues concerned with public and private viewing spaces and how such sites can be controlled and regulated. Recent moral panics about stars, celebrities and images of young children have focused on the role of the internet.

- *Audiences within media texts*. Certain kinds of popular televisual texts (such as game, talk, cookery, quiz shows) often include shots of an audience watching those performing in the 'text within a text'. They often have important functions in the show (approve, vote, hiss, boo, applaud, laugh, move from audience to participant etc.). The involvement of different types of audience within the show has been a key feature of more and more televisual shows as interactivity has become more important (e.g. studio audience, audience outside in the pub, street, home, meeting place etc.).

- *Organisational practices*. At the level of media organisation (as in film or magazine or poster production) decisions are made about what looks to employ.

- *Seduction/entrapment*. The viewer can be indirectly addressed by an offer or promise through the gaze though often this needs *anchorage* from the other elements in the representation.

- *A gaze of direct address* which represents a demand for the viewer (as the object of the look) to become involved in some way with the depicted person. Hence the importance of smiling for television newsreaders, and it is common in advertisements and posed magazine photographs.

Paul Messaris (1997) notes that historically, *'direct views into the camera have tended to be the exception rather than the rule in some ads aimed at men'*. However, *'during the past two decades or so, there has been a notable countertrend in male-oriented advertising, featuring men whose poses contain some of the same elements – including the direct view – traditionally associated with women'*. In conventional narrative films, actors only very rarely gaze directly at the camera lens. When they do it is often for comic purposes or a way of engaging with the internal thoughts of the character. Direct addresses to camera are much more common in the world of television than in the world of film. However, in television only certain people are conventionally allowed to address the camera directly, such as newsreaders, programme presenters and those making party political broadcasts or charitable appeals. The usual reason for this is that it connotes directness of approach and its attendant qualities of authority and reliability. However, other research proposes that a full-face shot suggests less expertise than a profile shot since in popular broadcasting those who address the camera directly are typically the reporters and link men, who transmit the news rather than initiate it. The expert, on the other hand, is more often seen either in interview or in discussion, and thus in profile. Unless the speaker may be assumed an expert on some other basis – which the conventional television reporter is not – the probability that he is expert and reliable in what he says will therefore be weighed as greater if he is seen in profile than if he addresses the camera directly. In modern television in the production of news this distinction breaks down slightly in that modern news reporters speak directly to camera not only in the studio where they anchor and link the story but on the spot where they are the expert commentator interpreting the images for the audience. It is important to remember that the same person in different situations can have multiple functions.

Baggaley also comments on the use of the autocue in relation to the full face: *'in the profile condition signs of autocue usage conveyed by a performer's eyes are less apparent'.* Even if an autocue is not being used, the 'unusual intensity' of the speaker's eye contact with the viewer may tend to diminish the speaker's credibility. Argyle (1988) suggests that the direct gaze can signify persuasive intent and an intention to draw the viewer to the represented person. It has an important function in advertising. Messaris (1997) suggests that a direct gaze is likely to enhance the likelihood of both empathy and identification.

The angle of the view, then, has been the focus of much research.

1. Where there are straight lines in a scene (such as in the outside or inside edges of a building or people standing in a line) the image-producer has the option of choosing a frontal angle in which such lines are parallel to the picture plane or of shifting the *horizontal angle* of the depiction to a more oblique point of view (Kress and van Leeuwen 1996).

2. John Tagg argues that frontality is a key technique of 'documentary rhetoric' in photography, offering up what it depicts for *evaluation* (Tagg 1988). He shows that historically the frontal portrait has been associated with the working class, and that frontality is a 'code of social inferiority'. However, in some modern media texts there is a greater sense of confrontation in the gaze especially from women challenging traditional representations. An example might be Robert Mapplethorpe's photographs of Lisa Lyons, the American bodybuilder.

3. High angles (looking down on a depicted person from above) are interpreted as making that person look small and insignificant, and low angles (looking up at them from below) are said to make them look powerful and superior. Kress and van Leeuwen modify this standpoint slightly, arguing that a high angle depicts a relationship in which the producer of the image and the viewer have symbolic power over the person or thing represented, while a low angle depicts a relationship in which the depicted person has power over the image-producer and the viewer. Messaris notes that a low angle combined with a frontal view and a direct gaze at the viewer may be interpreted as overbearing, intimidating or menacing, and that when the intention is to use low angles to suggest noble or heroic qualities, side views are more common (Messaris 1997).

4. Paul Messaris also notes about the view from the back, *'in our real-world interactions with others, this view from the back can imply turning away or exclusion'.* In travel advertisements where there are rear views of people this tends to be either in long-shots of landscapes or in mid-shots or close-ups of semi-naked bodies in seascapes. These function to locate the viewer in the scene, seeing what the subject sees in order to invite curiosity. However, in both, there is an implicit invitation to be part of what is being witnessed.

The Idea Today

T WO INFLUENTIAL WRITERS ON THE GAZE ARE JOHN BERGER (1972) AND LAURA Mulvey (1975).

John Berger

IN *Ways of Seeing*, a book based on a BBC television series, John Berger observed that *'according to usage and conventions which are at last being questioned but have by no means been overcome – men act and women appear. Men look at women. Women watch themselves being looked at'*. He argued that in European art from the Renaissance onwards women were depicted as being *'aware of being seen by a [male] spectator'*. Berger adds that at least from the seventeenth century, paintings of female nudes reflected the woman's submission to *'the owner of both woman and painting'*. He noted that *'almost all post-Renaissance European sexual imagery is frontal – either literally or metaphorically – because the sexual protagonist is the spectator-owner looking at it'*. He advanced the idea that the realistic, 'highly tactile' depiction of things in oil paintings and later in colour photography represented a desire to *possess* the things (or the lifestyle) depicted. This also applied to women depicted in this way. Berger insisted that women were still *'depicted in a different way to men – because the "ideal" spectator is always assumed to be male and the image of the woman is designed to flatter him'*. Such views have been challenged most notably by the art critic Peter Fuller (1980) who challenged the materialist basis to Berger's approach to high art. However, Berger's materialistic views of culture had enormous resonance in the field of cultural production. Writers on representations of women have used Berger's ideas in a variety of ways: Judith Williamson (1978), Gillian Dyer (1982), both on advertising, and Ellen McCracken on women's magazines (1997). Paul Messaris has noted that female models in advertisements addressed to women *'treat the lens as a substitute for the eye of an imaginary male onlooker,'* adding that *'it could be argued that when women look at these ads, they are actually seeing themselves as a man might see them'*. Such advertisements *'appear to imply a male point of view, even though the intended viewer is often a woman. So the women who look at these ads are being invited to identify both with the person being viewed and with an implicit, opposite-sex viewer'* (Messaris 1997).

Laura Mulvey – the male gaze

THE concept derives from a seminal article called 'Visual Pleasure and Narrative Cinema' by Laura Mulvey, a feminist film theorist. She did not undertake empirical studies of actual filmgoers, but declared her intention to make 'political use' of Freudian psychoanalytic theory (in a version influenced by Jacques Lacan) in a study of cinematic *spectatorship*. Such psychoanalytically inspired studies of 'spectatorship' focus on how 'subject positions' are constructed by media texts rather than investigating the viewing practices of individuals in specific social contexts. She declares that in patriarchal society *'pleasure in looking has been split between active/male and passive/female'* (Mulvey 1975). This is reflected in the dominant forms of cinema. Conventional narrative films in the 'classical' Hollywood tradition not only typically focus on a male protagonist in the narrative but also assume a male spectator. '*As the spectator identifies with the main male protagonist, he projects his look onto that of his like, his screen surrogate, so that the power of the male protagonist as he controls events coincides with the active power of the erotic look, both giving a satisfying sense of omnipotence*'. Traditional films present men as active controlling subjects, and treat women as passive objects of desire for men in both the story and in the audience, and do not allow women to be desiring sexual subjects in their own right. Such films objectify women in relation to 'the controlling male gaze', presenting 'woman as image' (or 'spectacle') and man as 'bearer of the look'. Men do the looking; women are there to be *looked at*. The cinematic codes of popular films 'are obsessively subordinated to the neurotic needs of the male ego'. Mulvey described this as 'the male gaze'. This article generated considerable controversy among film theorists. Many objected to the fixity of the alignment of passivity with femininity and activity with masculinity and to a failure to account for the female spectator. A key objection underlying many critical responses has been that Mulvey's argument in this paper was (or seemed to be) *essentialist*: that is, it tended to treat both spectatorship and maleness as homogeneous essences as if there were only one kind of spectator (male) and one kind of masculinity (heterosexual).

Ideology

W HEN THE TERM IDEOLOGY IS USED IN RELATION TO REPRESENTATION IT IS primarily concerned with 'ideas' and 'values'. Representation is concerned with how the producers and audience make things mean, and so is ideological through and through.

'Representation is a very different notion from that of reflection. It implies the active work of selecting, and presenting, of structuring and shaping: not merely the transmitting of already existing meaning, but the more active labour of making things mean' (Hall 1992).

Branston and Stafford (1996) offer three useful understandings of the term:

1. Sets of ideas that give an account of the social world, usually a partial or selective one.
2. The relationship of these ideas or values to the way power is distributed socially.
3. The way that such values are usually posed as 'natural' and 'obvious' rather than socially aligned.

These understandings draw attention to the fact that these ideas or values are not only present in the mediated world but also belong to our concrete experience of the world. To share in the space of the media text is to recognise the following:

- We may find similarities to our own experience of the social world. It may offer reinforcement and a sense of identity. The representations feel 'natural' and 'obvious' and we may recognise them and feel comfortable with them.
- We may add to our experience to the world through the information, values and ideas which are new to us or presented from a slightly different viewpoint. The representations may be transformative and offer us new ways of looking at the world.
- We may oppose or reject the representation of these values and ideas. They do not represent what we are prepared to accept. We may feel the need for correction of distortions of reality or the offering of alternative viewpoints.

- We may learn to recognise the gaps and silences in the textual construction. We can 'read against the grain' of such textual representations.

- We may not understand them because they are outside our experience socially or culturally. It is possible that that we could learn the codes and conventions of such representations.

I T IS NECESSARY TO RECOGNISE THAT IDEOLOGY PRECEDES MEDIA REPRESENTATIONS but is increasingly bound up with them as media technology impinges more and more on our social life. What media producers have to do in order to draw attention to their productions is to reduce the complexities of our identities in shorthand and condensed ways to constructions of reality that we recognise. In doing so the productions become the bearers of ideology. As such they necessarily trade in stereotypes.

Stereotypes

THE idea of stereotypes was defined by Walter Lippmann in 1922. In 'A Matter of Images' (1993) Richard Dyer described four functions of Lippmann's definition:

1. *An ordering process.* Stereotypes serve to order our reality in an easy-to-understand form, and are an essential part of making sense of the world and society. The fact that stereotypes offer an incomplete view of the world does not necessarily make them false; there is, anyway, no such thing as a complete view of the world. Having stereotypical knowledge about Cardiff is more useful for audiences watching a news story about the city or a feature film set there, than having no knowledge at all.

2. *A short 'cut'.* Because they are simplifications, stereotypes act as 'short cuts' to meaning. We can characterise London by using Big Ben or red buses as signs (metonyms) this will be sufficient for most purposes. The phrase 'chick flick' is a short cut to a more complex set of assumptions about a certain genre of film.

3. *A way of referring to the world.* They are social constructs and as such are a type of re-presentation. Stereotypes are most often used by individuals about people, or peoples, they do not know. It follows, then, that they must have received this information from others. The media, in its various forms, is one of the main sources of information and it is very likely that it is a crucial influence in stereotyping. Stereotypes serve to naturalise the power relations in society; they have a hegemonic function, so the fact that women are often stereotyped as subservient to men legitimises their inferior position. Stereotypes are not true or false but reflect a particular set of ideological values.

4. *An expression of 'our' values and beliefs.* Stereotypes are only effective if they are believed to be a view of a group which has a consensus. Of course, since many of the people who hold the stereotype actually derived their view from the stereotype, then the consensus is more imagined than real. Much of the power of stereotypes exists because they appear to have the status of consensus. What

stereotypes represent, however, are not the beliefs based upon reality but ideas which reflect the distribution of power in society – in other words, stereotypes are not an expression of value but of ideology.

The Idea Today

IDEOLOGY IS OPPOSED TO THE IDEA OF A FIXED REALITY AND HAS AS ONE OF ITS central aims the unmasking of the reality of representations. This clearly creates a mass of contradictions. Are the consumers of the media simply misled or duped by the media in some way? Do some people know that they are 'in the know' and can recognise ideological manipulation? Are some people then privileged insiders? Is everything ideological? The concept of ideology has tended to be replaced, some would say complemented or absorbed, into the concept of discourse. This can be an even more elusive and slippery term (see p. 71).

Identity

The Idea

WHAT REPRESENTATIONS DO IS TO MAKE SENSE OF OUR EXPERIENCE AND OF WHO we are. Further than that they can offer us more possibilities for who we are and for what we can become. Hence, as a cultural process it establishes individual and collective *identities*. The media offer us information which tells us what it is like to occupy a particular subject position. In drama, we can be positioned to be either the detective piecing the clues together, or the victim harassed by the predatory stalker who sees him off. In advertising we can be positioned by the representation to be the attractive male or female drawing the glances of the appreciative crowd or the upwardly mobile and technological savvy mobile phone user.

Representation is concerned with these forms of identification. We perceive ourselves as being similar or different to media representations on the basis of our concrete experience and cultural experience of the world. These can occur in relation to people or images so that we see ourselves in the images presented. These glimpses of ourselves are subject to change and the change that takes place is determined by our cultural experience.

The kinds of identities formed are contested. It is very common to hear the term 'identity crisis' in relation to media representations. The sense of ourselves can be affected by the processes involved with global change (as in the issues associated with the increasing use of the internet for information and entertainment), with questions of history (as in what does it mean to English, Black, Asian or Welsh), with questions of social change (as in the changing role of women in modern Western society), or with political movements (as in the anti-war protests).

The complexity of modern life requires us to assume different identities which sometimes conflict to create a crisis of identity.

- Are we the same person when we communicate with our parents, our friends or others in a chat room?
- What different representations do we make of ourselves in these multiple roles?

- Do you have to negotiate between them? Or do you keep them separate?
- Do you have an 'imaginary' version of yourself?

When you experience or interact with a media production such identities (they are extraordinarily fluid) can come into play. Such identities are rarely stable and are often subject to dramatic change. When we are recruited into subject positions by the text which offers glimpses of ourselves we are involved in a process of identification. The term used for this process by Louis Althusser (1971) is *interpellation*.

The process is both social (in that we recognise that we are being 'hailed' or addressed by the representations) and symbolic (in that we recognise and accept at an unconscious level the power of the sign).

The basis of this is ideology (see p. 64). This is based on both social and symbolic processes of thought. The key idea is that of the *unconscious*. This is based on Freud's theory of psychoanalysis developed further in the work of Jacques Lacan. The unconscious is made of powerful drives which are often unfulfilled and repressed. Where these find expression they do so in dreams, mistakes (Freudian slips) and nuances. Lacan suggested that by uncovering the laws that govern such instances it was possible to see the workings of the unconscious mind which operated in a different way to the conscious mind. The idea of a conflict between the conscious and the unconsciousness mind has had considerable influence on how we interpret media texts (see Psychoanalytic Approaches, p. 43).

The Idea in Action

Ethnicity

BRIGGS and Cobley (1998) point out that our notions of race have little to do with anything connected with biology, they are cultural through and through. In terms of identity they suggest it refers to a number of elements:

- the person's own' racial' identity (e.g. 'white');
- oppositions to that identity constructed through power relations (i.e. white versus Asian);
- a discourse that asserts the centrality of race as a defining feature of a person's identity (i.e. racism);
- other (non-racial) identities to which that person's 'racial' identity can be opposed/complemented in a power relationship (e.g. 'race' might be outweighed by 'gender').

Racial stereotypes are among the most readily employed in the media (see also Stereotypes, p. 65). Representation implies that the values ascribed are the natural order of things. The inherent view is that 'white' is normal. A simple binary categorisation which represents black as 'primitive' and 'savage' and whites as 'civilised' and 'developed' lies at its heart. A simple commutation test (or reversal of the two terms) can test the presence of ideology in a media text.

Typical stereotypes are:

- the black person as troublemaker or social problem;
- the black person as entertainer;
- the black person as dependent;
- the black person as exotic;
- the black person as threat.

There are senses in which the media (in Britain and the USA) have created many positive images and attempted to eliminate negative stereotypes; however, there is little reason to believe that the representation of black and Asian people will automatically improve as a consequence. There is still plenty of evidence that stereotypes continue to be recycled in Western cultures. Many feel that black and Asian audiences in Britain are not sufficiently well catered for and that there is still insensitivity towards issues of race and ethnicity.

In the engagement with media texts the issues can be problematised and made open and transparent. In areas like sport the representations can be positive or negative. On the one hand, the residual stereotype about blacks being naturally good at sport or Asians naturally good at cricket can still be encountered. On the other hand, it is possible to argue that that success in sport is good for the image of the represented group. By way of contrast, black footballers still have a hard time from white football supporters. The dialogic exploring of the 'richness' and 'diversity' of sporting representations can open opportunities for development.

Moral panics

THE term was used by Stan Cohen (Cohen and Young 1981) to reveal how the media represented youth culture in a stereotyped and negative way to create what he termed 'folk devils'. His work revealed how the media amplified such representations rather than reflecting the reality of youth culture. In doing so he drew attention to the media's role in creating audience response to such representations. He suggested that a moral panic occurs *'when a condition, episode, person or group of persons emerges to become a threat to societal values and interests'*.

This approach was then developed by the Marxist critics of the media. Such studies were used to demonstrate how the media help to avoid wider conflict in society by focusing our attention on the supposedly deviant behaviour of outsider groups, including 'black youth gangs', 'welfare scroungers', asylum seekers, 'single mums' and so on. By focusing attention in this way the media, it is claimed, contribute to creating and underpinning the social consensus on our society's core values. In the words of Naom Chomsky, an American academic, the media seek to 'manufacture consent'. That view is well summarised below by Fowler:

'Law and public opinion stipulate that there are many ideas and behaviours which are to be condemned as outside the pale of consensus: people who practise such behaviours are branded as "subversives", "perverts", "dissidents", "trouble-makers", etc. Such people are subjected to marginalization or repression; and the contradiction returns, because consensus decrees that there are some people outside the consensus. The "we" of consensus narrows and hardens into a population which sees its interests as culturally and economically valid, but as threatened by a "them" comprising a motley of antagonistic sectional

groups: not only criminals but also trade unionists, homosexuals, teachers, blacks, foreigners, northerners, and so on.' (Fowler 1991).

It is clear that without some of the moral panics some forms of youth culture (e.g. dance culture) would not have taken off in the first place without widespread media exposure. In addition, one of its effects is to create pressure groups or groups who have similar interests to which the media can give a focus. It is the highly effective media manipulation by pressure groups which leads to the suggestion that the moral panic model as presented by Cohen and Young needs updating. The pressure groups provide a constant stream of information and sound-bites and are always ready to wheel out experts to enter into television and radio discussions. Greenpeace, for example, have become at least as effective in their production of video news releases as major international corporations. Another group promoting 'Sarah's Law' have been just as effective in creating a moral panic and using the media to powerful effect. While cultural studies was about the struggle between different discursive practices for supremacy in their signification, there was often an underlying assumption that one set of discursive practices was 'wrong'; in other words, a view of ideology as a systematic distortion of the way things 'really' are. Current thinking suggests that we are more likely to see all representations as simply that – representations, none more 'right' than any other. As a consequence of the growth of technology and access to it, it is possible that such moral panics may become more widespread (see Postmodernism, p. 48).

Discourse

M OST OF THE THINKING ON THIS TERM DERIVES FROM THE WORK OF MICHEL Foucault (1972), the French intellectual.

Anything that has meaning is part of a discourse. This is the most general way to describe the term. Every kind of text or utterance is part of this definition (spoken, written, media etc.).

A discourse is made up of groups of texts or utterances which are in some way related to one another by patterns of similarity or difference. In some sense a discourse is coherent and recognisable. Hence it becomes possible for participants to talk about feminist discourse or film discourse from a shared understanding.

In the texts and utterances which form a discourse, clear ways of regulating or controlling what can and cannot be said in a discourse are used and understood by participants in it. There are rules that govern it which the discourse structures and makes coherent. A good example of this would be the phenomenon of news groups on the web where new participants can be 'flamed' for not understanding the protocols (or rules) of the news group.

The nature of discourse

DISCOURSE is social through and through. There is no reality as such, only competing discourses which struggle for the right to be heard or uttered. It is rooted in social practices and creates competition over meaning through the processes of challenge, change, adaptation of both the utterances produced by it and the ways in which the discourse categorises the meaning.

This emphasises that discourses are a site of perpetual struggle and that social institutions have a powerful role in circulating them.

Power, then, becomes central to discourse. It creates possible modes of behaviour (creates desire for them or legitimises them) and is complicit with these modes of behaviour. At the same time it seeks to close down or regulate or suppress other modes of behaviour through patterns of control. Foucault describes this as the 'power of desire' on the one hand and the 'desire of power' on the other. In society individuals are implicated in a diversity of discourses which both compete and complement at different stages of an individual's existence. Discourses, in such a view, are not fixed and stable but fluid and potentially dynamic.

The study of discourses

FOUCAULT uses the metaphor of 'archaeology' for the purpose of detecting 'fragments' of the construction of events in the real world, not in the sense of uncovering the essential or original meaning of these fragments, but more to reveal how these fragments are constructed to keep the discourse in place.

Key questions can help in the study of a discourse through textual representations:

1. How is the field delimited by the fragments uncovered? Hence you ask, what can't you do?
2. How do the fragments reveal the patterns of authority and legitimacy? Hence you ask, what can you do?
3. How does the discourse create events into narratives and categorise objectives for us? In general, what are the unwritten rules which govern it as revealed in its codes of construction?

The Idea in Action

Discourse analysis: linguistic texts

IN the 1970s attention to the linguistic structuring of media texts was relatively uncommon. Semiotics prevailed. Linguistic analysis of media texts, however, has exposed the assumptions and values that are involved in fairly simple linguistic forms such as headlines. Such analyses have shown how media language necessarily embodies relations of power and authority in society, which is the central focus of the term discourse. Social interactions are at its heart. In such a view text is both language and practice. All talk, all texts, are social in nature. *'Discourse analysis can be understood as an attempt to show systematic links between texts, discourse practices, and sociocultural practices'* (Fairclough 1995).

With regard to media texts, they do not merely convey information or establish the facts of a case. They argue, persuade and entertain. They are subject to patterns of control and regulation about what can and cannot be said, about what is acceptable and what is not, about tastes and preferences, needs and aspirations. Linguistic analysis can draw attention to these social issues by standing back and investigating from alternative perspectives, the 'common-sense' basis of much of our own communication and the media's communication with us.

At the basis of this investigation has been Halliday's 'functionalist' linguistics (see p. 31–2). By concentrating on function, Halliday created a model which could be used to look in a dynamic manner at the intended purposes of texts, their appropriateness to the audience and the ways they were encoded.

Central to the approach of such analysis is the term *transformations*. In essence this suggested that the same elements of language could function differently according to the context in which they were used. The term they use for this is *transitivity*.

Writers such as Fowler (1991) draw attention to a range of linguistic strategies in common use: nominalisations, passivisations, relexicalisation, overlexicalisation.

NOMINALISATIONS.   It is structurally possible and very common in English for verbs and adjectives to be realised as nouns. Fowler illustrates both how common these are in the discourses of reporting events and what the effects of such transformations are.

He suggests they act as a form of shorthand in that to spell out the consequences of the noun would take much longer. It is possible to hide who is doing what by such a strategy. So using a nominalisation such as 'allegations', there is no need to identify who is making allegations about whom. There may be institutional reasons for this to do with issues such as slander, court cases, protection of the names of participants etc. It could be that the writer does not want to make any form of judgement or attribute blame. As a consequence, the effect may be one of *mystification*.

Another ideological effect can be created by *reification*. Processes and qualities assume the status of *things*. They become less personal and inanimate. This can have a curiously deadening effect for the reader. The sense of event is dislocated and depersonalised by the language itself.

PASSIVISATIONS.   This turns active verbs into their passive forms, which can eliminate participants in the event. In the headline 'Boy shot' it is possible to eliminate the 'agent', that is, by whom? This can hide the activities of powerful groups. The focus of attention shifts from the 'agent' to the boy who is the 'acted upon'. There can be institutional reasons for this, that is, brevity, establishing the focus. So such transformations need to be studied for their function in the discourse. Through analysis it is possible to reconstruct the headline to reveal who is doing the shooting, which could have great significance.

Such syntactical transformations can be analysed by asking a series of questions:

1. Who is the agent or doer of the action?
2. Is this agent male or female, animal or human, natural or manufactured?
3. How significant is this in the written media text?
4. How was this agent behaving?
5. Who or what is the acted upon (the goal of the action)?
6. How are they behaving?

RELEXICALISATION.   Linguistic analysis examines the classificatory forms of language. It is concerned with how social experience is mediated through the written and spoken word. It seeks to analyse the ways in which individuals or groups are defined; the connotations associated with the descriptive labels attached to people and groups;

the ascription of status and respect. They explore how such classifications can structure inequalities by hiding them.

This is what relexicalisation involves. It is the process in which people, activities or groups are relabelled or reclassified. For example, there are different values and attitudes revealed in the names 'President Bush', 'George Bush', 'George W. Bush' and 'Bush', which can be analysed through the context (by whom? where? when?) in which they are used. Another way in which relexicalisation can take place is in the coining of new words and phrases. For example, 'drug taking' can be transformed by relexicalisation into 'substance abuse'; and 'refugees' into 'economic migrants' or 'asylum seekers'. It can be important in the analysis of encounters between guests and hosts on talk shows or news interviews in which contests over 'naming' can be a feature. For example, 'a policy' can be transformed in the course of an interview to 'a pipedream', 'a realisation', 'a perspective' or 'a notion'. It has obvious importance in political reporting as in this example: BBC staff are told not to refer to Israeli killings as 'assassinations'. *'In a major surrender to Israeli diplomatic pressure, BBC officials in London have banned their staff in Britain and the Middle East from referring to Israel's policy of murdering its guerilla opponents as 'assassination'. BBC reporters have been told that in future they are to use Israel's own euphemism for the murders, calling them 'targeted killings'. Israeli diplomats have been lunching with BBC officials and complaining that the corporation's coverage was anti-Israeli and pro-Palestinian'.* (Robert Fisk, Middle East correspondent, *The Independent*, 4 August 2001).

OVERLEXICALISATION.   This process involves the heaping up of synonymous words or phrases to designate items of significant interest to the experience of particular groups. For example, 'a debt' can be transformed into 'an overdraft', 'a credit deal', 'personal loan', 'bank loan' or 'low interest rate scheme' to suit the needs of bank customers and make them feel better about their debts.

The effect of the transformative process can be positive or negative. The questions to ask are those concerned with whose interests the transformation affects and whether it is positive or negative in terms of representation.

News reporting

Stage 1

THIS initial stage concerns the formal properties of texts such as news bulletins on television and radio or newspaper reports. This involves a recognition of the interplay between the 'traces' or 'fragments' of the process of production *as revealed in the text itself*, for example names, locations (inside/outside/on the spot/live), technology (video/audio/news agency etc.), news values, narrative structure (who, when, where, corroboration, quotes, evidence, argument, balance) and the 'audience cues' which are provided for the audience interpretation of events (the mode of address, identification, 'hailing').

Stage 2

IN this stage this interplay is more fully developed. Two areas require attention:

1. The immediate situation of the interaction between the participants in the communicative event. Increasingly, passive audiences (spectators/readers) are

being invited to partake in responses to news stories as participants, for instance, which can affect their reception.

2. The organisational values of the organisation producing the story as revealed in:

   a. 'branding' (logo, title sequence, choice of presenters/expert reporters, setting, mission statements, advertising and promotion, history etc.);

   b. 'competition' from other sources in terms of quality/entertainment, styles of presentation and typicality etc. Awareness of intertextual relations and genre.

Stage 3

THIS stage concerns the social order as a whole: what is the contextual influence of the society's prevailing attitudes and values?

Gramsci's notion of 'common sense' can be used. In his formulation it refers to the values, meanings and beliefs which are implicitly contained in everyday practical activity. Common sense is how the world is and how it is said to operate. It is a mish-mash of assumptions, ideas, conceptions etc. It is all that is taken for granted and unexamined. As such it creates unequal power relations in society and it works best when it is invisible and not foregrounded. It works by 'naturalising' the appearance of representations. Media texts can then be the site of struggles and conflicts to appropriate these common-sense meanings and turn them upside down, correct them, rework them (see Alternative Media, p. 106).

The discourse analyst is interested in how people use language to construct their accounts of the social world.

Visual representations

THIS is a useful approach with web pages, photographs, magazine covers and posters, in fact any media text in which design is important. It can be used to analyse individual comic frames and panels and frame-by-frame analysis of filmic texts, for instance. This section is adapted (and added to) from Gillian Rose's chapter in *Visual Methodologies* (2001).

Stage 1

TRY to forget all preconceptions you might have about the materials you choose. Look at them with fresh eyes. *'Pre-existing categories must be held in suspense. They must not be rejected definitively, of course, but the tranquillity with which they are accepted must be disturbed; we must show that they do not come about by themselves, but are always the result of a construction the rules of which must be known and the justifications of which must be scrutinised'.* (Foucault 1972).

It is important, therefore, to immerse yourself in the materials by revisiting them constantly. Study the inter-relation of elements of single images, for example:

1. What is the starting point of your look?

2. Where did your eyes follow next?

3. How much *movement* did your eye make before returning to the point at which you started? Trace or draw this movement so that you can identify each new place. Does it have a shape? Geometric? Flowing diagonally left to right, falling inward,

moving outwards, symmetrical etc.? Does it have compositional movement? List the use of curves, parallels, convergence, straight lines, strong verticals, textures, patterns, light and shade, human figures.

4. How is *depth* suggested in the arrangement of objects? Is perspective used? Three-dimensional fonts and figures? Use of colour?

5. *Humans and animals.* How is individuality and mood of the human subject expressed? Break this down into facial expression, body language, juxtapositions with other people/environment, props, clothed/naked, cut off/not cut off.

Stage 2

YOU need now to categorise across the range of your chosen texts. Your familiarity with the sources will allow you to identify key themes such as systematic use of colour combinations, recurring motifs, icons, symbols, patterns (antithesis, chiasmus etc.), distortions, typical modes of representation and so on. Make a list of these and then go through the sources, coding the material every time you have an occurrence.

You will be examining *'relations between statements (even if the author is unaware of them; even if the statements do not have the same author; even if the authors were unaware of each other's existence); . . . relations between groups of statements thus established . . . relations between statements and groups of statements of quite a different kind (technical, economic, political, social)'* (adapted from Foucault 1972).

You will question:

- how particular words and images draw attention to themselves;
- significant clusterings of images and their connotations;
- the connections between clusters;
- how they are related to common-sense notions in the social world.

This in turn will suggest new categories with which you can code your material and allow the materials themselves to guide the coding process.

Stage 3

HOW does the discourse generated from the study of texts work to persuade you to accept it as 'natural', 'the truth', or 'proof'? You need to examine its 'truth' claims. Do the texts offer points at which you can dissent from the discourse? (See Psychoanalytic Approaches, p. 43, for some discussion of this especially in relation to film spectatorship).

Stage 4

THE approach will inevitably raise complexity and contradictions in that intertextuality is at its basis. The aim is to uncover these contradictions to explore what can and cannot be said in a discourse; these can be deep-rooted assumptions within and outside the texts, which allow them to categorise in ways that appear to be unproblematical.

Stage 5

THE discourse can be read for what it does not say; for its gaps and absences, for its invisibilities and erasures. An example would be the discourse of 'the Cockney' in which 'whiteness' is the 'taken-for-granted' of the representation despite its obvious lack of relationship to the realities of London life. This erasure was clearly unsustainable after race rioting in parts of London in which it became clear that London was ethnically diverse. It might be possible to trace the fragments of this in character representation in the television series *East Enders*.

Stage 6

THE power of discourse often resides in the assumptions that are made about what is true, natural or real and in what is not created by the discourse. As a method it requires detailed reading and scrupulous attention to detail.

ONE OF THE DIFFICULT AREAS FOR SUCH ACTIVITY CONCERNS THE ROLE OF THE discourse analysts. What truth claims are made by the construction of their own discourse?

- The real aim, they argue, is to persuade rather than be truthful. As such, analysis becomes a form of discursive argument.
- As such, they produce a certain kind of text (appropriate to the social sciences and humanities type audience) which suggests the plausibility of the method. This can erase the institutional context of the discourse (education) with its needs for standards, levels, assessment, peer approval, the need to publish etc.
- If it is only a method, how does it relate to rational enquiry and the establishment of truth? (See Postmodernism, p. 48).

There are other difficulties with the method:

- Knowing where to stop in making intertextual connections. These can be so wide and varied as to seem meaningless. Why bother if all textual representation can be linked to other textual representations? It is like chasing shadows which free float on the surface of a sea of potential meanings. How the analysis can be justified is a key issue for practitioners.
- There is a tendency to neglect the social practices and institutions through which text and images are distributed and circulated.

Media Organisations

COMMUNICATION IN THE TWENTIETH CENTURY HAS CHANGED DRAMATICALLY AND that change has been accelerated in the early part of the twenty-first century. It is now more mediated through print or electronic technology with every chance that this change will accelerate further. This process is often referred to as 'mediasation'. The information and entertainment products of the media industries (film, television, radio, print-based, telecommunications and electronic) are brought to us in a wide range of products. Media organisations are seen as central to the understanding of the rise of mass communication because in the values implicit in them social and cultural practices are represented and accepted, ignored, misunderstood or fought over and challenged. Many argue that they should be seen as the prime focus for the study of culture and communication.

This is based on the following propositions about the media:

1. they are an agency of social control;
2. media productions contain representations which affect ideas about social groups;
3. the mass media have a relationship with the process of change in society;
4. media technology relates to the ways in which society develops.

The Idea in Action

T HERE ARE TWO VIEWPOINTS: THE RADICAL AND THE LIBERAL.

The radical

THIS suggests that there is a worrying concentration of power in the capitalist enterprise of the media. At the heart of this argument is the requirement to generate profit. There are two aspects to this. First, the creation of the maximum audience. Secondly, the need to create a scarcity value for the product.

Garnham (1990) proposed the idea of *cultural commodity*. The key features of this idea are:

1. *Novelty*. Audiences need to identify with commodities in order to use them. This leads to an emphasis on *branding* them to give them recognition. Novelty comes at a high production cost. Hence an emphasis on concentration of resources, driving down costs through strategic management such as internationalisation and cross-sector ownership. There is always a tension between the need to mass produce and the need to create scarcity value.

2. *The need to protect*. Media organisations aim to limit access to their goods from people who have not paid for them. This raises issues about brand protection and infringement, piracy, control of the means of distribution, intellectual property and copyright. This raises a whole set of issues to do with *ethics and the law*.

3. *The need to spread risk*. The creation of any media production is a risk in that audience response is unpredictable. Among the consequences are the need to research extensively in likely reception through audience research; the need to create an appropriate strategic approach to the distribution of the product; the need to diversify the costs of production and distribution in a variety of ways; and the need for a diverse portfolio of products. Key features of this have been internationalism (the need to sell in international markets) and the move towards cross-ownership through a process described as *vertical integration*. The creation of alliances, partnerships, mergers and acquisitions between media firms has been a central feature of the way in which media giants such as Disney, Time Warner, Viacom, Bertelsmann and News Corporation have developed profitability for their shareholders. In a process described as *synergy* (the combined effects of different elements adding up to more than the sum of their individual parts) Time Warner, for instance, could cross-promote its organisation via music, publishing, cable and multimedia. These have been 'anti-competitive' in the sense that they seek to close down opportunities for other media organisations. The *global* spread of these media 'empires' has been of great concern to cultural commentators, particularly as eight of the top brands in the world in 2003 were American. In their view, this reinforces the inbuilt tendency in capitalism to reinforce power and control of viewpoints and values in all parts of the globe.

'It is in the interests of the United States to encourage the development of a world in which the fault lines separating nations are bridged by shared interests. And it is in the economic and political interests of the United States to ensure that if the world is moving towards a common language, it be English; that if the world is moving toward common telecommunications, safety, and quality standards they be American; that if the world is becoming linked by television, radio, and music, the programming will be American; and that if common values are being developed, they be values with which Americans are comfortable' (David Rothkopf, academic and advisor to the Clinton administration, 1997).

The radical response is to find, uncover and lay bare the operations of power and the dominant vested interests implicit in such an approach. It aims to 'correct' these imbalances and distortions of power through the imposition of alternative ways through debate, challenge and confrontation. The radical approach raises ideas about cultural/ media imperialism.

The liberal

THIS is based on the idea that in the media all sorts of viewpoints are possible and desirable and that modern developments in technology need to be spread more widely and more equitably to achieve this. It proposes dialogue between these viewpoints which recognises patterns of similarity and difference. In such an approach all viewpoints are possible. Central to this are issues of *freedom of expression* and the *right to independent or alternative viewpoints*.

One of the areas in which this has been marked is in the development of technologies such as the internet, which allows users to communicate with each other through chat rooms, user groups and websites to set up their own ways of communicating through a set of shared interests. This can challenge the dominant view that audiences were passive consumers and texts rigidly determined. In the creation of websites and by intervention in debates passive spectators could be turned into active participants. The areas in which they could participate have raised many controversies particularly in relation to sexual matters and political viewpoints. Questions of *regulation and control* of new means of communicating are commonplace.

A second area is in the way in which media industries have developed. Strong relationships have been established between media organisations and independent producers in the form of networks. It is argued that this has allowed greater diversity of viewpoint within large centralised media organisations and more creativity. From 1990, for instance, the BBC and ITV networks had to contract 25 per cent of their programming to independent producers.

A third area has concerned itself with the way in which news and documentary production in particular has meant a greater diversification of viewpoint in that competition has a great impact on the range of approaches and viewpoints available to the modern consumer. An example would be the phenomenon of emailing news programmes, posting comments on websites etc., which in turn can become part of the news agenda which add to views of producers using traditional and non-traditional means of reportage (reports, expert commentators, interviews etc.).

The sources of information, it is argued, are changing. This approach raises issues about the *global and local reach* of media products.

Branding

The Idea

THE THEORY OF BRANDING IS BASED ON THE FOLLOWING:

- Create an *identity* in a variety of ways. Give it a *personality* that makes a promise. This identity will stand for a *set of values*. Harley-Davidson motorcycles might be said to connote the following values:

  1. functional value – big, heavy, powerful;

  2. emotional value – freedom-seeking, American-loving;

  3. Self-expression value – macho, tough.

  In the same way the BBC in a recent series of advertisements for its news programmes screened on air in 2003 can be associated with values like:

  1. functional value – bringing the latest news;

  2. emotional value – trustworthiness, getting it right;

  3. self-expression value – balanced, objective.

- Make it yours and establish your right to it legally.

- Use it to display and draw attention to your product(s) or service.

- Communicate it consistently throughout all the activities of your organisation. It is the primary focus.

- Grow and change with the marketplace and the consumer. In this way you will reflect social change.

- Become a way of life for a loyal franchise of customers and consumers. Build goodwill.

- Attract new users and grow unendingly by forming new relationships.

The Idea in Action

'THE BRAND' HAS MOVED IN THE 1990S TO THE CENTRE OF CORPORATE STRATEGY. Always important in advertising, increasingly it is becoming one of the most valuable assets in media organisations. Prior to this time media organisations had not given too much attention to it. Deregulation of broadcasting in the UK in this period (television and radio) meant that the tools and strategies of mass marketing and promotion (advertising, branding, packaging etc.) had to be used more and more in the face of competition from other sources of entertainment and information. Differentiation of the product became essential. Broadcasting needed to market and promote itself. Branding came to be seen as a primary strategic asset in terms of both competitive strategy and sustainable competitive advantage. Brand awareness for all the visual and aural manifestations of the media organisation's output became a vital component of this strategy: idents, trailers, teasers, stings, campaigns on screen, letterheads, logos, vehicle livery, posters, recruitment advertising.

The real wealth in a traditional business organisation is located in the intangible assets of that enterprise and not in the 'traditional (tangible) assets' such as real estate, plant, equipment, inventory, cash, and the like. An example would be the software company Microsoft. In 2000, with a market capitalisation of over US$423 billion, Microsoft reported revenues of only $23 billion. In its balance sheet it stated that it had conventional assets of $52 billion. This left $348 billion worth of market cap of unspecified value. What accounts for this $348 billion? Experts agree that this represents Microsoft's intangible assets or 'intellectual capital'. The brand represents these intangible assets and the intellectual capital wealth that an enterprise has created over time. It is the brand that investors buy into with the expectation of making profits for themselves through successful marketing of the products. It is not difficult to see why brands are so fiercely sustained and protected from those like software pirates who seek to plunder the brand. It also explains why Microsoft works to position itself in the market as a recognisable identity and develop its activity as the number one provider of software for the computer industry. In terms of broadcasting it is the way in which audiences are attracted to and stay with media organisations to ensure their survival in an increasingly competitive marketplace. Website designers use the term 'sticky' to describe this relationship with the user: they need to keep them on the site.

Mission statement

A mission statement is a short summative declaration of a corporation or organisation's philosophical ideals that subsume some combination of the corporate/organisational mission, vision and values. It portrays the organisational purpose, which is distinct from vision (future direction) and values (principles).

A mission statement stresses values, *positive* behaviours, and guiding principles within the framework of the organisation's *announced* belief system and ideology. As an increasingly popular genre of organisational communication, mission statements tend to be formally expressed and widely communicated to both internal and external audiences. They are a standard by which the organisation is supposed to measure itself and emulate, and whose demand for perfection it should strive to fulfil.

Marketing and Promotion

IT IS ARGUED THAT WE LIVE IN A 'PROMOTIONAL CULTURE' (WERNICK 1991) AND THAT consumers are 'advertising literate'. Wernick argues that the rhetoric of advertising has been extended throughout our culture so that we can regard such areas as school and colleges, churches and whole nations (such as Wales) as a brand which competes with other brands for the attention of customers. It is argued that the concern is about informed free choice. It is based on the view that consumers are aware of the degree to which they are addressed and able to make informed choices between different promotional approaches.

Brands associate meanings with products and services. These associated meanings have become increasingly complex and subtle. Particular texts in areas such as radio, television and the internet link consumers to wider systems of meaning. Hence, for instance, Pepsi can be associated with youth, Tetley tea with Britishness, Amstel beer with football, Tampax with freedom. Semiotics is the discipline that deals with the ways in which signs take on meanings. In general the process is one of demystification through analysis of codes and conventions (see Semiotics, p. 27). Advertising has been a particular area for critical analysis.

Myers (1999) lists the basics of advertising using the 'Four Ps' model:

- *Product.* The product or service needs to be distinctive and stand out from its competitors. It must meet a need, requirement or lack for the consumer/customer.

- *Placement.* The product needs to be where the point of need, requirement or lack is. As a consequence it needs outlets or distribution points (a cinema, videostore, supermarket, website etc.). There can be controversies over this as in the case of Tesco and designer clothes.

- *Promotion.* This process allows people to know about the brand. There is a huge range of promotional tools: celebrity endorsement, tie-ins, posters of all kinds, (normally in places where people congregate or which they pass but increasingly at the point of access for the consumer), film and television adverts, trailers of all kinds in a variety of media, product placement within other media texts, competitions, offers etc.

- *Price.* Goods and services must be priced according to what the customer is prepared to pay. Lower prices can help sometimes but premium brands often attract higher prices. They have 'added value' because of the brand. Some have associations connected with being 'reassuringly expensive'. A recent campaign (2003) for Volkswagen played on the idea that you would expect their cars to be more expensive as they cut their prices.

He goes on to add four Ps of his own which students will find useful in the analysis of advertisements:

- *Past.* Brands always draw on the past using a range of associative meanings or connotative meanings. They will often explicitly use the past in imagery to suggest tradition, departures from tradition and the ways things will be in the future. Cross-branding is commonplace as brands try to attract new customers from other brands. It aims to act for the benefit of both brands.

- *Position.* Brands often compete against other brands trying to attract the same type of customer. Brands often seek to be the market leader but increasingly many brands seek to create their own distinctive niche. In this sense they position themselves against other brands. It can be difficult for well-known brands to reposition themselves.

- *Practices.* Brands also need to explore how consumers use the products or services provided by the brand. Market research is essential to this process both at the development stage, the launch stage, in the post-launch phase and in any feedback related to its conditions of use. Levi's and Doc Marten boots are examples of the ways in which the use values changed from utility to fashion.

- *Paradigms.* A paradigm is the underlying, taken-for-granted set of relations in the brand. Common-sense ideas about ideal body shapes, modernity, health, for instance, can be detected in the brand and made to appear 'natural' or 'how it is'. Discourse analysis is much concerned with these paradigms (see Discourse, p. 71).

The Idea in Action

THERE ARE FOUR MAIN STRATEGIES OF ADDRESS IN ADVERTISING:

1. *Sincerity, authority and direct address.* This can be in the form of a person speaking and/or looking directly at you (see The gaze, p. 59). Intonation will give clues to the meanings that can be generated for the audience in the emphasis on key words, the use of pauses, the posing of questions, assertion of facts etc. It can be in the form of a voice-over.

2. *Setting.* This is a major component of advertisements. It can be done through the spoken word and non-diagetic sound or in visual images.

3. *Framing.* This is central to the point of view. Bodies can be segmented to draw attention to different parts of the body; increasingly reality is 'touched up' using digitalisation.

4. *Editing*. In filmic advertisements all cuts are 'motivated cuts' to draw attention. There is always a reason which should be obvious to the target audience. However, the consumer may only read part of the intended message or will ignore it altogether as so much 'moving wallpaper'. In print-based advertisements such as posters or the covers of magazines much attention is given to the *mise en scène* which is constructed through the layering of images and text.

Film promotion and distribution

THE following section is closely modelled on a conference presentation by Jill Poppy.

OBJECTIVES

- Create a 'buzz' about a specific film to make it a high priority in the consumer's mind.
- Make sure the film has an excellent opening weekend box office. The opening weekend is a good indicator to both distributor and exhibitor of how a film will run.
- Use word of mouth to ensure a long run on a large number of screens with high box office returns.

STRATEGY

- Advertising (press, radio, television, cinema, outdoor, world wide web)
- Publicity (news and press releases, star interviews, news stories about the making of the film etc.)
- Promotions (parties, press junkets etc.)
- Teaser campaigns
- Word of mouth (increasingly in web chat rooms).

TIMING.   This is critical. This all needs to be achieved within a specific time scale.

- Continual competition from new releases every week will try to steal the awareness created, and the screen space available.
- The nature of film-booking means that films which are not making money at the box office will be moved to smaller screens with fewer opportunities to generate income.
- The video window allows only six months between theatrical release and video rental, so every day counts.
- The post-launch period is also important if the film has been successful. The marketing objective then moves to maintaining a film's profile – generally through word of mouth, but this can be helped by advertising. Also, promotional and publicity opportunities will continue to be exploited.

PLANNING

- Setting the release date. This plays a major role in marketing as it determines competitive environment. The phased release of *The Lord of the Rings* trilogy is a good example (2002–2004). It has marketing advantages in that the film can benefit from Oscar nominations by playing at the right time, holiday playing time, media interest in subject matter and style, film festivals etc.

- Setting the marketing budget. There are two schools of thought. Some distributors set this by working to a percentage of the expected earnings of the film. Some determine what they think the film needs to make it work, and decide then whether it is realistic. The budget must cover all costs relating to a film, from direct media costs to production of posters, promotional materials and screening charges.
- Define the target audience. This will allow precise targetting, so that the advertising pound works to maximum advantage in informing those people most likely to be interested in the film. Most advertising builds in a wide range of potential target groups.
- Establish criteria for target groups. Analyse the subject matter to determine who the film 'talks' to:
  - is there a male or female bias to the film?
  - is there an age bias?
  - what type of audiences do the film's stars appeal to?
  - what genre is the film?
  - is there a specific audience that might be interested because it has a strong soundtrack or because it is based on a best-selling novel or true story?

  Once strong core groups have been identified, they will become the focus of the marketing campaign. It will be important to broaden out from these initial groups, however, if the film is to become a major mainstream success.
- Develop strategies to address the core groups.

BELOW THE LINE ACTIVITY

- Publicity
- Celebrity tours
- Press junkets
- Local articles
- Premiere launches
- Merchandise (including soundtrack, novelisations)
- Reviews

ABOVE-THE-LINE ACTIVITY

- Advertising. This will include either singularly or in combination, advertising on television, radio, in press, magazines, on poster sites and through dedicated websites and web users from the target group known to be interested who can link to the main site (fans in particular of stars, genres etc). This will initially be dictated by how much money is available to spend on the film's launch. Other factors that can determine what media will be used include the release date (media access is cheaper to buy at some times in the year); the amount of creative work involved as in the construction of website, posters, trailers etc.; and selecting the most efficient media to reach the core groups.
- Promotions. These will bring added awareness and reinforce the title in the consumer's mind (especially in non-traditional retail outlets such as nightclubs, gyms etc.). Promotional materials produced by the distributor such as posters, standees, leaflets, banners and so on can be used by the cinema in the cinema itself, or to create promotions within the locality.

IDENTIFY PROMOTIONAL PARTNERS

- Identify product or themes in the film.
- Link to manufacturers, retailers, third parties who might benefit from the association.

CREATE A LOCAL DISTRIBUTION STRATEGY. Local theatre managers implement marketing strategies through the community. They can use strategies like:

- Trailers to create pre-release interest
- Informing local papers
- Posters can be displayed in prominent positions
- Film-related merchandise can be used in photographs and press information can be displayed locally.

Local managers would ideally have unique access to local media, decision makers, retailers and the general public in order to exploit promotional ideas to gain additional coverage. They will be sensitive to the requirements of screening programmes in terms of local issues and be proactive in ensuring that the 'right' audience is invited for previews.

Local theatre managers (exhibitors) can greatly assist the distributor in five main ways:

1. Enthusiasm for the product.
2. Database of local contacts and the confidence to approach these people for editorial and promotional work.
3. Creative use of display material, and the ingenuity in organising displays outside the cinema.
4. Programme trailers with the right films to maximise exposure to the target audience.
5. Providing indicators about the type of audience attracted at various showings.

Target Audience

IN A PROMOTIONAL CULTURE MEDIA ORGANISATIONS NEED TO BE SURE THAT THEIR approach is effective. This raises a number of issues for them:

1. How precisely can the audience be targeted by region, socio-economic grouping, age, gender, or other demographic variables?
2. Are some media better at reaching some audiences than others?
3. How can the audience be measured?
4. Where are members of the target audience and what are they doing when they get the message?
5. How well is the message remembered?

Media organisations have turned to social sciences to understand consumer behaviour. The techniques have become very precise and very expensive. Some of the main ideas and theories associated with this are explored below.

Maslow's hierarchy

THIS is a theory of human needs suggested by Maslow in 1954. It suggests that groups in society have deep-seated needs, fears and weaknesses. Maslow organises these needs as a hierarchy:

1. *Physiological* needs. These are the basic requirements of life: food, water.
2. *Safety* needs. These are the freedom from danger and fear.
3. *Social* needs. These include companionship, belonging and friendship.
4. Need for *esteem*. These include esteem for oneself as well as the gaining of the approval of others.
5. Need for *self-actualisation*. Maslow describes this as the need 'to become everything that one is capable of being'.

Posed in this way, it seems to prioritise ambition over the need for basic needs. However, Maslow recognised that human behaviour was more complex than the model suggests.

Design approaches

CORPORATE business has developed more complex design approaches to the question of why a person engages with media products.

- The use of particular trigger words and phrases or the use of a particular mode of presentation.
- Editing techniques, visual style, the use of colour, type style and other visual elements to create 'hot' spots of attention.
- Musical and sound elements.
- Humour and surrealism.

The central aim is to create recall. It is the most important factor in persuasion. The memory process involves four stages:

1. The product must have attention paid to it. Web designers refer to this as 'sticky' while commentators such as John Berger, describing the effects of war photographs, suggests that they have the power to drag us out of our normal reality into the reality of their world.
2. The media image must be stored in the long-term memory.
3. It can be remembered over days, weeks, years.
4. It can be retrieved at the point of engagement at the point of sale.

These points help to explain the significance of genre and intertextuality as audience cues.

The RISC AmericanScan Programme

THIS is a marketing programme developed by Marshal Marketing and Communications in association with the International Research Institute on Social Change (RISC). Its mission is to help advertisers understand and adjust to purchasing behaviours of present and future customers.

Method

REPRESENTATIVE samples of people are questioned about relevant preferences and facts about themselves. The aim of the questionnaire is to capture the person's sociocultural characteristics.

A chart is created, which takes on the appearance of a compass:

- North – people who see change as a positive force.
- South – people who prefer stability, structure and consistency.
- East – people who are more independent and seek immediate pleasure.
- West – people with strong ethics who are more community orientated.

People are scored on about 40 characteristics which allow them to be placed on the compass. Each person is represented by a dot which clusters with other dots.

These clusters are divided into 10 territories of people with shared values and similar preferences.

Outcome

AN understanding of the cultural and social norms for any specific demographic group. For example:

- *Territory B2:* The key characteristics of such people are 'independent, experimental, interested in the new'.
- *Key attributes:* Exploring human potential, coping with uncertainty, personal growth, networking, pleasure, risk-taking, strategic opportunism, emotions.
- *Sociocultural profile:* intense, eager to explore, open and optimistic, invigorated by diverse, multiple connections, active and involved, always push to their limits, strongly individualistic yet open to a broad view of community, uncertainty equals a challenge.
- *Motivations:* culture, novelty, understanding, independence, fascinated by the avant-garde and unexpected, will pay more for what they want, intrigued by the one-of-a-kind and impossible, and the experiences which come with it.

Use

A voice actor preparing for the recording of an advertisement can adopt the tone of voice appropriate to this kind of demographic audience segment. In this case, it is suggested that the tone of voice will aim to seduce and enliven.

Public and commercial television

IN public service television there is an emphasis on freedom from pressures created by advertisers and from powerful vested interests, and a concern with quality programming and representation of national interests.

The principles of public service television are:

- Universal availability as a right of citizenship.
- Universal appeal with the consideration of as wide a range of tastes and interests as possible. This has led over the years to the diversification of programming available from the BBC, for instance (BBC1, BBC2, BBC3, BBC4, CBBC).
- Diversity and provision for minority audiences. In multicultural societies programming should emphasise plurality and diverse viewpoints.

- A concern to educate and inform its citizens.

- Independence from government and commercial interests.

- A concern with the public sphere in areas such as politics, law, consumer issues, national culture and the whole range of issues which affect the modern citizen.

In commercial television, freedom is used in a different sense. It means the freedom to maximise profits. The features of commercial television are:

- It emphasises freedom of consumer choice through diverse programming.

- The audience is seen as a consumer who is buying into the brand. This consumer is increasingly expected to pay for the privilege. As a consequence consumers enter into formal agreements with broadcasters and invest in certain types of technology to deliver the content.

- As consumers are in charge, they have freedom of choice and as a consequence can be regarded as sophisticated enough to know what they want from a media organisation. They do not need to be so regulated. Commercial broadcasters tend to argue for a lighter regulatory touch.

Both positions are criticised:

- Public service television acts in the interests of a dominant group to create élite programming.

- Opponents of a market approach say that it gives freedom to large multinational organisations to control media output. In the process they produce programmes which 'dumb down', are formulaic and lack range and diversity. They also argue that minorities are less well represented and the national culture impoverished.

Demographics

THE TERM 'DEMOGRAPHICS' IS A COLLOQUIALISM THAT DERIVES FROM DEMOGRAPHY, the study of the characteristics of human populations.

1. Demographics can be used to describe an audience. Such descriptive uses may be applied to an actual audience, as, for example: 40 per cent female, 62 per cent white, average age 30 etc. Or demographics may be used to describe a desired audience, as in older or children.

2. Demographics can be used to sort data about people for purposes of analysis. For example, data may be available from a study designed to assess people's evaluations of a newspaper's representation of an event.

3. Researchers may be interested in the average evaluation across people, in the evaluations of specific subgroups of people, or in the differences between the evaluations of specific subgroups. For either of the latter two purposes one would divide the data according to the demographic categories of interest and calculate averages within those categories. It would then be possible to report on how young women were affected by the presentation in a positive or negative way.

ADVERTISERS' INTEREST IN DEMOGRAPHICS ARISES FROM MARKET RESEARCH OR advertising strategies that emphasise certain types of people as the target audience for their advertising. Commercial broadcasters, then, who earn their living by providing communication services to advertisers, are interested in demographics because the advertisers are. Because advertisers are more interested in some demographic categories than others, the commercial broadcasters have a financial interest in designing programming that appeals to people in those more desired demographic categories.

Uses of demographics to define and generalise about people is an instance of social category thinking. The rationale is that the available social categories, such as age, gender, ethnicity, and educational level, are associated with typical structures of opportunity and experience that in turn produce typical patterns of disposition, attitudes, interests, behaviours, and so on. Age, for example, is easy to measure, amenable to being categorised, and associated with a great variety of differences in taste and activity. However, to generalise from this to the idea that certain types of people are affected in a particular way is problematic.

The demographics of gender

SOME researchers have divided women into four categories:

1. Women at home who do not plan to work in the future.
2. Women at home who plan to return to the work force.
3. Women for whom work is an economic necessity.
4. Women for whom work is a career.

Clearly the process of categorisation only works at a level of generalisation and can be in a constant state of flux. Women could be categorised in multiple ways and such categorisations are easily challenged by the lived experience of woman's lives. The process of categorisation clearly relates to the idea of stereotyping (see p. 65).

The demographics of social class

THIS is related to perceived spending power of different groups:

- *A households*: Successful upper professionals or business people. Includes doctors, lawyers and company executives.
- *B households:* Includes such categories as senior university academics, pharmacists, directors of small companies etc.
- *C households:* Lower middle class – trades people, owners of small businesses, white collar workers etc.
- *D households:* Categories such as clerical staff, apprentices, skilled and semi-skilled workers.
- *E households:* Manual workers – truck drivers, factory workers etc.
- *FG households:* People receiving welfare benefits, unemployed and retired pensioners.

The Idea Today

S UCH CATEGORISATIONS NEED HANDLING WITH CARE. FOR INSTANCE, THE SPENDING power of certain groups has changed significantly in recent years. In the UK, for instance, the rise in property values has raised the ability of the 'retired pensioner' to spend more. The term 'retire' has developed different connotations, as downsizing the workforce in the 1990s meant a second (or third) career for some 'retired people'. They are now sometimes relexicalised as 'silver surfers' or 'wrinklies' depending on the point of view taken (see Discourse, p. 71).

Share, Ratings and Scheduling

Share

SHARE is an audience measurement term. It can identify, for instance, the percentage of television households with sets in use that are viewing a particular programme during a given time period, or the number of readers for a newspaper in relation to other newspapers.

Share is a comparative tool; it allows media executives to determine how well their productions are doing when compared with competing productions.

Share is closely associated with rating, another measurement term. Share measures, for instance, the percentage of TV viewers who are actually watching a particular programme, while the rating for a programme calculates the percentage of *all* television households – both those using TV and those not using TV.

Share can also be used to illustrate programming trends. One network may average its share of successive programmes to illustrate its dominance on a particular weekday night. A new broadcast or cable network may average its share across an entire season to illustrate its increasingly competitive position over a previous season.

Share can be used to demonstrate industry trends.

A study of network share measures the competition between traditional broadcasters and their new technology competitors.

Ratings

RATINGS are a central component of the television industry. They are important in television because they indicate the size of an audience for specific programmes. Networks and stations can set their advertising rates based on the number of viewers of their programmes. Ratings enable publically funded organisations such as the BBC to justify the licence fee. Network revenue or funding is thus directly related to the ratings. In a general sense, the term is used to describe a process that attempts to determine the number and types of viewers watching TV. The general ratings process has varied greatly over the years.

THE PROCESS.   All audience measurement is based on samples. As yet there is no economical way of finding out what every person in an entire country is watching or indeed of measuring the global reach of a programme. However, the rating companies try to make their samples as representative of the viewing population as possible. They consider a wide variety of demographic features – size of family, sex and age of head of household, access to different modes of TV delivery (cable, satellite, terrestrial), income, education – and try to construct a sample comprising the same percentage of the various demographic traits present in the general population.

SAMPLE SIZE.   Statisticians know that the smaller the sample size the more chance there is for error. Ratings companies admit to this and do not claim that their figures are totally accurate. As access to interactive communication increases, it may be easier to obtain larger samples. Wires and radio signals from consumer homes back to cable or satellite systems could be used to send information about what each cable or satellite TV household is viewing. Many of these wires and wireless technologies are already in place. Consumers wishing to order pay-per-view programming, for example, can push a button on the remote control that tells the cable system to unscramble the channel for that particular household. Using this technology to determine what is showing on the TV set at all times can raise surveillance issues.

SAMPLE COMPOSITION.   Perhaps one of the greatest difficulties for ratings companies is caused by those who eliminate themselves from the sample by refusing to cooperate. Although rating services make every attempt to replace these people with others who are similar in demographic characteristics, the sample's integrity can be questioned. Even if everyone originally selected agreed to serve, the sample cannot be totally representative of a larger population. No two people are alike, and even households with the same income and education level and the same number of children of the same ages do not watch exactly the same television. Moreover, people within the sample, aware that their viewing or listening habits are being monitored, may act differently than they ordinarily do – this is a weakness in ratings procedures.

RATING TECHNIQUES

1. Households with 'Peoplemeters' may suffer from 'button pushing fatigue' thereby artificially lowering ratings. Additionally, some groups of people are simply more likely to push buttons than others.

2. Diaries. The return rate is low, intensifying the problem of the number of uncooperative people in the sample. Even the diaries that are returned often have missing data. Many people do not fill out the diaries as they watch TV. They wait until the last minute and try to remember details – perhaps aided by a copy of *TV Guide*. Some people are simply not honest about what they watch. Perhaps they do not want to admit to watching a particular type of television or a particular programme.

3. Interviews. People can be influenced by the tone or attitude of the interviewer or, again, they can be less than truthful about what they watched out of embarrassment or in an attempt to project themselves in a favourable light. People are also hesitant to give information over the phone because they fear the person calling is really a sales person.

4. Additionally, rating methodologies are often complicated and challenged by technological and sociological change. Videocassette recorders, for example, have presented difficulties for the ratings companies. Generally, programmes are counted as being watched if they are recorded. However, many programmes that are recorded are never watched, and some are watched several times. In addition, people replaying tape often scroll through commercials, destroying one of the primary purposes of ratings.

5. Ratings companies have yet to decide what to do with sets that show more than one picture.

Scheduling

THE scheduling of programmes is at the heart of a television station's business whether in the public sector (the BBC) or the commercial sector (see Figure 3). The line up of shows represents the brand of a station. Better ways of scheduling affect the bottom line especially in the commercial sector – more viewers create more revenue from advertisers.

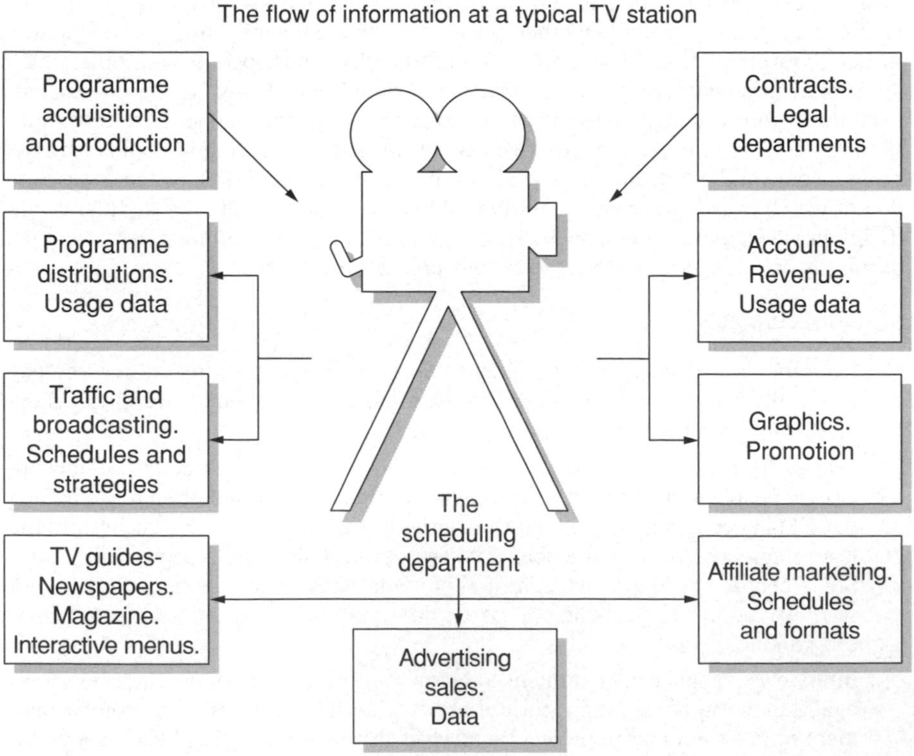

The flow of information at a typical TV station

| Programme acquisitions and production | | Contracts. Legal departments |

| Programme distributions. Usage data | | Accounts. Revenue. Usage data |

| Traffic and broadcasting. Schedules and strategies | The scheduling department | Graphics. Promotion |

| TV guides- Newspapers. Magazine. Interactive menus. | | Affiliate marketing. Schedules and formats |

| Advertising sales. Data |

Figure 3 The activities of a typical scheduling department

The television industry is very competitive. Attracting customers and keeping them is central to the mission of television organisations, especially as the audience, under the twin pressures of technological development and deregulation, has become increasingly segmented. Demographics are increasingly used to identify and attract potential consumers. Increasingly television companies are seeking to 'narrowcast' to specific kinds of audiences. At the same time they are seeking to expand their activity through a whole range of commercially inspired initiatives such as tie ins, sharing the costs of production, negotiating with independent producers, exporting their programmes and buying in programmes from other television companies etc. This raises a number of questions about the relationship with the customer. Will it mean endless reruns, formulaic television, reliance on the tried and tested, the use of well-known faces, the increasing development of pay-per-view television for major sporting and musical events?

Figure 3 illustrates the complex nature of scheduling, which is not simply concerned with the mechanics of putting programmes on in a particular order at a certain time of the day.

Stars and Celebrities

The Idea

STARDOM IS A KEY CONCEPT IN THE DEVELOPMENT OF FILM THEORY. PATRICK Phillips suggests that stars can be looked at from a number of perspectives.

A star is a real person. The cult of the star has depended on a simultaneous sense of the star's exceptional qualities and the fact that at some level of everyday living they have experiences just like we do and can be communicated with as friends we know. They could be part of our lives and when they die we feel the loss as if for a real person.

A star is a public performer of roles. The primary encounter with a star is with the roles they play. We come to know them through these roles, their bodies, their characteristic features such as voice, look, gesture. Through their roles we begin to associate them with particular attitudes and ideological positions.

A star is a persona. This involves a merging of the real person and the roles they play, particularly in cases where the star takes on the same type of role repeatedly. This is a figure constructed by fans, by publicists, by the media or all three working in combination. The persona may represent significant elements of the real person but not necessarily.

A star is an image. He or she becomes a sign, a cultural signifier of a particular concentration of qualities, most often relating to gender and sexuality. He or she may represent a particular male or female image. They are both likely to be objects of desire and to embody a set of values which are fashionable and which capture the *Zeitgeist* – the spirit of the time. The image can shift over time and can mean different things to different groups in society at the same moment (adapted from Nelmes 1999).

Stars are traditionally linked with success at the box office and traditionally their professional and personal lives attract enormous attention from the range of media. They function as an advance form of shorthand for the audience, to sell the film to the audience and become a commodity which can be promoted and marketed through meeting the needs, drives, values and aspirations of the spectator.

John Ellis (1992) describes stardom from this point of view: 'a star is a performer in a particular medium whose figure enters into subsidiary forms of circulation and then feeds back into future performances'.

Justin Wyatt (1994) adds to this organisational function of stars as follows: 'Economically stardom is a patent on a unique set of human characteristics . . . [which] include purely physical aspects'.

This clearly draws attention to the link between the economics of stars and their appearance. Jude Brigley (2002) develops this by describing the star as 'a glittering object of desire' which draws the spectator into the complexity of stardom and stresses the pleasure a star can bring to them.

Film stars are less significant in people's lives than they were. Developments in modern media production where there are more competing sources of entertainment mean that films are only a part of the wide-ranging media experience of audiences. They still have significance but share this with stars drawn from the worlds of television, music, sport and fashion. Stardom in film has to be seen in this context. The central concern at present is being famous across a whole range of entertainment formats. This means more exposure to allow the full exploitation of their qualities. Their private lives become the focus of attention. They need to sustain their star image to be in the public eye for longer and hence the sense of 'mystique' can be lost. The exploration of their private lives in magazines, videos, photography, interviews and appearances become the focus of concern. Stars have always been central to the publicity machine. However, with the increasing exposure of their private lives, they run a fine line between protecting their privacy and using their private lives to promote themselves and their products. It is one of the central tensions in the modern media which has strong historical roots in the studio system. Audiences are insatiably curious about private lives and as a consequence the details of lives so carefully concealed in the past are potentially open to scrutiny. Privacy has become a major area of attention in the modern media.

STAR SYSTEM. This was a method of manufacturing, developing and marketing stars that focused on the leading performer in a film. Associated with Hollywood and the major studios it is still a feature of Indian Bollywood films. Developments in other media industries have links to this. There are traces of it in the pop music of the 1960s with The Monkees as an example of a manufactured band. There are also traces in modern television programmes such as *Fame Academy* (BBC, 2002). The star system as such collapsed with the decline of the studio system in the 1950s. However, a key element was the creation of the persona of a star which could, by a process of synergy, be linked to other products: detergents, soft drinks, crisps, sweets, toys etc.

Celebrity

CELEBRITY is concerned with dissolution of the distinction between the private and the public. Celebrities are those who are brought into the public eye for one reason or another: '. . . the celebrity is a voice above all others, a voice that is channeled into the media system as being legitimately significant' (Langer 1998).

Once there, they become the object of curiosity and subject to intense speculation. They can be subject to speculation and gossip and become objects of attention for the paparazzi. They can be drawn from any area of life: business, sport, entertainment, the arts and so on. As such they are a ready source of news. In addition they can be turned into commodities. These can be marketed in their own right or used to market other commodities. They can become brand names as well as cultural icons. In order to do this they need to be involved in a commercial system of production that depends on publicity. As such they can reveal much about how values and attitudes are assembled and disseminated in the modern world.

Christine Geraighty (2000) suggests the following categories:

1. Celebrities whose fame rests on what happens outside their sphere of work. These people have lifestyles that attract attention. She offers Liz Hurley and Princess Diana as examples.

2. Professionals whose fame rests on their work. Examples would be newsreaders, chat-show hosts and sports commentators who address the public directly. She also suggests regular actors in soaps and situation comedy fall into this category.

3. Performers who draw attention to their skills in particular areas such as film, theatre, opera, rock music etc.

Chris Rojek (2001) suggests the following categories for the attainment of celebrity status:

1. *Ascribed status*. This depends on things that have little to do with the individual but have a status attached because of what they represent. The royal family in the UK who represent monarchical values is the example he gives.

2. *Achieved status*. This comes about as the result of accomplishment in a particular field of endeavour. In the Gulf War of 2003 a dog achieved such a status by sniffing out Iraqi armaments.

3. *Attributed status*. This is given to a person by virtue of becoming newsworthy by cultural intermediaries who sense an opportunity for publicity as a result of something which happened to them. He offers the publicist Max Clifford (UK) as an example.

He also offers two other useful terms:

1. *Celetoid*. These are generated by the media as objects of attention often for short time spans. He gives lottery winners and stalkers as examples.

2. *Celeactor*. A fictional character who is momentarily ubiquitous or who becomes a feature of mass culture. He offers Ali G and the characters of Harry Enfield as examples.

It is fair to suggest that these categorisations do not explore the full range of celebrity. It is difficult to describe, for instance, the real people featuring in docusoaps who have gone on to achieve celebrity status using these categories.

The Idea in Action

THE ACTIVITIES OF PUBLICISTS, AGENTS, MANAGERS AND OTHERS ARE CENTRAL TO the project of manufacturing celebrity. Often they remain invisible, though Max

Clifford would be an exception. He clearly prefers an active role in the construction of his own celebrity status as well as the people he represents. Presumably, keeping his name in the public eye through interviews etc. means that he can create his own reputation and therefore attract more work.

THE AGENT.   The aim of the agent is to book talent. For this the agent receives a fee, typically 10 per cent of the talent's fee. Many agents are increasingly global in their reach, aiming to secure work for their talent. They work in a highly competitive environment and need to promote themselves. Professional reputations are a crucial element. Hence industry experience can prove invaluable. Networking is seen as a key element in their activities. They also need to cross media boundaries in the search to secure work for the talent and sometimes persuade the talent to cross over from one media area to another. Kylie Minogue would be an example. They need to be in touch with the media industries and seek inside information on forthcoming productions. In addition they often make personal arrangements for their talent in terms of organising schedules and travel arrangements.

Agents also need to scout for talent and be proactive in the search for new people. In one sense they channel appropriate talent down the 'right' route while at the same time ensuring that the needs of the organisations they approach are met. The key factors for agents are 'looks' and 'voices'.

At the heart of the work is the contract. In television the fee is often not the most significant part of the contract, most income is earned from 'residuals': repeats and sales. Over-exposure is a problem for many celebrities and one of the agent's roles may be career building by seeking out the right opportunity at the right time. They often have to handle publicity and can be the first line of defence in the protection of the talent's privacy. Normally, though, this would be the responsibility of the manager.

THE MANAGER.   Turner et al. (2000) identify three types of manager:

1. *The classic manager.* These have an intense and ongoing relationship with the client. Typically they have few clients and those clients pay 15 per cent of their earnings. Given the payment of agency fees, clients need to able to afford this level of outlay. This kind of manager tends to grow with the client who has already established some form of public face. In that sense they help plan the client's career. This often causes the breakups that are such a common feature of this relationship.

2. *The role-specific manager.* These manage the engagements of the client especially in terms of interviews, speaker engagements and guest appearances as a regular part of the client's income. They emphasise the personality and appeal of the client in different circumstances to their performances which they may 'trail' in such appearances. They will often be engaged in press releases and the process of getting the client to the engagement. They ask for 25 per cent of the fee for the engagement. Often when initial public interest may have waned they offer the client new ways of exploiting their celebrity status.

3. *The impresario manager.* These are the managers who exploit trends in the media for particular types of entertainment and actively recruit 'acts' which are enhanced through contacts and engagements. Sometimes they achieve high status themselves and become publicity gurus who are able to advise on the trickiest of situations for their clients.

PUBLICISTS. These tend to be female, have often worked as journalists and are strong on networking. There are four main types of publicist:

1. *The freelance publicist*. These need to have excellent industry connections and as a consequence have often worked for major media corporations.

2. *The unit publicist.* This person is connected to an individual production. The work involves the publicity to be generated pre, during and post release. It will include such things as distribution of stills, on-the-set interviews and press kits (the guide distributed to newspapers, magazines and critics). Increasingly these are electronic allowing such features as video footage. There are clear objectives:

   a. *Newsworthiness* – creation of interest in star/celebrity/production and the generation of interest.

   b. *Placement* – the key to this is cross media application which highlights the production's content/issues/construction. Different media require different strategies.

   c. *Coordination* – time and place is always critical and has to be planned for. Productions are always time sensitive.

3. *Event publicists*. These people plan events inside events such as film and television festivals, or stand-alone events such as premieres or openings. The key to success is free advertising or editorial content. Generating 'hype' is central to their work. Contacts are critical to success. They are employed on a contract-by-contract basis and so need to be known in the trade.

4. *Media corporation publicist*. In large corporations there is a publicity department which has a range of staff. They provide an enormous amount of material for other media. All media, in this sense, feed each other. At the same time they seek to exercise control of the publicity generated for the stars and celebrities. Control of the image is central and leads to practices such as the agreement to tackle only certain kinds of issues in interviews and agreed agendas.

The Idea Today

PUBLICITY HAS BUILT THE CELEBRITY INDUSTRY. CELEBRITIES THEMSELVES ARE ALL spokespersons in one form or another for some further commodity than themselves. It is clear that in themselves they have become major selling devices for a range of goods, services and media organisations who need the endorsement which they give them. Celebrities help to position these through increasing media exposure. This needs to be managed.

Issues in media management

CLEARLY the media can build reputations, create reputations and destroy reputations. It is a highly volatile process. Becoming the object of intense scrutiny leads to a range of issues to do with how celebrities/stars can be enhanced, how they can be protected and how they might become 'victims'. Its effects can be very damaging. This raises a whole series of issues about private lives and what is and is not 'fair game' in terms of the coverage of celebrity. A central concern then is with regulation and control.

ETHICS.   In an aggressive, competitive media industry managers feel a clear need both to protect the interests of their clients while at the same time viewing them as a commercial product to be exploited through packaging. This can create tensions and conflicts about strategic management of the 'brand'. Does the manager or the client control the use which is made of the 'brand'? Can the 'brand' change?

DAMAGE CONTROL.   Stories can start from anywhere and its consequences can be very unpredictable. Often the aim of the publicist will be to keep certain stories out of the news. The fact that they tend to surface somewhere can often be explained by the highly competitive and often malicious nature of the tabloid press in particular. One phenomenon worth noting is how broadcasting is able to refer to 'tabloid gossip' through activities such as reviewing the daily papers. There are considerable dangers in unwanted publicity in that relatively inexperienced celebrities can be caught in situations which they do not have the ability to deal with. However, publicists are rarely averse to 'spinning' such stories to their client's interests rather than outright denial. Conversely, controversy is generally regarded as being good for sales. One of the difficulties comes with the generation of stories in different versions which tends to create a sceptical response among consumers. It becomes difficult to know the truth. Often young inexperienced performers are exploited and their stories revealed to generate publicity. Once exploited they can be discarded.

ACCIDENTAL HEROES.   It is clear that with the advent of reality television ordinary people living ordinary lives can be the focus of intense media speculation. The tactics used in documentaries and current affairs programmes – the adversarial interview, hidden cameras, door stepping – often mean that individuals can be caught in the media spotlight without any sense of redress. There is a sense that exposure equals guilt. The converse can be true. People can create stories that they know are newsworthy, which they feed to media to create some advantage to themselves. Part of this can be attributed to media deregulation, which means that more and more organisations are involved in the generation of stories for public consumption and in a competitive world ethical standards are less important than the need to attract an audience.

Alternative Media

R ADICAL CULTURAL THEORISTS HAVE ALWAYS BEEN CRITICAL OF MEDIA ORGANISATIONS.
Commentaries are full of terms with negative connotations: conglomeration,
commodification, 'dumbing down', a concentration of symbolic power in the hands of
a few powerful organisations led by powerful men. The concept of the 'public sphere'
is the ideal of a space for communication where people can participate equally, regard-
less of background, and where reason, rather than power has come under pressure
especially from feminists who argue that the balance of power in media organisations
still remains with men. There is also a strand of thinking which concentrates on the
potential of organisational change and technological innovation. In such a view alternative media *'have created new spaces for alternative voices that provide a focus both for
specific community interests as well as for the contrary and the subversive'* (Silverstone
1999).

This identifies two major concerns for alternative media: its oppositional nature and its
concern for communities.

Enzensberger in "Constituents of a Theory of the Media" sets up a series of oppositions
to define the difference between independent and mainstream which can act as a
starting point.

MAINSTREAM
*Repressive: Centralised: One transmitter: Passive consumer: Produces programmes
for mass audience: Depoliticised: Hierarchical: Industrial production: Objectivity,
balance: Conventional forms: Subject to legislative control e.g. taste and decency.*

INDEPENDENT
*Emancipatory: Decentralised: Everyone a potential transmitter: Individualised:
Interactive community audience: 'Integrated practice': Community of interest:
Political learning process: Collective production: Politically 'engaged':
Experimental forms: Pushing the boundaries: Transgressing/rule breaking.*

Atton (2002) offers a further definition: *'Alternative media . . . are crucially about offering the means for democratic production to people who are normally excluded from media production. They are to do with organizing the media along lines that enable participation and reflexivity.'* He goes on to define three foci drawn from the work of Raymond Williams (1980):

- *Decapitalisation*. The circulation and distribution of alternative media productions.
- *Deprofessionalisation*. The do-it-yourself ethic/everyone's a media producer now.
- *Deinstitutionalisation*. The problems associated with organising a medium within collective organisations.

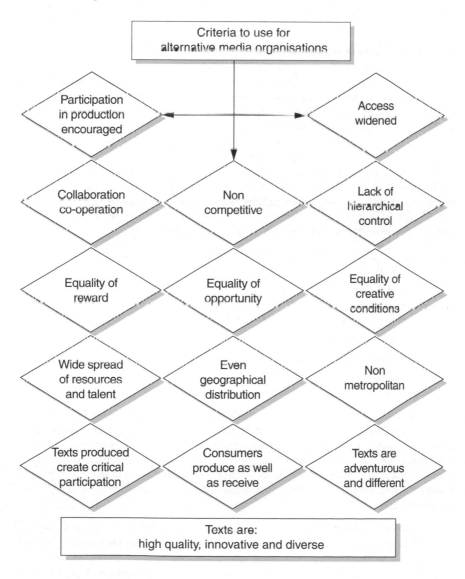

Figure 4 Criteria for alternative media organisations

The best way forward for the student is to explore a range of texts and organisations using a set of criteria which can test such a definition in a variety of contexts. (see Figure 4.)

Three such areas for exploration are discussed below: alternative and independent cinema, zines and the media organisation 'under*currents*' (founded in 1995).

The Idea in Action

Alternative and independent cinema

THIS section draws heavily on a conference presentation by Jill Poppy. Alternative and independent cinema would fit with the idea of 'contrary and the subversive' but would not meet some of the other proposed criteria. Such cinema sets itself against the style of filmmaking prevalent in Hollywood between 1930 and 1960, many aspects of which are still part of most commercial film production in the West: classical Hollywood cinema. This style of filmmaking prioritises narrative over any concern with alternative forms of creating stories. It aims to create a highly constructed reality that seeks to erase or make invisible the way in which it has been made. It achieves this through techniques such as continuity editing (invisible editing). Audiences are persuaded to accept the reality of what is depicted through an editing process which makes transitions between cuts appear seamless. The audience is 'sutured' or 'stitched' into the narrative. The narratives have clearly recurring patterns:

1. Stories with cause and effect plots: patterns of equilibrium, disruption and re-equilibrium.

2. Character-led stories that emphasise the individual: their drives, motivations, wishes, desires within social situations rather than analysis of that situation.

3. A high degree of closure: typically the 'happy ending' in that occasionally there is some space for moral or narrative ambiguity.

Its ideological function, it has been argued, is to naturalise issues of gender, race, sexuality and the economics of capitalism. It is subject to limited change under the influence of ideas from experimental and avant-garde film.

The film critic Peter Wollen (1982) identified key points of difference between mainstream and counter cinema, that is, cinema that somehow challenged or subverted the codes, conventions or ideologies of mainstream cinema. Such films are concerned with distancing the viewer from the reality portrayed in order to question what Jean-Luc Godard called '*the illusion of reality*' rather than the '*reality of the illusion*'. It was particularly influential in feminist film theory from the 1970s onwards. The key points of difference are:

• Narrative transitive/narrative intransitivity. In mainstream cinema narrative follows a clear developmental pattern of cause and effect. This happens, then this happens, because of this. Counter cinema often breaks the emotional hold of the narrative by disrupting its sequential flow (with interruptions, digressions and the absence of immediately apparent connections).

- Identification/estrangement. Counter cinema often uses deliberate mismatches between voice or sound and image, introducing actors as themselves or having them directly address the audience. This raises different kinds of questions for the audience: 'What is this film for?' rather than the usual 'Why did that happen?' or 'What will happen next?'.

- Transparency/foregrounding. In mainstream cinema we are not conscious of the act of filmmaking (we see through its construction) whereas counter cinema draws attention to the process of making a film, e.g., seeing someone with a camera, freezeframing, rewinding, etc. It seeks to make the invisible visible and part of the *mise en scène*.

- Simple/multiple diegesis. Mainstream cinema shows a consistent order of time and space (even when devices such as flashbacks are used). Counter cinema often introduces characters from different periods/fictions into the film so that the text does not appear necessarily as a whole. This audience is left guessing and unclear about the relationship between people or time or event.

- Closure/aperture. Instead of the closed self-contained text organised under a unifying vision that characterises mainstream film, counter cinema uses different voices and discourses which encounter each other and may conflict. The audience may be left with lots of questions rather than lots of answers, for example, who the murderer was in the thriller may never be made clear.

- Pleasure/unpleasure. Mainstream cinema seeks to entertain 'the consumer'. Counter cinema produces a collective working relationship between filmmaker and audience, in which the spectator can collaborate in the production/consumption of meaning. In this way the audience is empowered and turns into a 'citizen' rather than a customer.

- Fiction/reality. Mainstream cinema is a fiction. Counter cinema tends to distrust this as 'mystification and ideology', seeing representation as illusion and lies and seeking to put 'truth' in its place by challenging accepted stereotypes. It seeks to correct the distorted versions of reality produced by classical narrative with its emphasis on character.

Such texts are clearly diverse, different and create critical participation for the spectator whose preconceptions and view of the world may have been challenged, changed, modified or turned upside down.

Zines

ACCESS to alternative media encourages self-publishing. Zines are an example of this.

It is useful (Atton 2002) to distinguish between the 'fanzine', which are concerned with the reception of primary texts (films, characters, sport, books, genres etc.) by groups, and 'zines'.

Atton argues that zines are produced by people who *'turn to themselves, to their own lives, their own experiences, and turn these into the subjects of their writing . . . at the heart of zine culture is . . . the study of self, of personal expression, sociality and the building of community'.*

These 'zinsters' were empowered by the 'do-it-yourself' (DIY) philosophy of the punk revolt of the 1970s which itself was very much in the tradition of the kind of pamphleteering used in social protest in the earlier periods of the Civil War in England and

Chartist movements of the Victorian period. This also drew on models from the Dada art movement of the 1920s whose proponents produced journals in various European cities for their own pleasure and for the provocation of readers by making the world appear 'strange' and 'defamiliarised'. These publications were intended to be ephemeral and outrageous. The surrealists of the 1930s were also engaged in self-publication. The surrealists themselves paid for the publication, *Editions Surrealistes* without any indication of a publisher, bookseller or commercial organisation.

The key features of zines are:

- They are a cheap grassroots reaction to the crisis in the media landscape produced by corporate advertising, television programming, PR campaigns and its effects on consumer lifestyle. They attack the homogenisation of media culture from subjective viewpoints based on the general principle that consorting with the mass media has a damaging effect upon attempts at social revolution. As such they are intensely personal in orientation. They are often angry and polemic in their intentions.

- The zines are often produced by illicit means and often challenge copyright laws and ideas of intellectual property. As a rule the zinsters appropriate newspaper articles, magazine headlines and photos and use them without permission.

- They often reconstruct media messages by transgressions such as graffiti and cut-outs. Armed with a glue stick, scissors, a pen and a purpose they subvert dominant representations of reality to encourage activism.

- They are often threatened by legal action and have been prosecuted in criminal courts. Slander, piracy, obscenity, taste and decency etc. have occasioned such legal action.

- Modern technology has encouraged the growth of the 'ezine'. The proponents of this argue for its instant availability, easy updating, ecological advantage and cheapness. However, it has raised debates about the availability of computers and questions of access. It has also raised questions about the role of large software and hardware corporations such as Microsoft. The handling of desktop publishing also requires training which, it is argued, cut 'n' paste does not. It is sometimes suggested that the work of ezinsters is too clean and too well designed.

- Zines demand the personal communication inherent in a relationship. Hence this needs to be worked on and built. *'They're really about communication and ideas, not about selling other people's products. Zines are about creating culture and creating community'* (The Fat Girl Collective, http://www.fatgirl.com/). As Lynne Peril of Mystery Date, an American zine drawing on diverse sources (1950s' home economics textbooks, dating manuals, educational videos etc.) explains, *'Creating a zine is the best tactic for getting mail. I have been known to get extremely upset – even outraged – if I come home to an empty mailbox'*.

- One of its characteristics is the reflection of interests which the zinsters care about and often as such they have a short shelf life as interests develop in different directions.

- Costs can be a critical issue as low cost is good while 'free' is a better concept. The exchange of a zine can be considered a kind of 'gift relationship'. Readers are regularly expected to wait for its arrival and be patient.

under *currents*: an alternative news organisation

UNDERCURRENTS describes itself as an alternative news organisation and uses the slogan: 'Stop drinking from the mainstream'. Its starting point is frustration at what it calls the established media's *'lack of concern and analysis in reporting environmental and social issues'*. Its video footage is supplied by *'activists at the forefront of local and global campaigns'*. In many ways, then, it starts out from the same basis as a zine as a way of articulating a response to the mainstream media from personal and social viewpoints. Where it significantly differs is its engagement and use of the mainstream. Key notes about the messages and values of the organisation can be studied through the use of a range of sources. Most of these can be found on the website: http://www.undercurrents.org/.

Their own views: in press interviews

'BUT in the true DIY style of this movement, alternative outlets are being created. Video activists, internet hackers, radio pirates, digital photographers and text reporters are creating forums for the ignored and the marginalised. Undercurrents coined the phrase "video activists", but prefer the more flamboyant "video warriors" to describe this radical, hands-on form of journalism.

Slowly, they are infiltrating the mainstream media. "We started using video in a very strategic way then thought why not go to TV with these images? Eventually we bullied TV stations into considering them," he explains.

"They had never seen anything like it. This was the news they were missing. We go inside and get the views of activists, even if that means going up trees and down tunnels." Capturing such footage often puts them in sticky situations, to put it mildly' (In Focus: Amanda Castleman talking to Director Paul O'Connor, one of the founders of under*currents*, a video news organisation based in Oxford).

Such material needs handling with care. In a recent interview with Paul O'Connor (April 2003) he stated that he would never use a phrase such as 'video warriors' to describe participants in such activity. He regarded this as a typical misquotation by local media outlets. This suggests that sources cannot be accepted uncritically.

Their own views: in articles

1. *'Last month 12 environmental justice protesters and a video activist walked into Shell UK's London headquarters and occupied three offices. The first thing Undercurrents reporter Roddy Mansfield did was to set up his small digital camera and link it to a palm-top computer and a mobile phone. Despite Shell turning off the electricity and cutting the phone lines, within minutes he was broadcasting the protest live on the Internet, and e-mailing it to the mainstream press. By the time they were evicted a few hours later, five "broadcasts" had been made.*

Reportage of the future? A new tool of democracy? Or illegal, irresponsible behaviour? Take your pick, but just as sixties' students took over printing presses to further disseminate their political message, so today's activists have turned to new electronic technologies.

The Web and e-communications have revolutionised environmental and social justice campaigning and, arguably, helped to nurture a new North–South dialogue about democracy, social justice, development and human rights in an increasingly globalised world.

Many non-governmental groups now depend on the Web and e-mail to motivate, activate and communicate their uncensored messages. Most groups have camcorders and websites; all have e-mail.

The obvious advantage of electronic communication is the ability it gives campaigners to network quickly and cheaply. Using e-mail and "list servers" – where the same message can be sent to any number of electronic addresses – other groups can be alerted and global campaigns mounted quickly'.

2. 'From Belfast to Brighton, video activists are now editing on laptops and producing their own news. Screened monthly, via video projectors in solar-powered cinemas, the "News Reals", as they are dubbed, are attracting large audiences.

Undercurrents, along with other media activists such as Indymedia and the SchNEWS weekly newsletter, created a valuable platform for activists to bypass the corporate media by recording and circulating news of their own events. With just six agencies dominating the world's distribution of news, media campaigners are busy setting up working alternatives. Japanese video maker Matsubara Akira was so inspired while exchanging videos between Liverpool dockers and Japanese railway workers that he set up an organisation to distribute the works of video activists. Speaking at a festival in South Korea, he said, "I set up Video Act! to 'Create, Screen and Change'. I would like to make it go global and make a stronger network amongst the working people."

This desire to forge links is endorsed by Katharine Ainger, editor of the Oxford-based New Internationalist magazine. She argues: "As the economy globalises, we actually find out less and less about one another from the media. Cost-cutting means that coverage of international news in the west has fallen by an average of 50% in the last 10 years."

In reaction to the tightening grip of the media moguls, computer hackers created a unique "open publishing" network on the world wide web. By allowing anyone to publish their own text, audio or video reports online, Indymedia aims to "erode the dividing line between reporters and reported, between active producers and passive audience".

The price to pay for providing such an open platform is high. During the G8 summit in Genoa last month, paramilitary police attacked the volunteer-run Independent Media Centre. As hundreds of armed troops destroyed computers and cameras, a video activist from Undercurrents escaped on to the roof and recorded the brutal raid. Using a water tower for cover, Hamish Campbell had problems steadying his digital camcorder while listening to the screams of his colleagues being tortured below.

Bill Hayton, a BBC reporter, was so shocked by the raid that he published his own report using the independent media portal. He wrote: "The thought that a European police force can line protesters up against a wall and beat them until their blood literally flows across the floor chills me to the bone." Police assaults on the Independent Media Centres during the protests in Davos and Quebec received little or no mainstream coverage.

Outside the media centre lay the broken body of Marcus "Sky" Covell. Covell travelled to Genoa and volunteered his skills to ensure that the internet system worked for independent reporters. But after Italian police left him with snapped bones and lungs filling with blood, the Daily Mail penned reports accusing Covell of being the "mastermind", the "Briton who led rioters". These ill-informed reports provided yet another sad example of why activists have lost faith in the press.

American video activist Rick Rowley, who lost his camera equipment and tapes to the Italian state in Genoa, says the experience hasn't deterred him from video activism. Despite spending four days in jail before being released without charge, Rowley is still looking forward to being on the streets at next month's World Bank meeting in Washington DC.

He and his colleagues at the non-profit Big Noise Films co-produced 'This Is What Democracy Looks Like: The Story Behind the WTO Summit in Seattle'. As he explained: "It was pieced together from over 100 cameras and has sold nearly 10,000 copies, and last year, on the anniversary of the protests, the documentary was screened in 50 cities on five continents."

The alternative media are also providing a fuller record of the events in Genoa, a stark contrast to the daily news feeds distributed by the corporate agencies. Associated Press Television News (APTN) summed up the weekend of protests with a series of about 30 images, the overwhelming majority of which featured only the violent clashes.

Sam Wild remained in Italy to coordinate the distribution of "key moments of the protests" to alternative media outlets around the world. While sorting through the "sackfuls" of digital tapes, he says, "Because so much footage from so many people was contributed, we have ensured that we have a real overview of virtually every major and minor event that unfolded."

The alternative media take a much more inclusive view of protests. While not ignoring the street battles, we concentrate on giving a voice to the 300,000 non-violent demonstrators who travelled to Genoa.

Grassroots reporting is perhaps finally gaining acceptance within the mainstream. At the end of this month, Channel 4 will broadcast the pilot of a unique programme which, according to its producers, will offer "a radical new approach to current affairs and politics inspired by video activists". Alt-World will feature stories by video activists in Brazil, Australia, the United States, Yugoslavia and Britain.

Nina Simoes will present one of these segments, on the huge social movement in her birthplace of Sao Paolo. "In countries like Brazil, where an under-represented majority struggles to have its voice heard, video activism has been fundamental in raising aware-ness about many of the social problems."

. . . Pluto Press is releasing the Video Activist Handbook, detailing this growing movement and offering all the insider knowledge necessary for anyone to put a camcorder to good use' (Director and Founder Member, Paul O'Connor).

What becomes clear in such accounts is the way in which small media organisations can engage with the mainstream to get alterna-tive grassroots viewpoints expressed.

Their own views: in visual representations in posters and publicity

THE poster represents an interesting example of how the organisation works with its participants. A small group tends to lead sessions that explain how such publicity can contribute to the aims or mission of the organisation. This proved to be an interesting example for some participants in South Wales. A lot of time is spent exploring the appropriateness of certain kinds of approaches. This can lead to all sorts of splits and schisms within such organisations (though not in this case!). Central to the approach is dialogue and persuasion rather than control.

Their own views: in the events that it puts on

THE important thing to note here is the diversity of viewpoints that are represented. All kinds of people are involved.

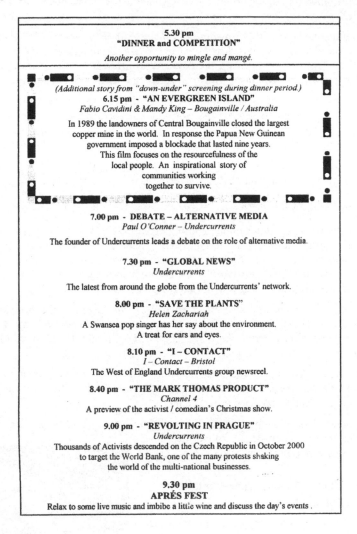

5.30 pm
"DINNER and COMPETITION"
Another opportunity to mingle and mangé.

(Additional story from "down-under" screening during dinner period.)
6.15 pm - "AN EVERGREEN ISLAND"
Fabio Cavidini & Mandy King – Bougainville / Australia

In 1989 the landowners of Central Bougainville closed the largest copper mine in the world. In response the Papua New Guinean government imposed a blockade that lasted nine years. This film focuses on the resourcefulness of the local people. An inspirational story of communities working together to survive.

7.00 pm - DEBATE – ALTERNATIVE MEDIA
Paul O'Conner – Undercurrents
The founder of Undercurrents leads a debate on the role of alternative media.

7.30 pm - "GLOBAL NEWS"
Undercurrents
The latest from around the globe from the Undercurrents' network.

8.00 pm - "SAVE THE PLANTS"
Helen Zachariah
A Swansea pop singer has her say about the environment.
A treat for ears and eyes.

8.10 pm - "I – CONTACT"
I – Contact – Bristol
The West of England Undercurrents group newsreel.

8.40 pm - "THE MARK THOMAS PRODUCT"
Channel 4
A preview of the activist / comedian's Christmas show.

9.00 pm - "REVOLTING IN PRAGUE"
Undercurrents
Thousands of Activists descended on the Czech Republic in October 2000 to target the World Bank, one of the many protests shaking the world of the multi-national businesses.

9.30 pm
APRÉS FEST
Relax to some live music and imbibe a little wine and discuss the day's events.

Its participants

Ken Moon 'FARMERS MARKETS'

KEN has memories of seeing hard-hitting journalism on the television. When he was shown an under*currents* video at college in Swansea he was inspired to have a go himself.

Now he has made a film about farmers' market, a subject dear to his heart.

'I did a degree in geography,' says 23-year-old Ken. 'Now I am studying for a diploma in permaculture design and sustainable land use through Kingston Moorwood College and horticulture at Carmarthen.

'I am interested in the farmers' markets because they promote sustainability. Customers buy goods directly from the producers. They know how the vegetables have been grown, for example, but it also means products will not have travelled far, will not be heavily packaged and should be much fresher than those bought in a supermarket.'

Although he comes from Cardiff Ken's roots are in Gower where his grandparents were avid gardeners. His love for the subject first took seed at an early age wielding a spade for his grandfather, Tom.

Now, as part of the Swansea Permaculture Group Ken plans to travel to Cuba to film. He explains that the government there is the only one in the world which has insisted on all food being organically grown. The Country has a special interest in being self-sufficient having suffered the effects of America's embargo on trade for many years. This makes the situation no less interesting from a permaculture perspective, says Ken. There are lessons to learn.

'Wales has missed the opportunity to go organic. It is moving in that direction but I would like to see it leading the way.'

It's time to lead the field then.

Al Coley 'MICROWAVE MADNESS' Mobile phone mast film

AL likes to make films that help people understand each other, to foster cross-cultural understanding. Having studied anthropology her film background is somewhat different from the usual journalistic style. She is used to getting to know those whom she is filming over a period.

'I am really against formal interviews, the use of tripod and asking people to do things again if they have done them once already so in a way this kind of journalistic film is new for me. It was quite a struggle as it goes against the tradition I come from,' she says.

'But now I'm seeing the benefits of knowing how to stucture something that way and you can bring in the style of filmaking you want within that structure.'

Her experiences with undercurrents have helped Al edit a film she made for her masters degree so it could be shown on Channel 4. Elvorian and the Fangmaker, about the death rock subculture, shows viewers a world which seems alien to many. The point is to help people tolerate and embrace diversity.

Apart from helping with editing other people's footage for the festival Al has made a film about the mobile phone masts protest. The film focuses on the scientific arguments about the dangers posed by their emissions rather than simply the aesthetic objections.

Al hopes to make a series of short films, in the Modern Times vein, called Tales from the City. Her plan is to find Swansea characters and let them talk. She feels the so-called Penlan Cowboys would make interesting subjects.

Al believes in Undercurrents, seeing it as an important and worthwhile organisation in itself. Apart from gaining experience for her own work she has been helping to train the would-be filmmakers of tomorrow.

Al worked on the video workshops provided for the young people's project, the Greenteam, at this summer's Eco Fest in Swansea's Singleton Park. It was one of the most popular activities on offer.

Its accounts

THE keypoints here are the smallness of the budget (in that massive amounts of money are not needed for highly effective campaigning) and the importance of being accountable to participants for the way resources are deployed. Openness and transparency are key features.

UNDER*CURRENTS* PRODUCTIONS PROFIT & LOSS		
Period Ending 31/12/96		
	£	£
Income		
Awards		1,206
Donations		1,148
Grants		4,623
TV Sales		13,686
Video Sales		11,421
Other		10

		32,094
Deposit Account Interest		.6

TOTAL		32,100
Expenditure		
Directors Remuneration	5,152	
Subcontractor staff	3,000	
Telephone	1,864	
Post&Stationary	3,717	
Advertising&Publicity	1,284	
Travelling expenses	2,829	
Computer expenses	-	
Filming costs	3,833	
Videotape costs	3,912	
Training	480	
Hire of Equipment	-	
Repairs & renewals	870	
Building Maintenance	-	
Property cleaning	-	
Sundry expenses	341	
Accountancy	800	
Legal fees	15	
Consultancy fees	-	
Commission paid	-	
Public relations	-	
Bad debts		-
Rents and rates	704	
Insurance	998	
Light and heat	-	
	-------	29,799

		2,301
Finance Costs:		
Bank Charges		153

NET SURPLUS		£2,148

Using such evidence (and other sources) it is possible to examine:

1. How alternative media organise themselves within this network: '*a network of active relationships between actors who interact, communicate, influence each other, negotiate, and make decisions. Forms of organization and models of leadership, communicative channels and technologies of communication are constitutive parts of this network of relationships*' (Melucci 1996). Questions about participation and control and the self-reflexivity of members/friends can be raised. How appropriate is the publicity to the messages and values of the organisation? Is it appropriate to work for a council? The network remains uncontrolled, non-hierarchical and open. Often decisions are made at a local level as in grassroots decision making.

2. Their tendency to move away from hierarchical models: consensus, cooperation and collective decision making are preferred modes of operation. However, a core group seeks to coordinate rather than control.

3. The ways in which the means of production are handed over through training, exhibition and distribution. Activists are never mere readers, consumers or specta- tors; they are encouraged to be organisers, workshop leaders, facilitators, producers and writers. It is essentially a creative enterprise with a point of view. Activists become communicators in their own right through being given a voice.

4. An irreverent take but involvement with the mainstream media in terms of getting airtime and coverage.

5. The use made of modern means of production such as the internet and the issues this raises for participants and for mainstream media organisations prepared to engage in dialogue with them.

Cultural Imperialism

The Idea

THIS THEORY ARGUES THAT THERE EXISTS A PROCESS WHEREBY ECONOMICALLY STRONG countries have imposed and developed their cultural control over other (often poorer) countries. The flow is always from the West, particularly the USA, to these countries and is generally argued to be one way.

'The cultural imperialism thesis claims that authentic, traditional and local culture in many parts of the world is being battered out of existence by the indiscriminate dumping of large quantities of slick commercial products, mainly from the United States' (Tunstall 1977).

This point of view is backed up by the commentators who state that capitalist countries have the power and influence to dominate media markets which are then used (in the main) to spread the capitalist ideals and values. This is a view which clearly makes connections between economic and political systems and which necessarily offers us a pessimistic outlook on the future. This relationship between the USA and the developing world, or Russia, or China or indeed France, is seen by many as a negative and the process whereby countries are dominated a relentless one. For the USA such countries become another market for their goods. People who resist such domination refer often to the fact that they are a people not a market to be exploited. People who argue this use words such as imposition and domination. Both imply a less than willing host country: consequently the term 'cultural imperialism' itself has become a somewhat emotive phrase, linked as it often is with images of enforced domination. O'Sullivan et al. (1994) after defining imperialism as a process whereby *'certain economically dominant nations systematically develop and extend their economic, political and cultural control over other countries'*, continue by offering us clarification on the cultural version of the term:

'cultural imperialism refers to . . . the ways in which the transmission of certain products, fashions and styles from the dominant nations to the dependent markets leads to the creation of particular patterns of demand and consumption which are underpinned by and endorse the cultural values, ideas and practices of their dominant origin'.

The *Fontana Dictionary of Modern Thought* goes a step further in its definition of cultural imperialism:' '*the use of political and economic power to exalt and spread the values and habits of a foreign culture at the expense of a native culture . . .*'.

It is clear that it is concerned with enforcing a version of what the world is like through the imposition of values and beliefs on native cultures through cultural products. The heavily mediated nature of the developed world which produces goods and services (e.g. Nike, Levis, Coca Cola, McDonald's) and a range of cultural products (e.g. Disney, Warner Brothers) and Western personalities (such as David Beckham, Eminem, Madonna, Denzil Washington) shows that there is clearly a concentration of organisations in the developed world, particularly the USA, seeking new markets and new labour forces to produce cultural products cheaply for the maximum profit. Media images and their stars are big business globally and have enormous impact. Their power clearly stems from the source of the money: the developed world, primarily the USA.

Thus, for many, the term cultural imperialism has become synonymous with the notion of cultural dominance, metaphorically a somewhat 'dirty' process linked with imposition of values and the contamination of indigenous cultures.

The cultural imperialism theory states that both an invasion and an imbalance of power combine to justify the term. Another definition of cultural imperialism can be suggested: when one country is subjected to substantial external pressure from the media interests of another country and when there is no exchange of media products. This absence of any exchange constitutes cultural invasion by another power and therefore an imbalance of power resources between the two countries.

The process more than damages, it is argued, it essentially obliterates local cultures.

Cultural triangulation

THERE is another version of this argument based in the culture's response to these media products. What happens if an external culture is welcomed, imitated or added to? Real audiences respond (often with great unpredictability) to the one-way flow of media products. It emphasises the fact that the media products may be meaningful to the host country but that the meanings extracted may not necessarily be the meanings they were encoded with.

The basis of the argument stems from a belief that people have preferences and that to prefer something that has not been an indigenous part of one's culture does not negate that culture or necessarily spell its demise. The tendency to prefer foreign media products is, as a result, because of a long period of familiarisation with those products. There are three levels of this process of familiarisation which incorporate political co-orientation, economic co-orientation and finally the level of cultural triangulation. The third level appears as a consequence of the other two. The imbalance of media flow is also inevitable, through the sheer volume of product produced by the West and by the West's unarguable control of the distribution. This view is aware that cultural triangulation, like imperialism, reflects a possible demise of native cultures; but the argument highlights the fact that all cultures eventually evolve and that any symbiotic relationship means change. Media technology is simply forcing the pace of that change. It is in essence an evolutionary version of how cultures develop.

The Idea in Action

A N EXAMPLE OF GLOBAL RESEARCH CAN BE FOUND IN WASKO ET AL. (2001), 'Dazzled by Disney?: The Global Disney Audience Project'. The project was designed to examine the way Disney products have proliferated globally and to identify the patterns of such expansion.

While the Disney organisation may individualise certain product offerings to specific countries, the core values of the company would remain remarkably consistent across cultures. Consumers would view such products as benign influences and tend to underestimate their own level of exposure to them. Parents in particular would see Disney as appropriate without realising the effects the company had on their own development.

The project involved researchers in 18 countries who took part in a three-pronged research design:

1. subject questionnaires and interviews;
2. individual country market analysis;
3. cross-cultural analysis.

The audience research segment used two research instruments: standardised question-naires and in-depth interviews. These explored the:

1. level of contact;
2. attitude to Disney at various age levels;
3. types and number of Disney products;
4. values that they attached to Disney;
5. the perspective from which Disney makes those offerings (American? Western? Global?).

The research reported widespread exposure to Disney products in the surveys and interviews. The average respondent was under 5 when first exposed. Less than 1 per cent reported having no contact; 99 per cent of respondents had seen a Disney film.

Eighty-five per cent of respondents agreed that Disney promotes core Disney values such as family, imagination, good over evil, happiness, magic and fun despite cultural and language differences. It was, then, possible to conclude that Disney had been remarkably successful in consistently implementing its brand values.

The interviews revealed that respondents recognised that Disney was a business with a priority to earn profits. Many referred with distaste to the organisational practices of Disney using terms such as greed, cultural imperialism, manipulation, monopoly etc. However, Disney as entertainment was still considered to be safe, wholesome and above all fun.

Attitudes to Disney varied greatly in the interviews. Often seen as typically American (which carried positive and negative connotations), some respondents felt that Disney represented their own culture. Some claimed that Disney was universal and crossed all borders and ages.

This study exemplifies what is often described as new audience research in that it looks at the international reception of Disney products. In common with many such approaches, while establishing the pervasiveness of the Disney brand, it begins to point out the complexity of such research into audience interpretation.

The Idea Today

THE THEORY OF CULTURAL IMPERIALISM IN MANY WAYS HAS BEEN OVERTAKEN BY theories about globalisation. The key developments in technology in the period since then have allowed for the multi-directional flow of information between countries as opposed to a uni-directional flow. Gaining prominence in the 1970s, a number of weaknesses have been identified by theorists.

- There are countries who are not dominated by foreign media organisations, for example, India, Brazil, Mexico. The term 'cultural proximity' has been used. This describes how audiences will tend to prefer programming which is close to their own culture, and so in some Middle Eastern countries, for instance, the cultural imperialism theory does not hold true in all cases. Hence the theory has limited scope in this sense.

- It is also limited in its ability to deal with the contexts of symbolic interaction with media products and how individuals respond to them. The theory proposes a passive audience and does not acknowledge the active audience member. Theorists of the active audience have rejected the theory: Liebes and Katz (1993), Ang (1985). Ang, in particular, sets out to challenge 'a stubborn fixation on the threat of American cultural imperialism'. Liebes and Katz argue that the messages imparted by media products depended on the viewer's values and varied according to the group to which the audience member belonged.

- The theory itself lacks precise definition.

- The terms that the theory uses lack precision. Culture is a word that has multiple meanings. The word is often used interchangeably with media. The two terms are not synonymous and need greater clarification in the contexts within which they occur. In some countries it may well be legitimate to argue about the centrality of media in the creation of culture, however that be defined; in others it may well have less significance.

The success of imported media products within the third world and the consequences of that success, remains a complex area for investigation.

'a moment's reflection will show that the practice of watching television cannot be deemed to be straightforwardly "imposed", that the intention of the broadcasters may not be directly to "exalt and spread" values and habits, and that the notion of the process being at the "expense of a native culture" is extremely ambiguous' (Tomlinson 1991).

Perhaps, then, people simply use what is available to them for their own ends. The transference of cultural values is a complex matter. But where does this lead this theory? The earlier theory that economically dominant countries saturated the developing world with their media products in order to achieve some kind of conscious culture dominance has lost most of its credibility. While few people would argue against the idea of economic supremacy, it is the notion of cultural supremacy that is being questioned at length.

Consequently it seems that a closer study of these local cultures is needed in order to discover whether there may be evidence to suggest the theories for assimilation and adaption have more credence than the more traditional theories of imposition and imperialism. For while the 'older generation' of academics have traditionally discussed the issues from a theoretical point of view, contemporary researchers are now undertaking detailed case studies within different world cultures.

Globalisation

T HE CURRENT APPROACH TO THE WORLD MEDIA DISCOURSE IS TO LOOK AT THE issue from a global position. Tomlinson (1991) states, *'what replaces "imperialism" is "globalisation"'*. The globalisation treatise *'emerged as a critical concept in the late 1980s'* (O'Sullivan et al. 1994) and is firmly rooted within the postmodernist school of thought. Globalisation can, according to Tomlinson, *'be distinguished from imperialism in that is a far less coherent or culturally directed process'*. He goes on to explain that the idea of imperialism was that it was a *'purposeful project: the intended spread of a social system from one centre of power across the globe'*.

Globalism, on the other hand, is less coherent; it is not about intent and although saturation of cultures may be a product of it, this is not its motivating force: economics clearly is. O'Sullivan et al. (1994) tells us that, *'central to this process has been the emergence of communications technologies and information networks which allow for faster, more extensive, interdependent forms of world-wide exchange'*.

What has happened, it is claimed, is that with the rise of the multinational conglom-erates, the media influences around the globe no longer emanate from any one partic-ular nation state. That is not to say that the individual programmes (for example) may not have been Western in origin. But it points out that these large corporations transcend national frontiers and provide the technological means to 'globalise' the media systems of the world. There is, however, little debate that these institutions emanate from a Western capitalistic perspective.

The term itself, like cultural imperialism before it, has many connotations and provokes much debate. One of these areas is the fear that global media networks are producing a homogeneous global culture. This is sometimes referred to as the 'McDonaldisation of the world'.

This seemingly negative attitude towards globalisation is frequently apparent in the approaches to the topic, because although the intent to imperialise may be absent within a system of globalisation many agree that technological advances and the opportunities that come with them, lead to a depressing case of 'sameness' around the globe. In fact the negative effects reach the established global cultures as well as the emerging ones. Tomlinson argues, '*The average European or North American probably no longer experiences the cultural security their national identity used to afford*' and '*their accompanying sense of belonging to a secure culture is eroded*'.

There is no doubt that at the beginning of the 1990s there was a heavy dependency on American programming to fill the hours available on satellite stations around the globe. It was felt that if everything was the same then the initiators of the message had as much to lose as the receivers of the message. Tomlinson remarked, '*the effects of globalisation are to weaken the cultural coherence of all individual nation-states, including the economically powerful ones*' .

It does not seem to matter that within a globalised system the power lies in the hands of the distributors (the multinational corporations) and not with (say) the American nation: the homogeneous nature of the message is all too apparent and, it is argued, benefits no one.

And yet this notion of negativity is not a universally held view. Many see the emergence of a global network, and the technology that accompanies it, as a time for opportunities – opportunities for resistance to sameness, opportunities for regional diversity within the global network, opportunities to use the technology to further the cause of local networks.

So although there appears to be a global concentration of power over media production and distribution it is obviously also important to look at and consider how international audiences make use of and interpret the products. Indeed it is essential to note that the flow of programmes tend to be those of a recreational nature and that they are bought simply because they cost a fraction of the price it would cost for 'home' produced dramas to dominate national screens. The economic logic for purchasing overseas programmes to fill schedules is quite clear. And so it is now perhaps far more important to consider the impact of a worldwide satellite system than to consider the impact of imported programmes. One line of recent research indicates that there is a clear resistance to blanket Western style programming.

In another area of media activity, the world wide web is opening up a world of different perspectives and viewpoints for users. In the area of news on world events, web users cast their net far wider in order to seek explanation and context of major events. This access to a diversity of viewpoints can lead to a more international viewpoint. However, it is worth noting that people still tend to gravitate towards sites which reflect their own views. When faced with millions of potential points of view, it becomes difficult to argue the case for media imperialism. Furthermore, the individual can get access to information and form communities of interest. This can be a good or bad thing depending on your viewpoint. A neo-Nazi group can exert an influence far beyond the members of the group while an anti-war group consisting of two people could potentially influence hundreds of people across a wide range of cultures. The proliferation of alternative news sources on the web is linked to an audience which is increasingly sophisticated in its use of the medium.

There can be patterns in which the global and the local are mutually constituting. Global and local are relative terms in the globalised world. Local can mean what is of concern in your community or it can mean what you experience at your desktop or mobile phone or in an internet cafe as you surf the web or enter a chatroom or contribute to a news group or use your webcam to communicate.

There is also the question of regional flows to consider: there is a significant flow of programmes around the globe that are not Western in origin; examples include the exporting of programmes from Brazil and Mexico, not only to South American neighbours but also to Hispanic-speaking Europe. Indian films and records achieve large sales throughout Asia and Africa and, of course, have a good market outlet in Britain, while Egypt is now the main producer of programmes throughout the Arab-speaking world.

So rather than characterising global culture as relentlessly one way and linear, it is envisaged as overlapping and complex. The global media world has led to a multiplication of viewpoints and leads multiple potentialities for conflicts, disagreements, antagonisms and contradictions on the one hand and a range of pleasures and gratifications on the other.

The Idea in Action

THE UNDERLYING PRINCIPLE IS THAT OUR IDENTITIES, THE NARRATIVES WHICH WE construct about ourselves, can be influenced by media representations in contexts such as television. Television is a major disseminator of such representations in modern society.

The concept of global television, following Barker (1999), has three related phenomena:

1. The ways in which public and commercial television are regulated, funded and viewed within the boundaries of nation states and/or language communities. These are the institutional or organisational factors which structure their activities.

2. The ways in which these organisations, through technology such as satellite, ownership as in the case of Rupert Murdoch, or through programme distribution as in the case of *Neighbours* and audiences as in the case of *Dallas*, operate across the boundaries of the nation state and language community.

3. The ways in which these cultural representations flow and the issues these raise about effects, power and identity in different cultures linked by electronic networks.

Television production is a global phenomenon. Sporting events such as the Olympics or the World Cup or world events such as the terrorist attacks on 11 September 2001 (9/11) draw huge audiences. The rise in the production of television sets bears witness to this phenomenon. There has been year-on-year growth of television ownership especially in the developing world (Africa and Asia). New televisions require new programmes regularly which in a symbiotic manner creates more demand: more televisions means more programmes means more televisions which are more up to date, easy to use with a wider range of options for the user. It is the dynamic of capitalism that drives their use. As televisions are produced in a capitalist system, whose primary objective is to pursue profit, markets must be expanded and new products and services developed. It is by definition an expansionist system.

This raises a number of key issues.

OWNERSHIP.   Who owns the companies that produce these representations, why they produce them and for whom they produce them matters. The ways in which they concentrate themselves into conglomerates has created global communication giants who have a mission in terms of profit and a set of values which they seek to promote as part of that mission. This process of the creation of conglomerates is aided by the radical changes in technology witnessed in recent years and which are likely to accelerate.

SYNERGY.   This is the bringing together of the various elements of television and other media at the levels of both production and distribution. The aim is to be more efficient, more cost effective, more competitive and create greater profits for shareholders.

CONVERGENCE.   This is the technological process of bringing together technologies which have been produced separately (television/PC/telephone) and linking them electronically through the process referred to as digitalisation. It refers in the first place, then, to the breakdown of technologies and secondly, to the way in which media production practices have created multimedia organisations through mergers and takeovers.

DIGITALISATION.   This allows information to be electronically organised into bytes using binary numbers. Such information can be compressed at source and decompressed on arrival in a variety of ways. The development of the digital transmission of information has been extraordinary as processing power has speeded up and more and more media devices are being developed for the consumer which bring together previously separate technologies.

SATELLITES.   The transmission of digital information is aided by the ability of satellites to offer an increased number of signals. They also have a higher quality than analogue transmission, hence sound and picture are better for the consumer. It has impacted on national television systems in different parts of the world in different ways. In Britain satellite in the form of BSkyB has gone head to head with the BBC and ITV. Its impact appears to be increasing even though both the ITV and the BBC have gone down the digital route, with varying degrees of success, through terrestrial technology (i.e. an aerial and a set top box).

CABLE SYSTEMS.   The development of fibre optic cable has allowed greater channel capacity and hence the ability to create more choice for consumers. In Britain NTL has been at the forefront of developments offering customers television, phone and 'always on' internet access through a single provider.

REGULATION AND DEREGULATION.   The growth of new communication technologies means that organisational convergence is required to provide the consumer with appropriate choice of media. Consumer choice is seen as an important goal. The new communication technologies were invariably expensive to develop. Governments, particularly in the USA and UK had a preference for funding television by commercial means. In the UK this also meant pressure on the BBC to operate with a commercial logic and compete vigorously with other providers for the audience.

GLOBAL AND LOCAL TELEVISION FORMS.   The narrative forms of soap opera (serial drama), news, sports, talk shows, quiz shows and music videos are found in most countries. The formats are endlessly copied and recycled for local audiences (as the ITV show *Tarrant on TV* testifies). At another level, the forms are exported cheaply for viewing in other contexts; sometimes this works, as with *Neighbours* in the UK or it doesn't work, as the same show in the USA.

POSTMODERN. The ability of modern technology to combine a huge variety of elements (news, gossip, views, drama, reportage, images, sounds etc.) together from different times and places has been termed postmodern (see Postmodernism, p. 48). What it suggests for the television audience is that their cultural identities are becoming increasingly more complex and varied through continual exposure to new influences.

The Idea Today

IT IS CLEAR THAT GLOBALISATION IS UNLIKELY TO PRODUCE A HOMOGENISED GLOBAL culture. There is little doubt that there is a drive towards consumerism and a greater emphasis on the exporting of successful brands in the interests of corporate share-holders. However, imposition is rarely a simple matter. It can and does create pressures in a global marketplace. On the other hand, it can equally open up spaces for margin-alised groups to assert sense of their own identity. Identity (see p. 67) is always fluid and subject to change under social, political and economic pressures. Taking control of that identity can be a positive or a negative process. It can reinforce the nationalist and ethnic conflicts between and within nation states or it can create conditions that allow local groups to take control of their own destiny. There are a whole range of difficul-ties and challenges that arise from the distribution of media productions in a globalised world. It seems unlikely that there can be too much optimism over the ability of technologies to smooth out inequalities or that dominant media organisations will not continue to 'penetrate' the global marketplace in order to grow 'for ever'. At the same time, there will always be resistance to such dominance and the spread of technology is likely to enhance that.

Regulation

The Idea

ALL MEDIA PRODUCTION IS REGULATED. AT A PERSONAL LEVEL THE WORK YOU produce for Media Studies is regulated in many ways:

1. Your own framing of the production based on your point of view suppresses some options while allowing others.
2. Your work will often be institutionally based, which can create more regulatory pressures about what you can and cannot do, what is acceptable and what is not.
3. It will be submitted under the regulatory framework of the assessment system in which you wish your work to be assessed, which will impose further restrictions.
4. Pressure from other people can regulate what you say and how you say it.

At the level of the country in which you live (your nation state), the central focus of regulation is the concern held by nation states in terms of protecting their culture and the rights and interests of their citizens.

Main terms

DEREGULATION is the process of removing or diluting the rules that govern the operation of certain companies or areas of industry. In the media, this refers to the move, especially in Western Europe, away from state-regulated broadcasting systems towards systems that are more open to market forces. In this it is following the American model. Because of this, in many countries it has been resisted. Regulation has been a constant concern for all governments even when they support deregulation. Some aspects of media production are judged to be too important to be left in the hands of an unregulated market. It is not just governments who are concerned about regulation: minority groups of various kinds seek to pressure the production and distribution of media productions – for example, feminists concerned with use of women's bodies; advocates of 'Sarah's Law' who want the media to publish details of known paedophiles; and the National Viewers' and Listeners' Association who want broadcasters to regulate their material in line with certain moral standards. Others argue that regulation is essential to promoting a public sphere that makes rational debate about different viewpoints possible.

Self-regulation is the process by which media organisations seek to control their own practices through codes of practice. Codes of practice establish a firm set of guiding principles and a consistent framework with which to address public concerns about media content. Media organisations argue that this is the best way of ensuring the individual citizen's or consumer's freedom of choice.

Reregulation is the process in which certain aspects of media production are ring-fenced as the deregulation of media organisations took place. In particular the protection of areas of media production are deemed important to the sense of national identity.

REGULATION IS AN ENORMOUSLY CONTESTED AREA SUBJECT TO A VARIETY OF SOCIAL pressures. The institutional significance of the media and entertainment industries will grow with profound consequences for everyday life. In what has been described as a new information age the central questions still remain:

1. Who has access?
2. On what terms?
3. How is it distributed?
4. What exactly are people being protected from?

Essentially these are debates about degrees of freedom within different societies and how modern technological developments are affecting this. It is clear that all nation states have different patterns of regulatory control over media content. In 2001, for instance, undue attention on a woman's breast and buttocks in advertising was restricted in Taiwan, China, Hong Kong, Malaysia, Indonesia, Brazil, the USA and Ireland but acceptable in the UK, France, Germany, Argentina. There are specific restrictions over the advertising of sanitary products in countries such as Kenya, Turkey, Indonesia (source: *The Global Media Atlas*, British Film Institute, 2001). These kinds of controls are not simply social, they are also historical. If you study the regulatory systems of different countries it is easy to see how in many parts of the world the regulatory media system is changing. The area of film classification is a very good example of the way in which the age categories for certain kinds of content are subject to change over time in different countries.

The Press Complaints Commission (PCC)

THE PCC is an independent body in the UK which deals with complaints from members of the editorial content in newspapers and magazines. It aims to provide a service that is free, quick and easy. Its central aim is to solve amicably disputes between a newspaper or magazine and the person complaining.

The Commission itself comprises 16 members with lay (non-press) members always in a majority whenever the Commission sits. The PCC is a self-regulating body and is independent of industry and Government. It has no statutory functions.

Its Code of Practice is wide ranging with 16 clauses covering four main aspects – accuracy, privacy, methods of news gathering and vulnerable members of society.

It deals with approximately 2500 complaints per year. It claims to be successful in solving about 90 per cent of cases where the Code of Practice may have been breached. On the remainder, the Commission reaches a final decision about whether the code has been breached or not. It claims to deal with complaints in an average of 30 days, which makes them the fastest regulatory body in the country.

Any individual or organisation directly affected by a story can complain within one month from publication of an article or one month from the last direct correspondence with the editor about the article.

The PCC does not deal with:

- Matters that are subject to legal proceedings on the subject or on contractual display.
- Advertisements, promotions and competitions.
- Matters of taste, decency and offensiveness.

The key benefits of the system of the self-regulation of the press and magazines according to the PCC are:

1. The PCC offers a service which is both *quick* and *free*; it costs only the price of a postage stamp to complain and there is no burden on the taxpayer either.
2. It has a tough *Complainants' Charter*. This, it claims, means that they are able to improve standards of service to the public year on year.
3. It is *accessible* to all sections of the community by:
   - operating a Helpline to assist members of the public in making complaints;
   - publishing literature in a range of dialects – including Welsh, Urdu and Bengali;
   - producing a tape for the blind;
   - maintaining an internet site so that information is available 24 hours a day;
   - operating a Textphone to assist deaf or hard of hearing persons with enquiries.
4. Self-regulation works because *the newspaper and magazine publishing industry is committed to it*. The PCC administers a Code written by editors and for editors. It claims that it is not simply a tool of the newspaper industry. Because the Commission has a decisive majority of lay members on it, this ensures that, although it is funded by the industry for the benefit of complainants, the PCC is clearly independent of it. The main evidence for this is:
   - Since the PCC started, every critical adjudication against a newspaper or magazine by the Commission has been printed in full and with due prominence.
   - When the Commission receives a complaint, editors now never do anything other than seek to defend themselves in terms of the industry's Code of Practice which is a sign of their commitment to it.
   - A further sign of this commitment is that adherence to the industry's Code is written into the contracts of employment of the vast majority of editors in the country. This is something which gives the PCC real teeth.

5. *It protects the vulnerable.* Central to the work of the PCC and to the Code of Practice is the added protection it gives to particularly vulnerable groups of people. The Code gives special protection to children, innocent relatives and friends of those convicted of crime, victims of sexual assault and patients being treated in hospital. It also includes rules on discrimination to protect individuals at risk of racial, religious, sexual or other forms of discrimination. The PCC from time to time issues special guidelines designed to add even further to this protection. In 1997, for instance, the Commission issued guidelines on the portrayal in the media of persons suffering from mental illness. Other specific areas the PCC has tackled include the identification, against their wishes, of lottery winners.

6. *It maintains a free press.* One of the central benefits of press self-regulation is that it combines high standards of ethical reporting with a free press. Statutory controls would undermine the freedom of the press and would not be so successful in raising standards. A privacy law, too, would be unworkable and an unacceptable infringement on press freedom. It would be of potential use only to the rich and powerful who would be prepared to use the Courts to enforce their rights and would be misused by the corrupt to stop newspapers from reporting in the public interest. Self-regulation has none of the problems of the law and yet still provides a system in which editors are committed to the highest possible ethical standards.

7. *The Code of Practice can be changed.* This means that changes in public and parliamentary opinion can be responded to quickly. Between 1997 and 1999 the following changes were made:

   • There was a new stipulation on the taking of pictures 'in private places'.

   • Pictures taken as a result of 'persistent public pursuit' are banned.

   • Protection of all school pupils from unnecessary intrusion and protection of the children of those in the public eye.

   • The use of inaccurate, misleading or distorted pictures to deal with photo manipulation.

   • Stories published at times of grief and shock must show sensitivity.

   • In cases involving children, editors must prove exceptional public interest.

In 2003 the offers of payments for stories by the press were tightened up in response to events in that year.

The public interest and the interest of the public

MOST of the debates about the press relate in some way to the distinction between these two phrases.

The public interest includes:

• detecting or exposing crime or serious misdemeanours;

• protecting the public health and safety;

• preventing the public from being misled by some statement or action of an individual or organisation.

The central concern is to protect the citizen. Allied to this is concern in a free society to protect freedom of expression.

The public are often interested in sex, scandal, gossip, lies, distortions, personal details etc., and it is clear that the press often pander to these interests to sell papers and magazines. However, the code suggests that editors, by assuming editorial control, will curb the excess of interest. Clearly this is an area of much contention with parliament, opinion formers, pressure groups, members of the public, within the organisation and across organisations.

The Advertising Standards Authority (ASA) and the Independent Television Commission (ITC)

THESE are the regulatory bodies responsible for the control of advertising in the UK. Their codes of practice have a central focus: advertising should be legal, decent, honest and truthful. The codes of practice they use are subject to constant change in the light of cases submitted to them by groups or members of the public. Advertisers constantly test the boundaries and public response raises the issues on which the panels adjudicate. The best source for the media student are these adjudications which give a clear indication of what society is prepared to tolerate at any one time. There is constant debate between the ways in which goods and services are promoted and their acceptance in the public sphere. It is important to remember that the goods and services themselves may not always be the issue but the associations and values that they raise for the consumer. This issue is further complicated by different patterns of regulation in different nation states.

Throughout its history, the self-regulatory system has had to adapt as external circumstances have changed. When the system began in 1962, it faced the challenge of getting to grips with inertia selling. A few years later, the ASA took on responsibility for monitoring direct mail. Later still, sales promotions were included within the ASA's remit.

Since the early 1990s, the self-regulatory system has had to get to grips with a range of new and developing media, including the internet. Codes do apply to advertising in paid-for space, such as banners and pop-ups, as well as commercial emails and sales promotions on websites. Admark is a membership scheme, open to all UK online advertisers and publishers, set up to boost consumer confidence in online advertising. Members are entitled to show the Admark logo on paid-for internet ads, demonstrating their commitment to keeping the Codes. Members have also agreed to abide by the ASA's decisions. With some of the UK's biggest online advertisers being among the founder members, Admark provides reassurance to consumers and a sign of best practice for advertisers.

Some regulatory issues in advertising

COMPLAINTS. The study of adjudications will make clear how few complaints there actually are. This does not mean that people were not offended. People can choose to respond in different ways and at different times to events. At a personal level, the author would not buy a 4×4 car because much of the advertising offends him. Such vehicles will be featured in places that in his view are inappropriate, such as deserts, forests and polar regions. Other consumers may decide to boycott French goods or certain banks or political parties for ideological reasons. Others will create subversions of advertising images through graffiti or parody to challenge their basic message and their values. Most of us do not complain formally but respond in a negative fashion to the goods or services by not buying into them. By way of contrast, pressure groups can affect the reception of an advertisement by campaigning about it and making it a focus for concern.

FALSEHOOD AND DECEPTION.   A major emphasis in advertisements is concerned with the truth claims that they make. This rests on a distinction between 'falsehood' and 'deception'. It is possible to say things in an advertisement which are false provided there is no intention to deceive the consumer. It is possible, therefore, to make all sorts of promises as long as they are vague and unspecified.

CONSUMER INFORMATION.   Products and services often come these days with disclaimers such as 'Read the label', and advisory information, 'Not suitable for children'. It can draw attention to the media production as in 'Not for boring old farts!', which was a subversion of such advisory advice to relate to a teenage audience. The disclaimer changes its function to become an audience cue. The growth of such infor mation is part of the pattern of regulation and is a feature not only of advertising but also of broadcast television where it is increasingly common to find continuity announcements about the content and language of programmes which are given an 'informal certification' by the broadcasters. These are nearly always to do with 'adult' sexual content or 'adult' language or levels of violence.

DECENCY.   Most complaints from the public concern this area, especially in relation to nudity, jokes and references to taboos. Sexual representations are a major area of concern and nation states have a variety of responses. In memorable advertisements humour is often a key feature and humour is a central area for testing out our assumptions of what is in good or bad taste. It can challenge or reinforce and draw attention to stereotyping.

USING AND SUBVERTING THE SYSTEM.   One of the methods for this is to create an outrage on the basis that any publicity is better than no publicity. The generation of complaints is a media strategy. Benetton, for instance, has made the attacks on their campaigns a part of the way in which they have built the brand. By creating synergy with newspapers, magazines and the broadcast media (news, talk shows etc.) they can create 'talking points' which draw attention to the brand through word of mouth. The exploration of the *Who Wants to Be a Millionaire?* trial and subsequent events will reveal many aspects of this: legal, ethical, promotional etc.

Censorship and film classification

CENSORSHIP means deciding whether or not a film, or part of a film (as in a trailer) may be shown in public or on television. It is clearly not self-regulation as it is imposed from outside the industry. It has taken many forms and moving image production is full of moments when certain films have been censored for a range of reasons. What such cases reveal are the social and political history of the times in which they were produced. The most obvious manifestation of this is the industry-centred system of film certification. In the UK every film is allotted a release certificate which indicates to distributors its official suitability for showing to children and young adults. The key areas of concern are violence, sexuality and language. The body responsible for this system in the UK is the British Board of Film Classification (BBFC). They give each film a rating based on the age when it is considered suitable for the film to be seen, either alone or accompanied by an adult in ascending categories. When an '18' rating is given to a film, it means that nobody under the age of 18 can be legally admitted. It has been traditional in the UK to award higher certifications to films appearing in video formats: this is related to the conditions of their use. It also means that different versions of films are available to the public. This can be another marketing opportunity, especially with DVD versions which often offer 'uncut' versions of films along with a variety of extra which can include scenes not available in previously released versions.

It is important to grasp that the BBFC does not police this system and so they do not bring prosecutions. This is left to local authorities and their officers.

In addition to certification, various other laws can be used to censor the screening of films. In particular the laws on obscenity, the creation of racial hatred, blasphemy and libel can control what can or cannot be screened. All of these have caused controversies because of the wide scope for interpretation which they offer. The creation of controversies is affected by the activities of powerful lobbying groups who use all the power of the modern media to get films banned. Such pressure can affect local politicians who feel they must act. In doing so they create a new level of censorship in a particular location. For instance, the Monty Python film, *The Life of Brian*, was banned in the author's area, which meant that filmgoers had to travel a very short distance to see the film in the next local authority area. Other locations for screening have often made use of such censoring as a part of their campaign to attract the widest possible audience to a film.

Another feature that has significance is the different forms of self-censorship when a film is conceived and eventually made. It happens at every level of moving image production: it can affect the original idea, casting, post-production and marketing. It is the same as your regulation of your own production work.

Children and the global media

SYSTEMS of media regulation vary from country to country, and operate with varying degrees of success. Most systems – those supervised by the state and the media industries – include special mention of the vulnerability of children and the need to protect them. On the one hand, there has been growing emphasis on protection of children from pornography and depictions of violence. On the other, there has been concerted pressure from within media industries for deregulation and increased opportunities for 'the market' to decide on what is, or is not, acceptable. Media organisations clearly have a part to play in this debate.

Campaigners for children argue that if children are to benefit from the opportunities afforded by the expansion of mass media markets, there needs to be both a recognition of their rights and a willingness to incorporate them in the media agenda. Ideally this should come from commitment and conviction from within the industry, rather than compulsion from outside. It proposes a global system of self-regulation.

The Oslo Challenge, 1999

THIS was issued on 20 November 1999 and acknowledges that *'the child/media relationship is an entry point into the wide and multifaceted world of children and their rights – to education, freedom of expression, play, identity, health, dignity and self-respect, protection – and that in every aspect of child rights, in every element of the life of a child, the relationship between children and the media plays a role.'*

Its aims were:

- to raise awareness in the media professions about the rights of children and how they can be protected and promoted by good professional practices or harmed through inappropriate policies or actions;
- to work ethically and professionally according to sound media practices and to develop and promote media codes of ethics in order to avoid sensationalism, stereotyping (including by gender) or undervaluing of children and their rights;
- to resist commercial pressures that lead to children's issues and the rights of children to freedom of expression, fair coverage and protection from exploitation, including as consumers, being given low priority;
- to work to enhance the relationship between children and the media so that both grow and improve in understanding of the positive and negative power and potential of the relationship.
- to recognise that an independent media is fundamental to the pursuit of democracy and freedom and that censorship and control are inimical to the best interests of both children and adults, and thus to create an effective and secure environment in which the media can work professionally and independently.

Among its challenges to various groups was:

1. The challenge to media professionals at all levels and in all media:
   - to raise awareness in the media professions about the rights of children and how they can be protected and promoted by good professional practices or harmed through inappropriate policies or actions;
   - to work ethically and professionally according to sound media practices and to develop and promote media codes of ethics in order to avoid sensationalism, stereotyping (including by gender) or undervaluing of children and their rights;
   - to resist commercial pressures that lead to children's issues and the rights of children to freedom of expression, fair coverage and protection from exploitation, including as consumers, being given low priority;
   - to work to enhance the relationship between children and the media so that both grow and improve in understanding of the positive and negative power and potential of the relationship.

2. The challenge to children and young people:
   - to know and understand their rights as laid down in the Convention on the Rights of the Child, and to find and develop ways to contribute to the fulfilment of these rights, including the rights of access to information and to diverse points of view, and to find ways to promote their own active participation in the media and in media development.
   - to learn as much as they can about the media so that they can make informed choices as media consumers and gain maximum benefit from the diversity the media offer;
   - to grasp opportunities to participate in production of media output and to provide feedback to media producers, both positive and negative;
   - to share their opinions about the media with those who can help to support a positive relationship between children and the media: parents, teachers and other adults and young people.

3. The challenge to the private sector, including media owners:

- to take into account the rights of children to access, participation, media education and protection from harmful content in the development of new media products and technologies;
- to make the best interests of the child a primary consideration in the pursuit of commercial and financial success, so that today's children become adults in a global society in which all people are protected, respected and free.

Ofcom

IN the UK the body taking up such challenges is Ofcom (Office of Communications). Ofcom will be the new regulatory body for the UK communications sector. It is the most powerful regulatory body Great Britain has ever seen. It is scheduled to be operational by the end of 2003 after the enactment of the Communications Bill. Ofcom at the time of writing has no statutory regulatory powers. However, in the Bill, Ofcom has a role to play in the promotion of what has been called 'media literacy' which has particular relevance to media students. It has been given the following role:

- Ofcom will be given the function to help people develop a better understanding of the different types of media service, both licensable and non-licensable and in particular the internet. This has the aim of enabling people to make more informed choices about what they and their children see and hear and, importantly, to think critically about viewing.
- Ofcom will also have the function to promote a better understanding of the systems which regulate access to media content, these include filtering and rating systems and other technological devices such as PIN based systems to control viewing.

Internet regulation

THERE are three myths surrounding internet regulation:

1. The internet is not regulated.
2. The internet cannot be regulated.
3. The internet should not be regulated.

In fact the internet has always been regulated. In the early years the USA military controlled its development and since then commercial regulation has emerged. To gain access we need an ISP (Internet Service Provider) and search engines are used to track down information (Yahoo, Google, Lycos).

Search engines play an increasingly powerful role in terms of what we access first. Media organisations need to maintain control by investing in search engine development from a commercial viewpoint. The increasing use of search engines in television broadcasting illustrates a similar point. Which programme appears first in programme listings has been shown to have an effect on viewer choice of station. Those who provide the service (BSkyB in the UK) clearly want their programmes at the top of the list while the BBC wants its programmes to have priority.

In the UK it is clear that bodies like Ofcom will seek to control these commercial activities through a framework of legislation. There is a range of media organisations wanting to effect the shape of this legislation and having an interest in the regulatory framework which emerges.

GreenNet: Civil Society Internet Rights Project, 2002

TWO hundred years ago the only means of communicating with a large number of people were the spoken word and the printed page (which had only limited circulation). Telecommunications, radio and television developed as mass media in the twentieth century and have become widely available over the last 50 or 60 years. The major debates on politics, social issues and social change now take place through the mass media.

The cost and complexity of the technology involved means that, until recently, only large public or private corporations have had the means to produce for and through these media. Today, however, internet and multimedia technologies are available on every computer, and ordinary people now have the opportunity to use mass media as both audience and producer.

Existing UK legislation relating to mass media reflects the media industry as it has been for most of the past 50 years. In the light of recent technological developments and with a new Communications Bill on the horizon, this legislative framework is set to change. New digital technologies offer immense potential for civil society and it is in the interests of civil liberties that the public's use of the new media should not be restricted.

Community interests

UK governments have traditionally been reluctant to expand community-based radio broadcasting (hence the pirate radio community that has thrived in the UK since the late 1970s). With the growth of digital media and the internet, many groups who previously sought broadcast licences are now realising the potential of *web-casting* (i.e. broadcasting via the internet) as a means to enable local community media.

If the government continues its effective ban on small-scale community media (the exception being short-term 'event' licences, a whole section of technologies available through the internet will be denied to the UK public. Small-scale online community media currently operate within a regulatory void and their situation is therefore precarious.

The communications white paper promises great change, but essentially it takes a purely commercial view of how media corporations will provide services to the public. It does not provide a framework to enable civil society to express itself, or to ensure that services provided by minor media groups are protected from the predatory actions of mainstream media organisations.

The white paper does, however, open up a space for debate. It gives civil society groups with an interest in the internet and community media a chance to promote alternative views on the opportunities for media and networking within communities (whether geographically or interest-based) that new digital media offer.

The ability of national governments may be limited in some respects. However, governments do seek to close access and certain types of conduct are properly regarded as being unacceptable on the internet as elsewhere. Many governments have developed net police squads. Many groups, as the above cases reveal, have an interest in how the internet is regulated rather than whether. Libertarians argue in favour of free access to information which includes, for instance, the legitimacy and legality of downloading copyright material from the web. However, these views tend to be less marked around issues of child pornography and international fraud.

The Idea Today

THE OPPOSITION BETWEEN INTERPRETATIONS OF THE CONCEPT OF FREEDOM UNDER-lies an increasingly complex debate about how to regulate a media increasingly dominated by economic forces. Media production is the site of a struggle over the term 'freedom': 'freedom to' as opposed to 'freedom from'.

When thinking about media regulation the following theoretical perspectives are useful:

1. Althusser's claim that ideology represents the *'imaginary relationships of individuals to their real conditions of existence'* (Althusser 1971). In this imaginary process individuals are called or hailed into subject positions. In other words, they have identities created for them. Central to the formation of these identities are the subject's experience of the media. To be Welsh, Irish, English or Scottish is to be called into an 'imagined community' of values, aspirations, hopes and dreams which the subject experiences in their daily life.

2. Gramsci's (1971) insistence that hegemony (ideological leadership) is only achieved when different cultural elements are knitted together to create a 'common-sense' way of looking at things which appears 'natural' and 'ordinary' or 'how it is'.

3. Foucault's (1975) view that discourses rather than ideology is the major focus. His discussions of the ways in which discourses are constituted and have effects on people are central to debates about 'customer choice' and 'deregulation'. He constantly poses the question, in whose interests are the media operating? He constantly questions all sorts of groups from this perspective and does not argue for one group to have control and impose its version on others. It leads to relativism: no one view is to be preferred. All discourse is driven by power and the desire for control.

The term 'regulation' is dynamic in that it is constantly changing. These changes are associated with:

* the convergence phenomenon (its technological underpinnings, the current developments in the market and their possible impact on the telecommunications, media and information technology sectors);

* the identification of actual and potential barriers which may hold back technological and market development;

* the existing regulatory frameworks;

- the possible future regulatory frameworks or approaches with regard to issues such as: market entry and licensing, access to networks, access to content, access to frequency spectrum, standards, pricing, individual consumer interests;
- public interest objectives (the need for a clear definition for public interest objectives, content related objectives, the role of public service broadcasting);
- options for a future regulation model (options for the structure of regulation, balancing EU and member state responsibilities, issues at an international level).

Hypermedia

The Idea

IT IS A FORM OF COMMUNICATION MADE POSSIBLE BY COMPUTER NETWORKS. IT IS information rich in that it has a range of methods of communication and data lean in that it is able to provide the most appropriate form of information at any given time because of the way in which the data can be compressed. Strictly the word 'hyper-media' comes from an acronym of the words hypertext and multimedia. The term 'cyberspace' refers to the worldwide computer mediated communication (CMC) network where words and graphics are shared and friendship and power relations are revealed.

Cyberspace is a sophisticated ensemble of audio, visual, digital and communication technologies used to produce and deliver written, visual, audio and, occasionally, kinesthetic narratives at light speed through fibre optic networks linked to satellite and computer systems. Some people use the term cyberspace and virtual reality inter-changeably.

Hypertext is text which is not constrained to be linear, and contains links to other texts, while multimedia refers broadly to information in different formats: text, still images, sound, music, video and animation.

The features of hypermedia are as follows:

- Interactive multimedia is the use of some or all of these in an interface to increase the level of communication with the users, add to the enjoyment of users and improve the environment of users.
- Used in a variety of different application types and is often recreational.
- An important aspect of hypermedia that defines a boundary between a collection of different types of media and true hypermedia is the ability to navigate within this vast collection of information.
- There are two classes of navigation: presentation (following links to information) and active/generative (allowing user input).

- A set of media elements (nodes) and the links that connect them. The links are usually triggered by user interaction. It is important to stress the word *interaction* as it is key in defining hypermedia. A multimedia presentation is not necessarily a hypermedia product. A presentation does not allow anything but a sequential display of the media elements. The user does not interact to decide what happens next.
- Narrative is a key feature of hypermedia.
- Experienced in a linear and non-linear manner. The user is required to participate in the order of the elements as they are presented.
- Hypermedia evolved from hypertext. Whereas in hypertext the writable elements were purely text, in hypermedia the writable elements can be pictures, text, sound, animation, music, full motion video.
- A hypertext is a database. The information is structured and also large, much like most information on most database systems. Although the structure of the information is different from that of the more common administrative databases, most current-generation database systems are capable of storing information used in hypermedia systems.
- Hypermedia is able to extend traditional forms of media by linking to other forms of media both within and beyond the document. It combines elements of print, television, radio, animation and live communication into a single media package, providing the user with a rich media experience.
- Hypermedia can be seen as an extension of hypertext by adding the element of time through video, sound and other media types.
- The rich content of hypermedia allows multiple perspectives and a variety of experiences from a single document. Well-crafted hypermedia allows a user to retrieve the information they want, and explore a hypermedia presentation in their own way.

The benefits of user activity in hypermedia include:

- ease of tracing references forward or back;
- ease of creating new references;
- information structuring;
- global views: outline, contents, page views;
- customised documents;
- modularity of information;
- consistency of information and references;
- task stacking, user multi-tasking;
- collaboration of authors.

The world wide web (www)

HYPERMEDIA is what might be described as the 'action' of the world wide web: it is how it works. The web is in essence, a 'hypertext', or a multiple, connective linking of various knowledge systems and conceptual hierarchies worldwide. Currently, the web is mostly writing (text) and images. These two are combined to interact via 'hot-links', with one another and give insight to a particular idea or feeling illustrated in a page.

What sets the web apart from other forms of media is interactivity. The user can be as much a creator of the content as the initial creator(s). The interactivity involved in using hypermedia allows users to tailor-make it for their own needs. In this sense, hypermedia is something which is moulded and shaped by both parties, with neither being solely creator or user. So what a person gets from it is dependent on what they are willing to put into it. The richness and variety of content allows a user/creator to express themselves in a way that was not previously possible through other mediums. The pictures, text, sound, animation, music and full motion video aspects allow it to be a highly personalised medium. It delivers for both a designer and user a multi-sensory experience. Its content could be seen as a reflection of a user's/creator's beliefs, talents, or even an extension of that person's personality and identity, while its diversity and non-linear layout provides a creator/user with a range of possibilities on what they want to create. It allows the user to drop in or drop out at any point. The user decides on closure.

There are five reasons why hypermedia is new:

1. It is a digital medium: it exploits the newness and latest developments of the IT and telecommunication technologies.

2. It is interactive: it requires active contributions from its users.

3. It is non-linear: there is no beginning, middle or end.

4. It employs multiple mediums: so it is a hybrid medium, portraying different combinations of old and new mediums.

5. The same technologies that use it are able to create it.

History of hypermedia

AMERICAN Scientist Vannevar Bush wrote in his paper 'As We May Think' in 1946: 'Now instruments are at hand which, if properly developed, will give man access to and command over the inherited knowledge of the ages. The perfection of these pacific instruments should be the first objective of our scientists . . . there should be a new relationship between thinking man and the sum of our knowledge'.

Vannevar Bush had ideas of harnessing man's knowledge into a system by which it could be more efficiently used and more easily accessible. His realisation of the potential that powers of data storage and automated document linking could have, were revolutionary considering they were made before the invention of the transistor. From this premise, Dr Bush went on in his paper to propose a hypertext engine called the Memex: 'a device in which an individual stores all his books, records, and communications, and which is mechanized so that it may be consulted with exceeding speed and flexibility. It is an enlarged intimate supplement to his memory'. Bush went on to describe something similar to a modern desktop computer system with multiple monitors.

Ted Nelson was the person who invented the term 'hypertext'. In his book *ComputerLib-Dream Machines*, he envisaged a system called 'Xanadu' where a vast database of information would be available to individuals. He described the importance of hypertext systems and expanded this concept by mapping out a distributed interlinked hypertext system, in which readers could follow their interests over a network to wherever relevant resources resided. Furthermore, anyone could publish their work in this interlinked system. Developments, however, were limited by the technology available at the time, but nowadays, the WWW bears an uncanny resemblance to some essential features of Xanadu. Some of the web's developers acknowledge that Nelson's ideas influenced them strongly.

Doug Engelbart implemented a number of hypertext features as part of the 'Augment' system. The aim of the project was to develop tools which would 'augment' the intellect of people. He stated in an interview that: *'I have always believed that the complexity of the problems facing mankind is growing faster than our ability to solve them. Therefore, finding ways to augment our intellect would seem to be both a necessary and a desirable goal.'*

His lab, NLS (which stands for oNLine System) first demonstrated in public at the 1968 Fall Joint Computer Conference in a remarkable 90-minute multimedia presentation, in which Engelbart outlined and illustrated his points, while other members of his staff linked in from his lab demonstrated key features of his system. This was the world debut of the mouse, hypermedia, and on-screen video teleconferencing.

The world wide web comes close to realising the dream of the early visionaries. It acts as a global distributed hypermedia system, and provides a standard for structuring applications, such as hypertext documents, that can be published on the internet. A user clicking on an anchor, can be directed to another hyper document or node. The links on a particular document can cause a jump to material held locally, or on a computer on the other side of the world. All documents on the world wide web are written in other languages, or using different communication protocols, such as Gopher. The Universal Resource Locator (URL) is a unique address for the destination, as well as the destination's name. Clicking on an anchor may download a picture, an audio fragment or even a (compressed) video fragment, each of which can be very large. The main advantage of this is that the basic authoring tool (HTML) is comparatively easy to create and distribute.

Hypermedia elements

THE various elements of hypermedia are:

TEXT

- Fonts
- Scanned writing
- TXT (scrolled, animated or user inputted)
- Hyperlinks.

GRAPHICS

- Standard formats : JPEG, GIF, PICT, etc.
- Used as backgrounds, pictures (photographs and drawings), image maps, animated graphics, rollovers.

AUDIO

- Standard formats : AIFF, WAV, etc.
- Voice-overs, music, FX.

FILM

- Video standard formats: MPEG, MOV, AVI, etc.
- Digitised video of live action, animation. The video elements can combine many technologies such as film, computer animation, cel animation and stop-motion animation.

In use the elements become functional:

- *Icons*. Images that represent the link or object clicked on. Icons are not symbolic but representative. They should accurately reflect the object they link to so that the user is not required to guess the object's identity.
- *Picons*. Picture icons are often better indicators of an object's identity as they are direct portrayals.
- *Micons*. Personalised icons. Users can adapt icons so that if a user finds that an icon is too symbolic it can be changed into something more meaningful. They are often seen as metaphors.
- *Image maps*. Parts of an image can be made into 'hot' areas. These can link to other relevant topics.
- *Rollovers*. When an image changes its visual form or adds a sound the user is alerted to do something. It is a form of user feedback.
- *Hyperlinks*. Text links can be established to other pages, text, images, etc. Despite the rise of other forms of linking, hypertext is still the most often used (often underlined and a different colour to draw attention of user).

Uses of hypermedia

THE unique and varied aspects of interactive hypermedia make it ideal to be used in disciplines such as presentations, references, entertainment, advertising, learning and simulation.

PRESENTATIONS.   Interactive multimedia presentations are very popular because of the interaction between the user and the information presented. Because of hypertext, hyperlinks, graphic pictures and sound, the user has a media rich presentation, which attacks a number of senses. The user has full control of what to view and when, allowing them to learn at their own speed, and in their own way. Interactive presentations offer the user a comfortable way of gathering information. Presentations are portable and can be conducted at trade shows, demonstration sites, or can be attached to email or websites. It also allows the creator to combine all of their elements into a single presentation medium with a non-linear access. In an online environment footnotes can link to complete documents.

INTERACTIVE VIDEO.   Within the home this enables online buying and selling. Interactive multimedia brings a meaningful visual component to online shopping. Consumers are given a clear vision of what they are buying. A wide variety of products can be sold, for example recreational goods, clothing etc. There are no time constraints as online shopping is available irrespective of the time. Because of the shift of control to shopper, successful marketing is highly dependent on the presentation. Hypermedia can also integrate video conferencing and messaging into any presentation, allowing people not present to take part in the presentation.

REFERENCE. The role of interactive multimedia (IMM) in presenting information sources and reference material such as encyclopaedias is extremely valuable. The senses, for example, of sight and hearing are utilised much more through media than would be in a paper-based version. In a multimedia encyclopaedia a bird can be seen in flight and its chirps can be heard. Cross-referencing and accessing information can be used in the same way as in paper versions.

ENTERTAINMENT. Leisure activities are supported by interactive multimedia. Games are central to many users' experience of hypermedia. Apart from games there are a vast amount of educational and information resources, which also provide entertainment. Hypermedia can take a relatively mundane subject, add sound, video, animation etc., and re-invent how that subject is perceived and presented.

ADVERTISING. Hypermedia is used for advertising using video clips, sound clips, animation etc. It is portable and attractive because it incorporates a combination of media. A product can be advertised using original, media rich packages, creating or updating a product's brand image. The way in which hypermedia is distributed also means that this is a particularly cheap method of advertising. It can also allow direct communication between advertiser and customer at the point of sale. There is a whole industry based on online advertising.

LEARNING. Interactive hypermedia can be used to aid different learning styles. A learning style can be defined as the individual's characteristic ways of processing infor-mation. Learning can be achieved by providing a series of linked lessons each of which is examined in relation to performance. Interactive multimedia has the potential to create a learning environment that utilises many senses, making the hypermedia presentation especially lively and engrossing. Within education hypermedia can be used as instructional aids, interactive tutorials, and reference work, allowing self-paced work, which will reduce classroom time. It also allows a hypermedia creator to centralise their training materials, and with these materials in one place, it becomes easy to change and update them.

SIMULATION. Simulation allows the visualisation of processes and helps with the construction of mental models, which aids the understanding and explanation of complex, abstract and dynamic processes. Simulation is especially helpful because it overcomes the barriers presented by whiteboards and overhead transparencies in the visualisation of complex processes. Simulated processes can be used as reinforcement tools at the pace of that student. Simulation is helpful in areas where the under-standing of the mechanical details of a process is hindered because it is not possible to use the real equipment.

COMMUNICATION. Hypermedia allows three types of communication:

1. Communication between individuals. It can create a very informal, friendly, personal form of communication and expression as in email, chatrooms, newsgroups or personal contact across space via videoconferencing.

2. Communication within an organisation. The use of intranets allows organisations to become more functional and more professional looking.

3. Communication between organisations and customers/potential subscribers/ members. The presentation of a formal, engaging and professional image is impor-tant in attracting different types of target group. It can convey company/brand image.

THINKING.   Through allowing people to communicate in such a rich and varied way, hypermedia could well influence the way people familiar with this technology think, communicate, and perceive things:

- Linking information and ideas, and connecting them with the various mediums which make up hypermedia, makes the user think in terms of image, sound, video, text, animation etc. when wishing to express ideas and feelings. The personal will be thought of, and considered, in these media elements.

- Through providing multi-sensory simulations, users are able to interact in an equally rich way, creating different kinds of understandings and relationships. It could allow people to understand each other better, and work on the same wavelength.

- Expressing ideas using multiple media will engage more aspects of our minds in solving problems.

- Finding creative ways of thinking and understanding, and collaborating in different aspects of problems and ideas, and channelling them into new forms and expressions.

- Multi-sourced information can allow a user to think about and tackle problems differently, as well as being informed in newer ways.

Advantages of hypermedia

THERE are several advantages:

EASY TO LEARN.   It allows access to information by incorporating the notion of navigation, annotation and tailored presentation. Users are quickly able to understand the most basic commands and navigation options and use them to locate wanted information. It lets users feel they are in control. The user can enjoy the session without having to familiarise themselves with the entire structure.

EFFICIENT TO USE.   Given that the user wants to find a certain piece of information, they will either get to it quickly or soon discover that it is not in the system. When users arrive at a link, they are quickly able to orient themselves and understand the meaning of the link in relation to where they are in the system.

EASY TO REMEMBER.   After a period of not having used the hypermedia system, users have no problem in remembering how to use and navigate once they return to it.

FEW ERRORS.   Users will rarely follow a link only to discover that they really did not want to go to wherever the link leads. In case users have erroneously followed a link, it is easy to return to their previous location. Users can in general easily return to the location where they have been before.

PLEASANT TO USE.   Users prefer using a hypermedia system to the existing alternative solutions such as paper or other non-hypertext computer systems. They are rarely frustrated with using the hypermedia systems or disappointed about the result of following links. Users feel that they are in control with respect to the hypertext and that they can move about freely rather than feeling constrained by the system.

TIME SAVING.   Hypermedia applications can often save time by allowing the users to browse through information without having to pay attention to details. This technology offers a quick way of retrieving linked or cross-referenced information without stepping users through a series of intermediate menus. In essence, hypermedia offers the ability for users to have direct manipulation of the information at hand. The overall result is a saving of time by making more efficient the task of pinpointing and retrieving relevant information.

AIDS DISCOVERY.   Hypermedia can also aid in the discovery of new ideas or relevant information by indicating links to information that might not have been originally sought. These meta-text elements help to locate information in a layered fashion and provide an avenue to view a subject or topic by just clicking on it. This fosters a greater degree of exploration of the text than was possible before the preprocessing and hyper-text indexing was accomplished.

NAVIGATION.   The ability of hypermedia to offer better user navigation or control of a system accounts for most of the technology's popularity to date. The reasons for this are that until hypermedia surfaced, program control was always in the domain of the developer. Menus, hierarchies, and linear sequences of questions or directories kept users on course throughout a working session. Usually, the only flexibility offered was going back to the previous screen or returning to the beginning of the program. Hypermedia, however, offers non-linear access to information and program control that open up avenues not only for exploration but for user-defined system navigation.

EASE OF USE AND PORTABILITY.   It is useful to contrast physical media with digital media.

Physical media:

- has high storage requirements as in video or film boxes, or books;
- is editorially 'locked' in their physical distribution medium and therefore is subject to time constraints and dependent on other distributors;
- has a high distribution cost – the quantity of information is limited by the distri-bution format;
- the end user has to collect and store physical atoms of information and then sift through them.

Digital media:

- requires no storage space except for the masters;
- is editable at any time in its life cycle;
- has a low distribution cost;
- the quantity of information is limited only by the authoring process and hyperlinks;
- the end user edits the material in real time to their own specifications.

Disadvantages of hypermedia

THERE are also some disadvantages:

- It is not completely portable because some internet connection is required. This is currently changing (April 2003) as wireless networks proliferate.
- There is a complex authoring stage which users need to go through to be able to participate fully. There can be a steep learning curve for the end user.

- Reading from a screen for long periods of time can be difficult. There is evidence to suggest that users regularly print off hard copy.
- Hypermedia is constrained by developments in IT especially in terms of speed and processing power.
- The quality and power of a user's computer will have a very significant effect on a user's hypermedia experience, while hypermedia transmitted over the internet will be constrained by a user's 'bandwidth', or the rate at which it is able to receive data. A person who is able to receive information at 56 kilobytes per second will have a very different hypermedia experience to that of a person who is able to receive information at 1 megabyte per second.
- The expense of computer equipment for casual users.
- The unequal distribution of resources globally.
- The costs of development mean that large software companies dominate the commercial market. Commercial imperatives are placed before issues of equal access.

The Idea in Action

Navigation

WHY is navigation a central issue in the design and implementation of a hypermedia system?

Navigation is important because it determines if the application has been developed or authored at a high level. Hypermedia is a system where communication is the key element in accessing vast amounts of information. For this reason if good navigation tools are interpreted appropriately then the program will be able to perform at its best.

The types of input communication devices vary from traditional mouse to touch screens, which are becoming more and more popular, and also voice commands. Developments are afoot (sorry!) to use the whole body as an input device. It is therefore important that navigation plays a large role in implementing and designing a hypermedia system for the future, where new input devices may be introduced. As well as input devices, it is essential that navigation works effectively in extracting information in whatever form. The user, or general public, expects from a hypermedia system fast response as and when they need it. There is no use having poor navigation tools when the response time may be 1–2 minutes, when it can respond in seconds. Navigation will shape the whole hypermedia experience for the user, and determine what the user is able to get from the package. Bad navigation will ruin the effect good content could have on a user, and affect how long a user will use a particular package.

All hypermedia users navigate. When they click from one website to another, they are navigating in hyperspace. The problem is being able to get (or get back) to where the user wants to be. Users often complain about being lost in 'hyperspace'. The nature of hypermedia dictates that there are many links leading away from any one node. Clicking on the wrong node can cause the user to become lost down the wrong path.

Tools are programming elements that can find data according to type, location, similarity, etc. They are presented to the user via an interface *metaphor*. A good metaphor will indicate the function of the tool it represents. Some of the more common (and most useful) metaphors are:

- *Bookmarks.* Bookmarks can be placed at points of interest so that the user can return to that position at a later time. Essentially, they serve the same purpose as real bookmarks: to find the location where the last session ended, or find a point of particular interest.

- *Indices.* Indices are also borrowed from books. An index can be searched using a single keyword or combinations of keywords. They are useful when looking for a specific or detailed topic.

- *Contents listing.* Contents lists divide media into related topics or groups. They are useful when looking for general information about a subject. The bookmarks provide no information about the structure of the information. They are a central feature of index pages (home pages).

- *Maps.* Maps provide a structural overview of the information and how it links to other information. Search tools allow maps to be created by criteria. This will produce a reduced map (more focused, less disorientating) but the structure and relationships are still shown.

- *Tracks/trails.* Tracks and trails are basically retrospective maps. They appear as maps or with track or trail marks where the user has already been. The tracks and trails do sometimes display relationships between nodes.

- *The navigational toolbox.* Recent developments in tracking methods have extended the metaphor to include a guide to direct users along a safe path that will take them where they want. This is possible by logging the labels of nodes or node elements as users trek through them.

The integrated design of metaphors should involve a consideration of:

- the user's role through user familiarity with what is being represented;
- the essence of the product: a condensation/distillation;
- the type of information that is being represented (its genre);
- what the product is used for;
- the map metaphors to appropriate functions through repetition.

User experiences

ORIENTATION. A semi-structured or assisted approach to browsing has eased user frustration and increased user enjoyment. This is particularly important if the main user task is information retrieval or research. Orientation is usually established at design level: how to structure information, what links should exist, how they can be reached.

DISORIENTATION. Users who complained of being 'lost in hyperspace' felt disorientation as they progressively lost track of their original search. It is generally accepted that in the workplace this is a bad thing. User frustration often leads to poor performance and mistakes. However, there is some debate as to whether disorientation is a bad thing. Sometimes, disorientation can shake the user out of a lull of successive click-and-skim cycles. Disorientation can awaken a bored user or a mundane hypermedia experience. One important area of the disorientation debate is whether people actually learn through retrieval or exploration.

LEARNING THROUGH INFORMATION RETRIEVAL. This kind of learning is 'factual learning'. It is memory based, that is, search contents for information, remember it and recall it at a later date. This learning method does not incorporate thinking, it merely aids recall.

LEARNING THROUGH EXPLORATION. Disorientation can force exploration into an unknown area. The information is not presented in a linear cohesive way so the user discovers, pauses, thinks and then goes to another subject, which may or may not be related. This allows the user to build up his or her own view or perceptual model. The user can add more information at will, therefore, develop an understanding incorporating the user's views and thoughts can be formed. The obvious problem with this is the scope for misinterpreted knowledge.

STRUCTURAL LINKS. The information contained within the hypermedia application is usually organised in some suitable fashion. This organisation is typically represented using structural links. These are most often sequential but increasingly information accessed is hierarchical. Structural relationships, however, do not imply any semantic relationship between linked information.

ASSOCIATIVE LINKS. An associative link implies a semantic relationship between information elements. In other words, completely independently of the specific structure of the information, there are links based on the meaning of different information components. It is like cross-referencing in books. It is these relationships – or rather the links which are a representation of the relationships – which provide the essence of hypermedia, and in many respects can be considered to be the defining characteristic.

REFERENTIAL LINKS. A third type of link which is often defined (and is related to associative links) is a referential link. Rather than representing an association between two related concepts, a referential link provides a link between an item of information and an elaboration or explanation of that information. A simple example would be a link from a word to a definition of that word.

The Idea Today

ALTHOUGH THE UNDERLYING IDEAS OF HYPERMEDIA ARE STILL BEING ACTIVELY refined, debated and improved, many of the technical limitations associated with handling various forms of media, such as image, video, animation, and audio, have been removed to some extent. However, the provision of broadband in the UK is still patchy and expensive, which can make reception of information-rich texts tedious. Similarly there is an understanding of how to manage the various technologies in a reasonably cohesive fashion (much of this has been a result of the development of the WWW over the last few years).

The effective location of information is still a problem area and search engines are still fairly primitive. They are also driven by commercial imperatives. In order to be able to use information users must be able to identify or locate the information they need. Current applications typically rely on primitive manual authoring of static links, with little subsequent assistance to a user. Similarly, current applications rarely attempt to develop an understanding of the user's context and how to respond to this. Conventional hypermedia can only do what the user tells it to do. If a user knows what they are looking for, the hypermedia works fine. It is when the user doesn't know what information is required, or does know but doesn't know how to find it then 'intelligent' links need to be added. This suggests a greater need to research how the user responds to the material.

Information publishing will change. Currently this involves five different stages:

1. Creating the content
2. Editing the content, including the selection of the authors
3. Manufacturing copies of the resulting product
4. Distributing copies of the product through the sales channels
5. Advertising and promoting the product.

Clearly (Stage 3 onwards) manufacturing physical copies of the information product will gradually go away for hypermedia publishing because the users will be creating their own copies on demand as they download information from the internet. Production, distribution and promotion limitations have caused the publication of paper-based information products to be concentrated in the hands of a number of publishers that is much smaller than the number of potential authors or providers of information. With the move to distributing information products over the internet, distribution will go away as a limiting factor for information publishing, supporting a trend towards having more publishers. Essentially, everybody with a workstation and an internet subscription can become a publishing house and sell information products over the net. Indeed, with the WWW, the trend so far has been for a large number of people to set up their own individual 'publishing houses' in the form of their home pages and associated hyperlinked material. Promotion and advertising will still tend to favour larger publishers with more resources, but the most effective type of promotion for internet hypertext will be having others link to your material; and an author can potentially be linked to by many others without being affiliated with a major publisher.

Difficulties with the freedom to publish and distribute include:

• information overload;
• people's ability to check out new websites is more constrained than is often suggested;
• with more and more information placed on the internet there is potential for confusion. In addition, many users prefer to stay within safe websites that are known to offer high-quality material.

With the move from simple text-based hypertext to multimedia-oriented hypermedia production values become steadily more important. For a text-only hypertext product, an individual author can craft a good product, but a full-scale multimedia product with video and animation takes a crew of graphic artists, set designers, actors, make-up specialists, camera-people, a director, etc. It remains true that professionally produced multimedia titles with good production values look so much better than amateur productions but they require a lot more funding. This is only available to a fairly small number of companies. Major computer companies hire specialised production staff and graphic artists to dress up the home pages of smaller companies with boring pages (or worse, ugly graphics designed by a programmer). All products have to battle for attention.

Reputation has to be earned and it is hard to break through. Few people or companies are particularly well known, and the more people read or hear about someone famous, the more famous that person becomes. In a promotional culture 'name' matters.

Hypertext products derive significant added value from links and add-on information. Synergy is as important in this area as in the production of other media.

It is currently impossible to predict whether the claims to freedom to publish, which many developers hope for, will materialise or whether there will be an inevitable take-over by large monopolies.

Intellectual property rights (for example, copyright)

CHANGES in the legal system always trail behind technological changes. The case of Napster makes an excellent example. File sharing was technologically possible but the music publishers eventually went to court and did a deal with Napster. 'Information wants to be free' as any self-respecting hacker will tell you. The administration of permissions and royalties adds significant overheads to the efforts of people who work within the rules. Under current law, hypermedia authors are not allowed to include information produced by others without explicit permission. Getting this permission is costly, both in administrative costs such as tracking down the copyright owner, writing letters back and forth, and possibly mailing a cheque with the royalty payment. If designers want to assemble a large number of smaller information objects the costs can be prohibitive.

It is possible to establish barriers to information dissemination, either by legal and moral pressure ('Don't copy that CD' or licence agreements) or by actual copy protection. Users tend to resent such barriers and have been known to boycott vendors who used particularly onerous copy protection mechanisms. An alternative would be to eliminate copyright protection of the information itself and let information providers be compensated in other ways. It is already the case that software vendors generate most of their revenues from upgrades and not from the original sales of the software, so it might be feasible to give away the software and have the vendors live off upgrades and service. Moving software from a sales model to a subscription model (possibly with weekly or daily upgrades) would make it similar in nature to magazines and newspapers where people pay to get the latest version delivered as soon as possible.

It is also possible for intellectual property owners to get compensated, not from the information itself, but from a derived value associated with some other phenomenon that is harder or impossible to copy. It may be that fame and reputation may be more important. The downloading of music is encouraged by no less a figure than Robbie Williams and it might be that this augments his reputation. Copyfree has been important in the internet community where the freedom to exchange products and services is highly valued if there is no commercial aspect to the transaction.

Hypermedia and human memory

WE often remember information via association. That is, a person starts with an idea which reminds them of a related idea or a concept which triggers another idea. The order in which a human associates an idea with another idea depends on the context under which the person wants information. That is, a person can start with a common idea and can end up associating it to completely different sequences of ideas on different occasions. Physical media such as newspapers and magazines and videotapes only allow us to represent information in an essentially linear manner. Thus the author has to go through a linearisation process to construct his knowledge or his story to a linear representation. This is not natural. So the author will often provide additional information, such as a table of contents, an index, title sequence, chapters, sections to help the reader/viewer understand the overall organisation of information.

Readers automatically break the information into smaller chunks and rearrange these based on the reader's information requirement in different ways. Readers skim and scan for information, rarely reading the whole text sequentially. They tend to browse through the information and then follow the information trails that are of interest. Hypermedia users, using computer-supported links, partially mimic both the writing and reading process as they take place inside our brain. Readers create non-linear information structures by associating chunks of information in different ways using links. Further, by using a combination of media consisting of text, images, video, sound and animation to enrich the representation of information the eye can be drawn to different points at different times. This can create a sense of control over the information and a greater sense of engagement.

It is not necessary for an author to go through a linearisation process of the author's knowledge when writing. Also the user can have access to some of the information structures the author had when writing the information. This will help the readers to create their own representation of knowledge and to integrate it into existing knowledge structures. In addition to being able to access information through association, hypermedia applications are strengthened by a number of additional aspects. These include an ability to incorporate various media, interactivity, vast data sources, distributed data sources, and powerful search engines. These make hypermedia a very powerful tool to create, store, access and manipulate information.

It can also be a recipe for mindless, sensation seeking and titillation. It is possible to click until the user finds something worthy of attention, which may not impart any useful information. The screen can become the equivalent of 'moving wallpaper' or a source of endless stimulation employing a range of senses (synaesthesia) in the domestic sphere. CMC has the potential to permeate all social spheres (work, education, leisure consumption, interpersonal, sexual) all areas of knowledge (economic, artistic, scientific, religious, political, technical), and all user characteristics (age, gender, ethnic origin, activity, location) while cutting across national borders.

What is clear is that participants in CMC do not simply use them for the gathering of information but also use them for a range of entertainment reasons. As the technology develops, this aspect may become increasingly important.

Andrew Darley (2000) categorises the broader, distinctive mode of spectator experience in the following ways:

1. Intensity of direct sensual stimulation. Spectators are seen as *'seekers after direct visual and corporeal stimulation'*. The emphasis is less on what is being said and more on how it is represented. The emphasis is on spectacle and diversion. The surface is more important than the content in visual digital genres. There is less concern, therefore, with the interpretation of meaning and more concern with play and seeing what happens next if . . .

2. The element of playfulness. This is particularly evident in computer games where competition, skill and perseverance are critical features. It is also evident in the spectacle of films (especially in terms of special effects which are increasingly a key component of marketing), television advertisements and music videos which 'play' on appearances in a range of ways. Shock, disorientation and astonishment are key to a 'good' spectator/user experience. Central to this is the foregrounding of the image in relation to the spectator who increasingly becomes a participant. Hence the importance of the subjective point of view in visual digital culture. The search is to be a part of the spectacle by influencing its direction and shape. However, that urge is an illusion in that the boundaries are established by the designer.

3. This raises the question of control. Exactly how active is the spectator in such a rich and stimulating environment? They certainly have a sense of playing with the reality in front of them but how passive are they really? The idea of users being intoxicated by sensation or even 'drugged' or 'addicted' to sensation might need to be revisited in this context. One participant in my own research on uses of multi-media referred to the idea that 'users get greedy': they expect more and more to happen in multimedia productions. They may be 'hooked' on sensation and may become voracious consumers of images. Or do they 'resist' as some cultural commentators suggest (Fiske 1994). (See Media Audiences, p. 155).

4. The key difference between other kinds of visual spectacle experienced previously is in its mode of consumption. Such content is delivered and experienced privately in the home. The emphasis is less on communication and more on style, decoration, ornamentation: the 'wow' and 'phwoaw' factor. It is life as experienced through images.

5. This clearly has links to how we experience reality. If it is in terms of images experienced at a local level those images can come from anywhere on the globe. The look or the gaze of the individual spectator becomes an important part of the experience. The fact that in hypermedia these images can be recycled, manipulated and played with suggests real complexities in the 'active spectator' role of the user of hypermedia.

Media
Audiences

ORIGINALLY, AN AUDIENCE WAS A SET OF SPECTATORS OR LISTENERS FOR PERFORM-ances of some kind. Its use in Media Studies has been extended beyond the role of spectator (though this is important still in film and television) and listener (though this remains important in radio) to encompass the roles of 'user' (as in computer games, multimedia or the internet) and 'reader' (as in the case of magazines and newspapers). In more general terms the metaphor of audiences 'reading' media productions has been used to explain how audiences both interact with texts and produce 'readings' or 'make meaning' from them.

Media audiences can be defined broadly as follows:

- *Location*. Media audiences are primarily located in domestic circumstances except for the cinema audience, though even here the advent of DVD and the use of laptops and home cinema systems have changed the traditional viewing place for films. The advent of the internet has also changed the nature of film spectatorship through interactivity and the playback possibilities inherent in modern technologies also allows the revisiting of scenes of particular interest (often from a different point of view). The domestic consumption of most media productions raises a key set of issues about their regulation and control.

- *Consumption*. Audiences can be defined to some extent from the media products that they consume or use. Those who use the radio can be broadly defined in this way in that they may be different from consumers of woman's magazines. Audiences, therefore, may be audiences for a particular genre, medium or text. Fans can be defined in this way as groups who have a passionate and often well-informed sense of particular media stars or programmes.

- *Community*. Audiences can be followers of particular media organisations (such as S4C in Wales) or media technologies (such as the internet). Subscribers to particular media organisations (such as BSkyB or to newsgroups on the internet) fall into this category.

- *Size*. It is useful to distinguish between the mass audience and 'narrow casting'. The twentieth century has seen a breakdown of the mass audience under the pressures of increased competition from an increasing variety of media organisations for the audience. Increasingly media organisations target their products at narrow segments of the audience as a starting point from which to attract attention.

- *Subjectivity*. Audiences belong in pre-existing groups. Hartley (1982) defines these subjectivities as follows: self, gender, age group, family, class, nation, ethnicity. Fiske (1989b) adds to these categories: education, religion, political allegiance, region, urban versus rural background.

Passive Audiences and the Effects Tradition

The Idea

'*W*HO SAYS WHAT IN WHAT CHANNEL, TO WHOM WITH WHAT EFFECTS?*' (LASSWELL 1948).

One perspective in audience studies stresses the power of the text (or message) over its audiences. This position is most obviously represented by the whole tradition of effects studies, mobilising a 'hypodermic' model of media influence, in which the media are seen to have the power to 'inject' their audiences with particular 'messages', which will cause them to behave in particular ways. One view is to see the media as causing the breakdown of 'traditional values' as a consequence. Another perspective sees the media causing their audience to be 'cultural dopes' who are easily influenced and who inhabit some form of 'false consciousness'. There are many theories as to how this is supposed to happen, many of which exist at a common-sense level in society. For the student researching the effects that media has on audiences, these are important as they often surface in the responses of audiences to their questions about their use/consumption of media texts.

The magic bullet theory (Harold Lasswell, 1930s)

THE simple metaphor envisages the way in which media content penetrates, as a bullet might the body, the human psyche powerfully, uninhibited by other factors. Its effect is direct. The audience are seen as victims who are affected similarly and uniformly. It is 'magic' in that the audience is unable to resist and can be 'enchanted', 'spell-bound' and 'captivated'. Though a simple idea, it has much power when we think of how we often respond to, for instance, films and film stars or when we meet celebrities in real life.

The hypodermic needle theory

THIS metaphor is slightly different in that it proposes that media content is injected from a hypodermic needle which represents a particular media, such as television, with direct effects on the group which receive the 'drug'. Hence, for instance, values in a television programme or rap music lyrics or aggressive attitudes in computer games or violent behaviour in films could be 'injected' into the audience. The effect is direct and powerful and alters the audience perception of things by either creating a change of attitude (nearly always for the worse) or creating acceptance of the message. One of the most influential versions of this kind of 'hypodermic' theory of media effects was that advanced by Theodor Adorno and Max Horkheimer, along with other members of the Frankfurt School of Social Research (1970s). This 'pessimistic mass society thesis' stressed the conservative nature of 'mass culture' for the audience. Mass culture was seen to suppress 'potentialities', and mask the real world with its contradictions and tensions from them. Implicit here was the 'hypodermic' model of the media which were seen as having the power to 'inject' a repressive ideology directly into the consciousness of the masses who were powerless to resist. Out of this developed the familiar metaphor of the 'plug-in drug' that could be applied to television. Metaphors associated with addictive behaviour and mindlessness can be traced back to this theory.

Two-step (later multi-step) flow theory (Paul Lazarsfeld, 1944)

PAUL Lazarsfeld and his colleagues suggested that opinion leaders or people who are looked upon as leaders, or who are popular (such as stars and celebrities) or who are more vocal, get information, ideas, attitudes about things from mediated experiences and then in interpersonal situations they share what they have experienced from the media. They suggested that the interpersonal medium was more persuasive than any mass communication medium. This theory would attach much importance to word-of-mouth strategies of distributing messages and values involved in media texts. It therefore proposes a less direct relationship between the media text and the audience.

Consistency theories (Festinger, 1950s)

PEOPLE want their beliefs and judgements about things to be consistent with one another. In order to reduce dissonance created by inconsistencies in belief, judgements and action, people expose themselves to information that is consistent with their ideas and actions, and they shut out other communications. It is clear that the appeal of particular newspapers and/or increasingly sources of news such as those found on the internet, aim to fit with the lifestyles and values of their users. Just as the daily paper is delivered to the doorstep so the news can be delivered to the desktop in a form acceptable to the users.

Agenda setting theory (1970s)

THIS theory is concerned with the ability of the media to influence the significance of events in the public's mind. The media might not tell us what to think but they tell us what to think about. The media set the agenda for what we talk about. The media may mentally order and organise our world for us. The theory can be related to the word 'consensus' (which means a generally shared agreement). The media are complicit with common-sense views of groups and issues in society. The term is used in particular by Marxist critics of the media, who argue that the media operate to create a consensus in society (or at least an illusion of consensus) that the norms, laws and rules in our society are the only 'right' ones, which any right-thinking member of our society must accept. Thus, for example, those who might operate outside the consensus, such as 'eco-warriors' or 'economic migrants' do not normally have their ideas and views presented by the media as if they are 'reasonable' points of view. In order to strengthen the consensus the media periodically whip up moral panics against those who are deemed to lie outside the central cultural system. In this process such groups are labelled and stigmatised. Alternative media organisations will often seek to challenge and correct what they regard as the 'distorted lens' of the mainstream media in terms of the issues they choose to prioritise and the point of view they take.

Conspiracy theory

THIS view assumes that a small and powerful, and often hidden, élite are able to use the mass media to condition and persuade passive audiences into conforming to the powerful élite's wishes. It depends very much on the notion of all-powerful media and easily duped audiences. It is a very common theme of many films and television series though it is hard to find the evidence in the real world of the media. Much political criticism of the media is very close to this theory.

Copycat effect

THIS is also called the contagion effect or imitation effect. It refers to the supposed power of the media to create an 'epidemic' of behaviour based on what has been seen or heard in the media. In many ways it is very clear that as consumers and users of media we consciously imitate many of things we find there – dress codes, appearance, music etc. There is plenty of evidence of media patterns of behaviour being copied in the real world. The difficulty comes when this is applied to the theme of media violence. It seems to be generally agreed among media researchers that it is very difficult to find any clear evidence for the copycat effect in relation to the representation of violence.

Desensitisation

SOME theorists argue that the constant media diet of violence desensitises audiences (makes them less sensitive) to real human suffering. It is hard to find proof for the theory, though the practice of systematic desensitisation in behaviour modification may lend incidental support to the theory. Belson's 1978 study of over 1500 teenage boys did not find any support at all for the desensitisation hypothesis. The effect of the 'distant violence' presented in the news was virtually nil and the effect of directly experienced violence was even slightly negative, which, if anything, suggests increased sensitisation to real-world violence.

The manufacture of consent

THIS view, formulated from a political economic perspective on the media, is especially associated with Noam Chomsky. He suggests that the media serve to mobilise support for the special interests that dominate the state and private activity. They are powerful agents of 'thought control' (a term derived from George Orwell): they manipulate public opinion towards a particular point of view favoured by the establishment. In doing so they suppress, falsify and manipulate in the interests of the most powerful members of society. The activities of 'spin doctors' who seek to massage 'reality' into acceptable forms with whom media organisations collude, the training of reporters and journalists in media organisations using conventional ways of doing things (experts, spokespeople, the location of reporters in centres of power), the ownership of media by a few powerful men whose interests need to be taken care of, all contribute to the 'manufacturing' of a particular way of looking at events in the world.

Cultivation theory (George Gerbner)

ESSENTIALLY, the theory states that heavy exposure to mass media, in particular television, creates and cultivates attitudes more consistent with a media-constructed version of reality than with what the reality actually is. Cultivation theory asserts that viewers who have a constant diet of television have attitudes that are cultivated primarily by what they watch on television. Gerbner views this television world as reality itself. It is not a window on or reflection of the world. This constructed version of the world makes viewers assume things about violence, people, places, and other fictionalised events which do not hold true to life. Television, as a consequence, acts as a socialising agent that educates viewers to a new reality. The concrete base behind the cultivation theory states that viewers tend to have more faith in the television version of reality the more they watch television. It is important to emphasise that the theory is only concerned with people who use television constantly.

In order for cultivation theorists to prove their ideas, they must continually conduct research to demonstrate television's effects. Through a technique called cultivation analysis, involving the correlation of television content with data accumulated from surveyed audience members, the media world of television is characterised. From the data obtained, theorists attempt to prove how violence, swearing, nudity among other characteristics (love, infidelity, cheating, crime etc.) is more prevalent in the television world than in the 'real world'.

The Idea in Action

ALL OF THE ABOVE APPROACHES FOCUS ON THE MEDIA TEXT, WHICH IS USED AS A starting point. Because of this, content analysis becomes an important research method. It seeks to identify, analyse, categorise, describe and quantify public beliefs, attitudes, opinion and behaviour in media texts. It is well suited for analysing and mapping key characteristics of media texts from the point of view of content especially over time or across cultures.

ANALYSING THE VISUAL IMAGE. Content analysis can count the frequency of certain visual elements in a clearly defined sample of images in order to analyse them. If the results obtained are to be valid then a certain number of requirements need to be met.

FINDING APPROPRIATE IMAGES. The key here is the research question. If, for instance, the focus of the study is representations of women, then a question needs to be formulated in relation to this. This could be focused, for instance, on the types of gaze used by women in a particular context in a range of magazines. The focus could then be further narrowed to the use of particular types of magazine which were of interest to the researcher within a specified time period or across two or more cultures. The key question then becomes, 'How representative are these images?' Clearly it will not always be possible to deal with every appropriate image and some form of sampling will need to take place to ensure that the sample is significant (and therefore useful). There are a number of possible sampling strategies:

- *Random*. Number each image from one. Decide on any of the numbers which you will sample in a random manner (you could make a number table).
- *Stratified*. Break the sample into appropriate subgroups. In our example, direct gaze, eyes to right etc., or by age or ethnicity. Choose a representative image from each subgroup.
- *Systematic*. Select every third or fifth or *n*th image within a subgroup.
- *Cluster*. Choose groups at random and sample from them only.

These may be mixed and matched depending on the research question. The key issue is concerned with manageability of a large body of data and the importance of maintaining the focus of the study.

CATEGORY CODINGS. These must be exhaustive in the sense that they must deal with every aspect of the image under study. They must not overlap. They must be relevant to the research question. This is probably the most difficult part of the study in that the diversity of what is available has to be controlled and in that process some of the richness of the material may be lost. It is here that the importance of earlier work will be most evident. In our example there is an existing body of work about the gaze which can be used to structure the study and therefore the categories. In this sense there will be something to *test against*: a knowledge of this will be central to the validity of the conclusions reached.

IMAGE CODING. In an ideal world, when the images are coded more than one person would have to agree that a particular image could be coded in a specific manner. Idiosyncratic coding of images means that the study is not replicable. The images then need to be systematically organised into their relevant coding categories. This needs to be done carefully (and can be boring). Index cards or spreadsheets are useful tools in this systematic analysis.

ANALYSIS. This requires counting to produce quantitative data. The most obvious analytic procedure is concerned with the frequency of a certain coding. The significance of this needs to be assessed against the literature (existing body of work). If the material is drawn from different time periods then frequency can be tested against the knowledge of the social context of the time. If the basis is cultural then knowledge of the cultures will be essential. Content analysis requires, therefore, a wider knowledge of the context in which the images occur. This will allow interpretation of the data.

The Idea Today

WHILE IT WAS CLEAR THE MEDIA HAD SOCIAL EFFECTS, FOR SOME COMMENTATORS these effects were neither all-powerful, simple, nor even necessarily direct.

'A homogeneous, externally produced culture cannot be sold ready-made to the masses: culture simply does not work like that. Nor do the people behave or live like the masses, an aggregation of alienated, one-dimensional persons whose only consciousness is false, whose only relationship to the system that enslaves them is one of unwitting (if not willing) dupes. Popular culture is made by the people, not produced by the culture industry. All the culture industries can do is produce a repertoire of texts or cultural resources for the various formations of the people to use or reject in the ongoing process of producing their popular culture' (Fiske 1989a).

One key advance was concerned with the idea that different people looked at or used media texts in a variety of ways and as a consequence were involved in complex and diverse interactions at different times.

David Gauntlett (1998) suggests that there are ten reasons why the effects model is flawed:

1. By using media texts as the starting point the problem is tackled backwards. He suggests research needs to start with the people themselves.

2. The model treats children (often the basis of effects research) as inadequate and incapable of rational judgement. He suggests that there is research which reveals the young person as discriminating and knowledgeable.

3. Many effects researchers have a conservative ideology which suggests the malign influence of media. Many researchers reveal a continuing willingness to impute *effects* from a count-up of content in media texts.

4. The effects model inadequately defines its own objects of study. By this he means that the category codings employed are based on spurious interpretations of what the behaviour/image represents.

5. Studies are often artificially based and do not consider the effect the researcher has on the selection of material employed and the situation in which the participants in research find themselves.

6. Many of the studies are not replicable and the use of the same kind of approach can come to very different conclusions.

7. The effects model is selective in its criticisms of media depictions of violence. These criticisms are often based on questions of taste.

8. The effects model assumes superiority to the masses. The relationship between the researcher and the researched is related to a presumption that the researcher is in some way neutral or above the 'problem' being researched.

9. The effects model therefore performs the double deception of presuming (a) that the media presents a singular and clear-cut 'message', and (b) that the proponents of the effects model are in a position to identify what that message is.

10.   The effects model is not grounded in theory. It is based on the assertion that certain types of media content will causally produce certain types of effects.

He argues, 'With the rise of qualitative studies which actually listen to media audiences, we are seeing the advancement of a more forward-thinking, sensible and compassionate view of those who enjoy the mass media. After decades of stunted and rather irresponsible talk about media "effects", the emphasis is hopefully changing towards a more sensitive but rational approach to media scholarship'.

Active Audiences and Reception Theories

Uses and gratifications

THIS approach focuses on why people use particular media, rather than on content. In contrast to the concern of the media effects tradition with 'what media do to people' the theory can be seen as part of a broader trend among media researchers which is more concerned with 'what people do with media', allowing for a variety of responses and interpretations. However, some commentators have argued that gratifications could also be seen as effects.

Denis McQuail (1987) offers the following typology of common reasons for media use:

INFORMATION

- finding out about relevant events and conditions in immediate surroundings, society and the world
- seeking advice on practical matters or opinion and decision choices
- satisfying curiosity and general interest
- learning; self-education
- gaining a sense of security through knowledge.

PERSONAL IDENTITY

- finding reinforcement for personal values
- finding models of behaviour
- identifying with valued other (in the media)
- gaining insight into one's self.

INTEGRATION AND SOCIAL INTERACTION

- gaining insight into circumstances of others; social empathy
- identifying with others and gaining a sense of belonging
- finding a basis for conversation and social interaction
- having a substitute for real-life companionship
- helping to carry out social roles
- enabling one to connect with family, friends and society.

ENTERTAINMENT

- escaping, or being diverted, from problems
- relaxing
- getting intrinsic cultural or aesthetic enjoyment
- filling time
- emotional release
- sexual arousal.

The Idea in Action

SURVEY RESEARCH AIMS TO PROVIDE EMPIRICAL DATA FROM RESPONDENTS. AS such, it is good at finding out about individual opinions, attitudes and behaviour towards a whole range of topics and issues. The main tool is the questionnaire, which allows the standardisation and organisation of the collection and processing of information. It is particularly useful in uses and gratifications research. Large numbers of people can be accessed using identical or very similar questions.

They can be used:

- face to face in the home or in a public situation with the interviewer responsible for filling in or recording the responses;
- handed out or posted for self-completion in the respondents' own time;
- completed by phone by answering questions read out to the respondents;
- completed on the internet.

The type of questionnaire used will be determined by what is being investigated and the availability of resources; the questions will be dictated by the need for quantitative responses for factual information and qualitative responses for opinions or attitudes. Factual information requires closed questions while opinions and attitudes requires open questions allowing a variety of responses.

HYPOTHESIS.   The starting point is always interest in a media text, media organisation or type of audience (otherwise you are working outside the 'box' or 'framework' of Media Studies). Researchers need to develop this interest by expanding their knowledge and understanding of it. Normally this would be by exploring previous research in the area or, increasingly for media designers, the exploration of forms and genres, the knowledge of other practitioners through their products or through increasingly news and user groups on the internet where new insights, attitudes and approaches can be explored and developed. The issues which arise from this developing interest will create the kinds of questions and approach to questions which will need to taken.

WHAT INFORMATION?   This is concerned with what to ask and who to ask. One of the key principles of survey research is to generate enough data from sufficient people to ensure reliability and representativeness. This implies the need to select the participants in the research on some basis and to select appropriate questions to ask them. Choices have to be made. There is a distinction between large-scale surveys and those surveys which have a more limited scope. Limited scope surveys tend to use more qualitative questions than larger scale surveys unless these are carried out as longitudinal studies (i.e. over time). Questionnaires typically do not allow space for an on-going, in-depth investigation of attitudes and opinions. They do not go in for in-depth analysis of responses or seek out contradictions. Hence clarity of purpose is an essential skill in the posing of the questions.

These are based on:

- The nature of the research.
- The types of people to be canvassed and their location.
- The type of questionnaire.
- The type of research method – postal, telephone, internet – and its implications in terms of time.
- How will material be collected and stored?

TYPES OF SURVEY

1. *Face-to-face.* These are time intensive, often require a large budget and often require assistance. Filling in responses manually will take a long time and even recording responses will require later transcribing. Travelling may well be an issue especially if respondents are in different physical locations.
2. *Self-completed questionnaires.* These could be delivered manually, by post or electronically. Each approach might have a different response rate and this will need to be taken into account. Length becomes an issue in that most people don't like to fill in forms but the target group of respondents might have specific interests in your research topic. Response levels tend to be fairly low, which could affect the distribution of the questionnaire.
3. *Telephone surveys.* These are less frequently used. Though the increasing use of mobile phones and dedicated call centres may change that. They are easy to administer once a respondent agrees to be interviewed (though this is a difficult task in itself because of problems of identification and the ethical issues raised). Interviewers may well need to inform respondents that they will telephone through other means, such as a letter prior to the phone call.

LENGTH OF QUESTIONNAIRES.   The best guides are other surveys and some personal experience of what it is like to be approached either at home or in the street or electronically. Anticipating likely responses is a key skill. Being thoughtful and professional is nearly always worthwhile.

SAMPLING.   This is critical to ensure 'representativeness' and a sense of validity in the conclusions reached.

- *Random sampling*. This occurs when each person or address has an equal chance of being selected. Very often lists are used (telephone directories, websites etc.). Appropriate numbers can be selected (1, 5, 10,15, 20 etc).
- *Stratified sampling*. This allows for the representation of different types of groups in the sample by attempting to ensure an equal balance of males and females, or adults and children, students and office workers, for instance.
- *Quota sampling*. This is like stratified sampling except that the interviewer can select non-randomly. An example would be stopping for questioning fashionably dressed teenagers to find out about the programmes they watched.
- *Purposive sampling*. It may not be important for the sample to be representative. It may be that the sample is chosen simply to test a particular hypothesis or to compare rates of media usage in particular groups. This points to the importance of being clear about the respondents who are chosen.

QUESTIONNAIRE DESIGN.   Choices have to be made between questions which *must* be asked, which *have* to be included, which *ought* to be included, which *can* be included if time permits. It is nearly always important to have basic socio-demographic data (gender, age, income, place of work, type of work etc.). It is important to grasp the importance of ethical considerations at this point in the responses made. There are ways around difficult issues like salary but central to all of this work is respect for people's right to privacy. This will act as a primary limitation on the types of questions you can ask.

- *Question wording*. The questions should be clear and unambiguous. In addition they should require the minimum amount of effort to fill in or respond to. The responses need also to arrive in a form amenable to codification. This is especially important in self-completed questionnaires in which the respondent has no access to help or clarification. The key skills are clarity and logical organisation (because the respondent's thoughts should not be forced to jump around too much).
- *Question order*. Where questions come in a sequence is very important. It can create greater participation through a sense of being personally engaged and drawn into the final completion. It is important that respondents do not lose their way or feel they are losing control of the questions. It is often useful to have a gentle introduction.
- *Pre-testing*. This is a useful way of piloting the questions on a small number of people prior to the full implementation of the questionnaire.

THE QUESTIONNAIRE.   Key features of the questionnaire should include:

- Introduce the researcher/interviewer in some way. Identification of person and reason for the questionnaire is central.
- Ensure that each response can have an identifying code number.
- An easy set of questions to start off.
- Related questions should follow one another in a logical manner.

- Respondents may need to miss sections out and this should clearly be flagged using appropriate graphical or auditory means.
- Help sheets or menus (in interactive presentations) are essential. Tips at the point of need are also useful.
- Always include a response which allows respondents to say they don't know or the question is not appropriate. Unanswered questions are always tricky.
- Vary the style of questions but do not change style too quickly.
- Place questions at the end that are rather more tricky for respondents to deal with.
- Make sure you can handle the data generated.

Reception analysis

THIS focuses on the way that audiences resist the constructions of reality preferred by the mass media and construct their own, often oppositional, meanings for media texts.

In reception analysis, audiences are seen as *active producers of meaning*, not consumers of media meanings. They decode media texts in ways that are related to their social and cultural circumstances and the ways that they individually experience those circumstances. The new emphasis on this approach has led to it being called the 'New Audience Research'. Rather than using solely the questionnaire technique generally used in uses and gratifications research, reception researchers will normally also use qualitative methods on a smaller scale. For example, in-depth interviews and group interviews as a means of uncovering the meanings which small groups of readers generate for media texts, focusing on the audience's 'situatedness' within a particular socio-historical context.

Broadly speaking, reception analysis has developed from a combination of traditional qualitative research strategies in sociology with some of the ideas of reader response theory in literary criticism. Over the past few years, as reception analysis has come to reveal more of the fine detail of our reception of media messages, *an ethnographic approach* to audience studies has become steadily more popular, using interviews and participant observation, a methodology owing much to the research of David Morley, and Michel de Certeau's theorising on the practices of everyday life, both in the early 1980s. This has been supplemented by the use of Stanley Fish's notion of the 'interpretive community'. Fish (1980) suggests that members of a community have common interpretative (the British spelling of the word) strategies. He describes their use in the following way: *'these strategies exist prior to the act of reading and therefore determine the shape of what is read rather than, as is usually assumed, the other way round'*. It clearly suggests that what the audience bring to the text is at least as important as the text itself.

Action research

THE idea of such research is based on the ethnographic principle that people's responses to their culture are worthy of study. Such research deals with the subjective reactions of people in their situated cultures and this has particular relevance in the context of the media. For students of the media such research can be used in a variety of ways to extend their knowledge and understanding of the three study areas by exploring response to media products such as: violent films; simulated combat games;

understanding effects of watching too much television; experiencing violent cartoons; and exploring the values and interests of young girls through their response to magazine images of supermodels.

Media producers have always recognised that the reactions of audiences matter: from the letters page in the newspaper, to the chatroom, to the telephone vote, to the email or text to programme presenters, to the street online interview (vox pop), to the ability to control aspects of the media production itself through personal interactions (as in interactive TV or computer games). While traditionally ethnography has been used to generate an understanding of other cultures from the viewpoint of the dispassionate observer, newer understandings of ethnography have emphasised the relationship between the observed and the observer in relations to issues of power and have applied it exploring, for instance, how people make sense of the media environment, how they react to new products, how certain kinds of issues affect them. Beverley Skeggs (1998) makes the point: 'What is relevant to note is the repositioning of ethnog- raphy from colonial method to liberation strategy. It is the shift from positioning others to authorising others.'

One of its main features is that it allows different voices to be heard in the process of both media production (the testing of media products in the planning phase) and in terms of media response (reactions to different types of media products). The relation- ships between the observer (the person(s) doing the research) and the observed (the people who are being asked for subjective responses) are dialogic and hopefully emancipatory for both by leading to better products or practice or understandings. These relationships are often usefully described as 'field relationships' in the literature on participant observation (Hansen et al. 1998).

Action research literature (Lewin 1947a, b, Calhoun 1994) suggests that there are four common characteristics to such an approach:

1. an orientation to action and change with a desire to make a difference or improve a situation;
2. a focus on a problem or need;
3. an 'organic' or 'dialogic' process involving systematic stages which are sometimes iterative;
4. collaboration among participants.

The ideal domain of such research is characterised by a social setting where:

- the researcher is actively involved, with expected benefit for both the researcher and the researched;
- knowledge gained can be applied immediately in a practical manner by all partic- ipating;
- research seeks to link theory and practice in a cyclical and ongoing developmental manner.

This is often described as 'participatory action research' (Wadsworth 1998). She defines such research in the following ways by deconstructing the formulation into its compo- nent parts. Starting with action, she argues, 'All research seems to me to be implicated in action', in that to explore existing situations in new ways always has consequences. It allows participants a voice. She describes it in this way: 'action research is the way *groups of people can organise the conditions under which they can learn from their own experiences and make this experience accessible to others.'*

She goes on to outline the roles of the participants in the research:

- *The researcher.* This could be, for example, an academic researcher researching the effects of computer games on young people or their response to certain types of films; a product designer testing out design ideas; a product tester wanting to find out reactions to a new product with a view to improving it.
- *The researched.* Typically these will be representative groups, that is, the young, adolescents, senior citizens, young women and the more that such groups can be narrowed down the more effective the outcomes are likely be. So, for instance, 10-year-old computer games players can be subdivided into novice, intermediate and expert users for whom, it might be hypothesised, the experience of a new game will be different and who will suggest different types of improvement.
- *The researched for.* (1) In media terms this would often be the client commissioning the research. They need things such as better information about likely responses so that they can improve the product/idea/service. They are likely to be engaged at all phases of the production cycle.
- *The researched for.* (2)These might, for instance, include the group who are perceived as having a problem which the research might ameliorate. If, for instance, such research established a causal link between the ownership of guns and a wide-ranging knowledge of 'rap' culture, it might be able to create a case for certain kinds of legislation.

An academic approach

Annette Hill, *Shocking Entertainment: Viewer Response to Violent Movies* (1997)

THE aims of this study were:

- to learn why people choose to watch violent movies;
- to talk to consumers of violent movies to explain their appeal;
- to use qualitative research to achieve this.

RESEARCH METHOD.   The study found the consumers through pilot studies using interviews and questionnaires. These methods were mainly unsuccessful in eliciting the data except for the individual interviews. However, what they lacked was the interaction of ideas.

The study then concentrated on self-contained focus groups. These allowed for lively and informal conversation which was able to explore specific topics and reveal cognitive processes at work. *'Focus groups are useful when it comes to investigating what participants think, but they excel at uncovering why participants think as they do.'* (Morgan 1988).

The data from these groups formed the primary method of data collection.

DESIGN OF FOCUS GROUPS.   The group members were all active consumers of violent movies. The movies chosen were films which at the time of the study had a theatrical

18 certificate release and available on video (except one). They had not been screened on terrestrial television. They viewed the films either in the cinema or in the home environment.

Participants had to be over 18 years old. They must have seen three or more films on the list. They must not be engaged in any research on this area. Male and female participants were recruited equally to ensure that all male, all female and mixed gender focus groups contained a balanced mix of participants.

In the end, there were 20 male participants and 16 female participants. The participants were not representative in terms of class or ethnicity.

CONDUCTING THE FOCUS GROUPS.   Groups of 4–6 met in London in 1995 on Saturday afternoons in a safe neutral environment. The environment was made deliberately social and included alcohol.

The format was standardised. Participants were invited to provide brief biographical details, invited to offer their opinions concerning the target films followed by a more focused discussion using questions led by the researcher. Three cues were used by the researcher: the list of films and two film clips related to the questions.

Discussions lasted two and a quarter hours with an interval approximately half way through the session. The female researcher (the moderator of the group) was assisted by an assistant male moderator.

DATA COLLECTION INSTRUMENTS AND ANALYSIS.   The moderator acted as a neutral observer, posing the same questions, in the same order, with the same cues, to each group at the same time in the discussion.

Discussions were audio recorded and the responses of each focus group fully transcribed. Preliminary readings of the audio material assessed the emergent themes and categories for analysis. Short written reports were produced after each focus group was conducted. Discussions with the assistant moderator and the supervisors of the research also took place.

For ethical reasons participants are not identified.

RESULTS.

- Violent movies test the viewers, and the consumers are aware of this. They have an understanding of the aesthetics of violence and want to make up their own mind.
- Viewing violence is a social activity.
- Anticipation is a key factor in determining responses to violence.
- Consumer choice influences the way consumers relate to characters; they control their response to characters.
- Thresholds are part of the way that consumer reactions are tested and reaffirm social taboos and individual experience.
- Viewers use a variety of methods to self-censor violence.
- Boundary testing is part of the process of viewing violence.
- Real violence is not entertaining. Fictional violence can be for reasons not causally connected to the violence per se.

- Violent movies offer a safe environment to experience their responses to violence.
- Consumers build up ways of interpreting and understanding violent movies which allow them to respond in diverse ways. They are active readers.
- The author concludes the findings with a complex model of the viewing process.

POLICY RECOMMENDATIONS. As is common with action research approaches, the researcher offers policy recommendations to improve attitudes to screening violent movies. In essence, they seek to move the debate about effects from the movie to the consumer.

The debate about 'violence' needs to recognise the complexities of response when watching violent movies. Violent movies are part of the entertainment industry and consumers choose to see them because they are entertaining. Centralised censorship needs to be accountable and clear to the public. The role of self-censorship needs to be acknowledged by the legislators and self-appointed 'moral watchdogs' and, in particular, regulators such as the British Board of Film Classification (BBFC), and the Independent Television Commission (ITV).

A product design approach

Mike Edwards, *Testing and Developing a Media Product* (2002)

THE product is an interactive introduction to GCSE Media Studies. Using action research techniques, the research tests the effectiveness of a multimedia learning tool designed to introduce teachers new to the requirements of and concepts involved in the GCSE Media Studies specification.

In order to do so it presents the version of the materials with a discussion of its 'preferred meaning' (that is, the meaning which the author intended to create) and tests them against the subjective responses of a range of participants involved in the field of GCSE Media Studies using interview and focus group methods.

It presents the data from the methods used and discusses the emergent themes and categories which arose from the internal triangulation of the participants' viewpoints.

The researcher finally presents recommendations that will make a full implementation of the materials possible and briefly discusses the use of such research techniques in the design of multimedia materials.

THE FOCUS GROUP. The focused group interview has become a very popular research method for studying the responses of media audiences. In recent years it has been of particular importance to researchers who aim to explore how audiences interpret, make sense of, use, interact with, and create meaning out of media content and technologies. *'Meaning was seen as intra-textual (requiring analysis of textual structures), inter-textual (requiring analysis, among other things, of genres and relations between them) but finally and decisively interpretative (requiring research into the situated practice of "receptive" understanding)'.* (Corner 1991).

The main reason for using focus groups is that they offer dynamics and ways – not available in individual interviews – of generating, stimulating and elaborating potential audience reactions. *'The hallmark of focus groups is the explicit use of the group inter-*

action to produce data and insights that would be less accessible without the interaction of the group' (Morgan 1988).

The result is a more information-rich basis for action. However, Liebes and Katz (1993) make this point: *'Group dynamics are such that opinion and participation are not equally weighted; some people have disproportionate influence'.*

In focus group research, the researcher has to act as the moderator for the group. He/she assumes responsibility for the issues, topics and foci to which they wish to draw attention; the balance of contributions; and the direction of the discussion into avenues relevant to the study. The discussion is not an 'open ended free for all' but is always carefully focused by the moderator who must ensure that participants can contribute effectively.

INTERVIEWS.   The study also used individual interviews. These are useful when issues can be explored in some depth, issues pursued and confidentiality can be dealt with. In this case, the occupational backgrounds of the participants on both sides were important: both in different ways were subject to strict controls (though often informal controls) over whom they could speak to and the remarks that could be attributed to them. The interviewers' fields of specialist expertise, while having similarities to those of the participants, revealed marked differences in terms of these patterns of regulation. This clearly has implications in an informal open interview situation that is being recorded. The convention of 'open' interviews is that no formal schedule of standardised questions is used, rather maximum space is given to interviewees to speak of their responses to the material and its suitability. Thus, Hammersley and Atkinson (1995) note, *'Ethnographers do not usually decide beforehand the exact questions they want to ask, and do not ask each interviewee exactly the same questions, though they will usually enter the interviews with a list of issues to be covered. Nor do they seek to establish a fixed sequence in which relevant topics are covered; they adopt a more flexible approach, allowing the discussion to flow in a way which seems natural.'*

One of the key issues which needed to be addressed in the interview in relation to the status of the participants was that of accountability for observations made in the interviews. It was essential with these participants that they gave their permission for their observations to be used and that they had the power to veto any quotations attributed to them in the research.

Issues raised by research methods

THE research methods outlined raise a number of issues in relation to what might be called the 'plausibility' of the data. There are two main areas of concern. First, there are potential problems about what may be termed the status of the data generated by the investigation. Can the interviews be read as more the product of micro-social interactions which tell us more about the participants reacting to something new than about the usefulness material as a learning tool? Secondly, there are issues relating to the way in which the participants shape themselves to the perceived needs of, or are in other ways affected by, the research process.

In relation to the first question, for instance, Robert Dingwell (1980) has argued, *'the data produced by interviews are social constructs, created by the self-presentation of the respondent and whatever interactional cues have been given off by the interviewer about the acceptability or otherwise of the accounts being presented . . . Interview data cannot offer us literal descriptions of the respondent's reality . . . [they] are fraught with problems because of the activity of the interviewer in producing them.'*

In response to the second issue, reactivity on the part of the participants is an essential part of the research if it is to remain a genuinely creative and formative activity. While essential, it has to be acknowledged that it is a temporary resting place from which the maker will need to move on. The aim of such research is to suggest new routes and avenues for development.

Indeed the central point about participatory action research that the social interaction produces unforeseen approaches and suggestions which are clearly motivated by the range of interests exhibited by the participants and which may have been produced by the activity itself. If its aim is to ameliorate situations or propose new solutions, then by definition it needs to be left behind. Such insights cannot be gained in any other way. What Bahktin (1981) argued was that language in any form was inherently a social activity and language was how we became human. Terry Eagleton (1983) describes his theory as laying the ground for a materialist theory of consciousness itself: *'Human consciousness was the subject's active, material, semiotic discourse with others, not some sealed interior realm divorced from those relations: consciousness, like language, was both "inside" and "outside" the subject simultaneously. Language was not to be seen either as "expression", "reflection" or "abstract system", but rather as a material means of production, whereby the material body of the sign was transformed through a process of social conflict and dialogue into meaning.'*

Hence all discourse is necessarily inflected with relations of power and involved competing versions of reality. It was a theory that emphasised meaning making through active engagement. This would define the central thrust of this kind of research in that it seeks to explore the creative process through the interaction of key participants: it is a messy and random process which needs to invite dialogue from interested parties in order to establish successful approaches to a complex task. In this research it allows the participants to contribute and add value to the final production.

The Idea Today

ACTION RESEARCH IS OFTEN DESCRIBED AS NEW AUDIENCE RESEARCH IN THAT IT addresses the question of where the generation of meaning takes place. There is an assumption underlying much of what is often referred to as the transmission model of communication that the 'transmission' of meanings from 'sender' to 'receiver' is a relatively unproblematic process. Somehow the sender puts meanings into symbols which he or she then transmits to the receiver, who somehow takes the meanings out again.

The approach from semiotics is quite different. The semiological approach is to see meaning as a social construction. If you follow that approach through to its logical conclusion, then you have to ask to what extent it is possible to make the claim that meanings are somehow 'in' the signs we use at all. It could be that it is not sensible to look for meaning within media 'texts' at all, but rather to look at how meanings are constructed at the point of encounter between texts and readers. Both the examples in different ways explore this encounter for very different purposes. The 'new audience research' can be a useful corrective to the tendency of some semiotic analysis to assume that meanings inhere within the text, a useful corrective also to the tendency of some students of the political economy of the media to assume that ownership of media organs equates to ideological power. However, some reception analysis simply passes from enumeration of audience responses to a banal conclusion that we don't all understand things the same way. Action research as a subset of qualitative research by way of contrast seeks to offer accounts from individuals with a view to ameliorating or improving the situation for those involved.

Media students need to be suspicious of anything which describes itself as 'new' and this is true of audience research. In it can be found traces of a whole range of attitudes. The movement from text (1960s) to audience (1980 onwards) as a seamless transition is often represented as a progression towards a more enlightened view of the activity of engaging with media meanings. This needs care. The media student does not have to be tied down in this way as whole range of approaches can be mixed and matched to create understandings of the complexities of media production and often the best place to test those complexities lies in the activity of media production itself. What is clear in the millennium is that in developed countries at least this is a realistic objective as technology is becoming cheaper, more portable, easier to use and more accessible. What is also clear is that the 'media literate' student does not just make things, they need a wide experience of media texts and a willingness to research and find out more.

References

An asterisk (*) after an author's name indicates a useful text for students.

ALTHUSSER, L. (1971) *Lenin and Philosophy, and other Essays*, translated from the French by B. Brewster, New Left Books, London.

ANG, I. (1985) *Watching Dallas: Soap Opera and the Melodramatic Imagination*, Methuen, London.

ARGYLE, M. (1988) *Bodily Communication*. Methuen, London.

ATTON, C.* (2002) *Alternative Media*, Sage, London.

BAHKTIN, M.M. (1968) *Rabelais and his World*, translated by H. Iswolsky, MIT Press, Cambridge, MA.

BAHKTIN, M.M. (1981) *The Dialogic Imagination*, edited by M. Holquist, translated by C. Emerson and M. Holquist, University of Texas Press, Austin.

BALNAVES, M., DONALD, J. AND HEMELRYK, S. (2001) *The Global Media Atlas*, British Film Institute, London.

BARKER, C.* (1999) *Television, Globalisation and Cultural Identities*, Open University Press, Milton Keynes.

BARKER, M. (ED.) (1984) *The Video Nasties: Freedom and Censorship in the Media*, Pluto, London.

BARKER, M.* (1989) *Comics: Ideology, Power and the Critics*, Manchester University Press, Manchester.

BARKER, M. (1993) Sex Violence and Videotape, *Sight and Sound*, 3.5, May.

BARTHES, R.* (1972) *Mythologies*, Cape, London.

BARTHES, R. (1981) *Image – Music – Text*, translated by S. Heath, Noonday, New York.

BARTHES, R. (1990) *S/Z: An Essay*, translated by R. Miller, preface by Richard Howard, Blackwell, Oxford.

BELSON, W. (1978) *Television Violence and the Adolescent Boy*, Saxon House, Farnborough.

BERGER, J. (1972) *Ways of Seeing*, BBC/Penguin Books, Harmondsworth.

BLANDFORD, S., GRANT, B.K. AND HILLIER, J.* (2001) *The Film Studies Dictionary*, Arnold, London.

BOYLE, T.* (1997) *Design for Multimedia Learning*. Prentice Hall, London and New York.

BRANIGAN, E. (1992) *Narrative Comprehension and Film*, Routledge, New York.

BRANSTON, G. AND STAFFORD, R. (EDS)* (1996) *The Media Students' Book*, 3rd edn, Routledge, London.

BRIGGS, A. AND COBLEY, P.* (1998) *The Media: An Introduction*, Longman, Harlow.

BRIGLEY, J. (2002) *List of Terms in Media Studies*, WJEC.

BUCKINGHAM, D. (1993) *Children Talking Television: The Making of Television Literacy*, The Falmer Press, London.

BUCKINGHAM, D. (1996) *Moving Images: Understanding Children's Emotional Responses to Television*, Manchester University Press, Manchester.

BURTON, G.* (1999) *Media and Popular Culture*, Hodder and Stoughton, London.

BUSH, V. (1945) As We May Think, *Atlantic Monthly*, available online at http://www/isg.sfu.ca/~duchier/misc/vbush

CALHOUN, E.F. (1994) *How to Use Action Research in the Self-renewing School*, Association for Supervision and Curriculum Development, Alexandria, VA.

CHANDLER, D.* (2001) *Semiotics: The Basics*, Routledge, London.

CHANDLER, D. AND ROBERTS-YOUNG, D. (1998) The Construction of Identity in the Personal Homepages of Adolescents', http://www.aber.ac.uk/media/

COHEN, S. AND YOUNG, J. (1981) *The Manufacture of News: Social Problems, Deviance and the Mass Media*, revised edn, Constable, London.

CORNER, J. (ED.) (1991a) *Popular Television in Britain: Studies in Cultural History*, British Film Institute, London.

CORNER, J. (1991b) Meaning, Genre and Context: The Problematics of 'Public Knowledge in the New Audience Studies', in J. Curran and M. Gurevitch (eds.), *Mass Media and Society*, Arnold, London.

CREEBER, G. (ED.)* (2001) *The Television Genre Book*, British Film Institute, London.

CURRAN, J. (ED.)* (1999) *Media Organisations*, Arnold.

DARLEY, A. (2000) *Visual Digital Culture*, Routledge, London.

DEACON, D. ET AL.* (1999) *Researching Communications*, Arnold, London.

DINGWELL, R. (1980) Ethics and Ethnography, *Sociological Review*, 28: 871–91.

DYER, G. (1982) *Advertising as Communication*, Methuen, London.

DYER, R.* (1993) *A Matter of Images: Essays on Representation*, Routledge, London.

EAGLETON, T. (1983) *Literary Theory: An Introduction*, Basil Blackwell, Oxford.

EDWARDS, M. (2002) Investigating the Role of Multimedia Presentation of Information for Teachers of Media Studies in the Context of the General Certificate Secondary Education (GCSE). Unpublished MSc thesis.

ELLIS, J. (1992) *Visible Fictions*, 2nd edn, Routledge, London.

ENZENSBERGER. H.M. (1976) Constituents of a Theory of the Media, in *Raids and Reconstructions: Essays on Politics, Crime and Culture*, Pluto Press, London.

FAIRCLOUGH, N. (1995) *Discourse and Social Change*, Polity Press, Cambridge.

FISH, S. (1980) *Is There a Text in this Class? The Authority of Interpretive Communities*, Harvard University Press, Boston.

FISKE, J. (1989a) *Reading the Popular*, Routledge, London.

FISKE, J. (1989b) *Understanding Popular Culture*, Routledge, London.

FISKE, J. (1994) *Television Culture*, Routledge, London.

FOUCAULT, M. (1972) *The Archaeology of Knowledge*, Pantheon, New York.

FOUCAULT, M. (1975) *Discipline and Punish*, Penguin, Harmondsworth.

FOWLER, R.* (1991) *Language in the News: Discourse and Ideology in the Press*, Routledge, London.

FULLER, P. (1980) *Seeing Berger: A Revaluation of Ways of Seeing*, Writers and Readers, London.

GARNHAM, N. (1992) The Media and the Public Sphere, in C. Calhoun (ed.) *Habermas and the Public Sphere*, MIT Press, Cambridge, MA.

GAUNTLETT, D. (1995) *Moving Experiences: Understanding Television's Influences and Effects*, John Libbey, London.

GAUNTLETT, D. (1997) *Video Critical: Children, the Environment and Media Power*, John Libbey Media, Luton.

GAUNTLETT, D. (1998) Ten Things Wrong with the 'Effects Model', in R. Dickinson, R. Harindranath and O. Linné (eds), *Approaches to Audiences: A Reader*, Arnold, London.

GAUNTLETT, D. (ED.)* (2000) *Web.studies*, Arnold, London.

GERAIGHTY, C. (2000) Rethinking Stardom: Questions of Texts, Bodies and Performances, in C. Gledhill and L. Williams, *Reinventing Film Studies*, Arnold, London.

GERBNER, G. (1994) The Politics of Media Violence: Some Reflections, in O. Linné and C.J. Hamelink (eds), *Mass Communication Research: On Problems and Policies: The Art of Asking the Right Questions*, Ablex Publishing, Norwood, NJ.

GERBNER, G., GROSS, L., MORGAN, M. AND SIGNORIELLI, N. (1986) Living with Television: The Dynamics of the Cultivation Process, in J. Bryant and D. Zillmann (eds), *Perspectives on Media Effects*, Lawrence Erlbaum Associates, Hillsdale, NJ.

GRAMSCI, A. (1971) American and Fordism, in *Selections from the Prison Notebooks*, Lawrence and Wishart, London.

GRAY, A. (1992) *Video Playtime: The Gendering of a Leisure Technology*, Routledge, London.

HALL, S. (1992) The Question of Cultural Identity, in S. Hall, D. Held and T. McGrew (eds), *Modernity and its Futures*, Polity Press, Cambridge, in association with The Open University.

HALL, S. (1999) Introduction: Looking and Subjectivity, in J. Evans and S. Hall (eds), *Visual Culture: The Reader*, Sage, London, in association with The Open University.

HALLIDAY, M.A.K. (1975) Talking One's Way in: A Sociolinguistic Perspective on Language and Learning, in A. Davies (ed.), *Problems of Language and Learning*, Heinemann, London.

HALLIDAY, M.A.K. (1994) *An Introduction to Functional Grammar*, Arnold, London.

HAMMERSLEY, M. AND ATKINSON, P. (1995) *Ethnography: Principles in Practice*, Routledge, London.

HANSEN, A., COTTLE, NEGRINE, R. AND NEWBOLD, C.* (1998) *Mass Communication Research Methods*, Macmillan, Basingstoke.

HARTLEY, J. (1982) *Understanding News*, Methuen, London.

HEBDIGE, D. (1979)*Subculture: The Meaning of Style*. Routledge, London.

HILL, A.* (1997) *Shocking Entertainment: Viewer Response to Violent Movies*, John Libbey Media, Luton.

HODGE, R. AND KRESS, G. (1988) *Social Semiotics*, Polity Press, Cambridge.

JENKINS, H. (1992) *Textual Poachers: Television Fans and Participatory Culture*, Routledge, London.

KELLNER, D. (1995) *Media Culture*, Routledge, New York.

KRESS, G. AND VAN LEEUWEN, T. (1996)* *Reading Images: The Grammar of Visual Design,* Routledge, London.

KRESS, G. AND VAN LEEUWEN, T.* (2001) *Multimodal Discourse: The Modes and Media of Contemporary Communication*, Arnold, London.

KRISTEVA, J. (1980) *Desire in Language: A Semiotic Approach to Literature and Art*, edited by L.S. Roudiez, translated by T. Gora, A. Jardine, and L.S. Roudiez, Columbia University Press, New York.

LACAN, J. (1977) *Ecrits: A Selection*, W. W. Norton, New York.

LACEY, N. (1999) *Image and Representation: Key Concepts in Media Studies*, Macmillan, Basingstoke.

LACEY, N.* (2002) *Media Institutions and Audiences*, Palgrave Paperback, Basingstoke.

LANGER, J. (1998) *Tabloid Television: Popular Journalism and the 'Other News'*, Routledge, London.

LASSWELL, H.D. (1948) The Structure and Function of Communication in Society, in L. Bryson (ed.), *The Communication of Ideas*, Harper & Row, New York.

LÉVI-STRAUSS, C. (1973) *Anthropologie Structurale Deux*, Plon, Paris.

LEWIN, K. (1947a) Frontiers in Group Dynamics, *Human Relations* 1.1: 5–41.

LEWIN, K. (1947b) Frontiers in Group Dynamics II, *Human Relations* 1.2: 143–53.

LIEBES, T. AND KATZ, E. (1993) *The Export of Meaning: Cross-Cultural Readings of 'Dallas'*, Polity, Oxford.

LYNCH, P.J. AND HORTON, S.* (1999) *Web Style Guide: Basic Design Principles for Creating Web Sites*, Yale University Press, New York.

LYOTARD, J-F. (1988) *The Differend: Phrases in Dispute*, University of Minnesota Press, Minneapolis.

MANOVICH, L. (2002) *The Language of New Media*, MIT Press, Cambridge, MA.

MASLOW, A. (1954) *Motivation and Human Personality*, Harper & Row, New York [1970].

MCCARTHY, H.* (1993) *Anime! A Beginner's Guide to Japanese Animation*, Titan Books, London.

MCCLOUD, S.* (1993) *Understanding Comics: The Invisible Art*, Kitchen Sink Press, Northampton, MA.

MCCRACKEN, E. (1997) *Decoding Women's Magazines*, Macmillan, Basingstoke.

MCQUAIL, D. (1987) *Mass Communication Theory*, 2nd edn, Sage, London.

MEDHURST, A. (1998) Sexuality, in A. Briggs and P. Cobley (eds), *The Media: An Introduction*, Longman, London.

MEDVED, M. (1992) *Hollywood vs. America: Popular Culture and the War on Traditional Values,* HarperCollins, London.

MELUCCI, A. (1996) *Challenging Codes: Collective Action in the Information Age*, Cambridge University Press, Cambridge.

MESSARIS, P.* (1997) *Visual Persuasion: The Role of Images in Advertising*, Sage, Thousand Oaks, CA.

MILLUM, T. (1975) *Images of Woman: Advertising in Women's Magazines*, Chatto & Windus, London.

MITCHELL, W.J.* (1994) *The Reconfigured Eye: Visual Truth in the Post-Photographic Era*, MIT Press, Cambridge, MA.

MORGAN, D.L. (1998) The Focus Groups' Guide Book, Volume 1, in D. Morgan and R. Krueger (eds.), *Focus Group Kit*, Sage, Thousand Oaks, CA.

MORLEY, D. AND ROBINS, K. (1997) *Spaces of Identity*, Routledge, London.

MULVEY, L. (1975) Visual Pleasure and Narrative Cinema, in Screen, *The Sexual Subject: A Screen Reader in Sexuality*, ed. M. Murck, Routledge, London.

MYERS, G.* (1999) *Ad Worlds: Brands, Media, Audiences*, Arnold, London.

NEALE, S. (1990) *Genre*, British Film Institute, London.

NELMES, J. (ED.) (1999) *An Introduction to Film Studies*, 2nd edn, Routledge, London.

NELSON, T. (1987) *ComputerLib-Dream Machines*, Tempus Books/Microsoft Press, Redmond.

O'SULLIVAN, T. ET AL.* (1994) *Key Concepts in Communication and Cultural Studies*, Routledge, London and New York.

PHILLIPS, P.* (2000) *Understanding Film Texts*, British Film Institute, London.

POOLE, S.* (2000) *Trigger Happy: The Innerlife of Videogames*, Fourth Estate, London.

PRICE, S.* (1997) *The Complete A–Z Media and Communication Handbook*, Hodder and Stoughton, London.

PROPP, V. (1968) *Morphology of the Folktale,* University of Texas Press, Austin.

ROJECK, C. (2001) *Celebrity*, Reaktion Books Ltd, London.

ROSE, G.* (2001) *Visual Methodologies,* Sage Publishing, London.

SAID, E.W. (1985) *Orientalism*, Vintage Books, New York.

SAUSSURE, F. DE (1966) *Course in General Linguistics*, translated by W. Baskin, McGraw-Hill, New York.

SCHANK, R.C. AND ABELSON, R. (1977) *Scripts, Plans, Goals and Understanding*, Lawrence Erlbaum, Hillsdale, NJ.

SCHODT, F.* (1996) *Dreamland Japan: Writings on Modern Manga*, Stone Bridge Press, Berkeley, CA.

SILVERSTONE, R. (1999) *Why Study the Media*, Sage, London.

SKEGGS, B. (1998) Seeing Differently: Ethnography and Explanatory Power, *Australian Educational Researcher*, 26.1 (1999): 33–53. AARE, Camberwell.

TAGG, J. (1988) *The Burden of Representation: Essays on Photographies and Histories*, Macmillan, Basingstoke.

TODOROV, T. (1981) *Introduction to Poetics*, translated by R. Howard; introduction by P. Brooks, University of Minnesota Press, Minneapolis.

TOLSON, A.* (1996) *Meditations: Text and Discourse in Media Studies,* Arnold, London.

TOMLINSON, J. (1991) *Cultural Imperialism*, Pinter Press, London.

TUNSTALL, J. (1977) *The Media Are American*, Constable, London.

TURNER, G., BONNER, F. AND MARSHALL, P.D.* (2000) *Fame Games: The Production of Celebrity in Australia*, Cambridge University Press, Cambridge.

WADSWORTH, Y. (1998) What is Participatory Action Research? Action Research International, Paper 2. Available online: http://www.scu.edu.au/schools/sawd/ari/ari-wadsworth.html

WASKO, J.* (2001) *Understanding Disney,* Polity Press, Cambridge.

WASKO, J., PHILLIPS, M. AND MEEHAN, E.R. (2001) *Dazzled by Disney? The Global Disney Audience Project*, Leicester University Press, London.

WATSON, J.* (1998) *Media Communication*, Macmillan, Basingstoke.

WELLS, P.* (1998) *Understanding Animation*, Routledge, London.

WERNICK, A. (1991) *Promotional Culture: Advertising, Ideology and Symbolic Expression*, Sage, London.

WILLIAMS, R. (1980) Means of Communication as Means of Production, in *Problems in Materialism and Culture: Selected Essays*, Verso, London.

WILLIAMS, R. AND TOLLET, J. * (2000) *The Non-Designer's Web Book*, 2nd edn, Peachpit Press, Berkeley, CA.

WILLIAMSON, J. (1978) *Decoding Advertisements*, Marion Boyars, London.

WOLLEN, P. (1982) *Readings and Writings: Semiotic Counter Strategies*, NLP, London.

WYATT, J. (1994) *High Concept: Movies and Marketing in Hollywood*, University of Texas Press, Austin.

Useful websites for students

http://www.aber.ac.uk/media

http://www.cultsock.ndirect.co.uk

http://www.popcultures.com

http://vos.ucsb.edu

http://www.Theory.org.uk

http://www.NewMediaStudies.com

Index

Action
  code 14
  research 168–74
  spheres of 13
Adorno, T. 158
Advertising 84–8, 93, 132–3, 145
Advertising Standards Authority 132–3
Agenda setting theory 158
Agent 103
Allusion 49
Althusser, L. 45, 68, 138
Anchorage 31, 60
Animation 32, 56
Anthropomorphism 36, 57
Antithesis 36, 76
Aperture 109
Aporia 47
Arbitrary meaning 28
Attention, forms of 58
Audiences, media 25, 93, 155–6
  active 157–63
  measurement of 96, 156
  passive 164–75
  target 89–92

Bahktin, M. 33, 50
Barthes, R. 14–15, 31
Bernstein, B. 33
Binary opposition 13, 36, 45, 68
Body
  female 58
  representation of 56–7
Bookmarks 149
Branding 75, 80, 82–5, 105
Bricolage 50

Camera, positioning of 11, 60
Carnivalesque 50
Cartoons 32–3, 56
Categorisation 94
Cause-effect relationship 13, 108
Cel animation 56
Celeactor 102
Celebrity 59, 101–2
Celetoid 102
Censorship 133
Chiasmus 36, 76
Children, media and 33, 134
Cineliteracy 32
Cinema 62, 108–9 see also film
Class, social 94

Closed stories 7
Closed text 6
Closure 109
Cluster sampling 161
Codes 2–4, 16, 20, 27, 31, 84
  linguistic 33
  narrative 14, 31
  of practice 129–30, 132
Coding 161
Comics 18–20
Common sense 1, 75
Communication 140, 145
Community 137, 156
Competition 75
Complaints 129, 132
Computer-generated imagery (CGI) 36, 56
Computer-mediated communication (CMC) 140, 153
Computers 39, 83, 140
Conglomerates 123, 126
Connotations 1, 3, 29
Consciousness 44, 174
  false 13, 157
Consensus 69, 158–9
Consent, manufacture of 69, 159
Consistency theory 158
Conspiracy theory 159
Construction, textual 2, 10
Consumer 133, 156
Contagion effect 159
Content analysis 53, 160–1
Contents lists 149
Continuity editing 108
Conventions 2–4, 16, 20, 27, 84
Convergence 126, 138
Copycat effect 159
Copyright 152
Cross-ownership 80
Cultivation theory 160
Cultural commodity 80, 102
Cultural imperialism 118–22, 123
Cultural proximity 121
Cultural theorists 106
Culture 50, 57, 118–19, 121
Cyberspace 140

Decency 133
Deception 133
Decoder 1, 3
Deconstruction 2–4, 10, 47

Defence mechanisms 44
Demographics 89, 91, 93–5
Denotations 1, 3, 29
Deprofessionalisation 107
Deregulation 26, 126, 128
Derrida, J. 47
Desensitisation 159
Desire 46, 72
Diagetic sounds 12
Diegesis 109
Digitalisation 126
Discourse 71–7
Disney 56–7, 120–1
Disorientation 149
Documentaries 6, 53–5
Docusoaps 55, 102
Dominant reading 6
Domination 118
Dreams 44, 68
Drives, biologically based 44, 68
Dumbing down 26, 92, 106

Editing 9, 12, 85, 108
Effects tradition 157–63
Eisenstein, S. 14, 48
Encoder 1, 3
Enigma code 14
Entertainment 53, 145, 165
Essentialist view 49
Estrangement 108
Ethics 105
Ethnicity 68
Ethnographic approach 168–9

Falsehood 133
Familiarisation, process of 119
Fantasy 46
Fanzine 109
Feministic aesthetic 57
Fiction 109
Film 6, 9–12, 43
  classification 133, 172
  documentary 9
  narrative 9
  promotion 86–8
  spectatorship 43, 62, 76
Focus groups 170–3
Foregrounding 109
Foucault, M. 71–2
Four Ps model 84–5
Fragments 72, 74
Frame 8, 34, 85
Frankfurt School 158
Freedom, degree of 129, 138
Freud, S. 43, 47, 68
Freudian slips 44, 68
Functionalist linguistics 31–2, 73
Functions 12, 73

Gaze 45, 57, 59–61, 161
  direct 60–1, 85
  male 62–3

Gender 94
  representation 50
Genre 16–26
  characteristics of 16
  film 20, 53
  of integration 21
  of order 21
  speech 33
Globalisation 81, 121, 123–7
Grammar 31–2
Gramsci, A. 138
Grand narratives 49
Gratifications 164
GreenNet 137

Halliday, M.A.K. 31–2, 73
Hegemony 138
Hermeneutic suspicion 53
Home pages 22–4, 149
Hyperbole 36
Hyperlinks 144
Hypermedia 140–54
  advantages and disadvantages 146–8
  elements of 143
  history of 142–3
  uses of 144
Hyperspace 148
Hypertext 140
Hypodermic needle theory 158
Hypothesis 165

Icon 30, 39, 144
Iconography 16–17
Ideational function 32
Identification 108
Identity 67–70, 82, 127, 138, 164
Ideology 52, 64–6, 138
Image 34–5
  analysing 160–1
  coding 161
  maps 144
Imitation effect 159
Independent Television Commission (ITC)
  26, 132–3, 172
Indexical sign 30, 39
Indices 149
Infotainment 26, 53
Integration, vertical 80
Intellectual property rights 152
Interaction, user 141, 165
Interactive video 144
Internationalisation 80
Internet 22–4, 81, 136–7, 140–54
Interpellation 68
Interpersonal function 32, 158
Intertextual relay 16
Intertextuality 5–6, 38, 49–50
Interviews 168, 173
Intransitivity 108

Lacan, J. 43, 45, 62, 68
Language 28, 32

children's 33
Learning 145, 150
Liberal view 81
Linear theory 13, 140–2
Linguistics 28–31, 72
Links, network 144, 150
Litotes 36

Magazines, women's 58, 161
Magic bullet theory 157
Male subject position 45
Manager 103
Manga comics, Japanese 18–20, 56
Maps 144, 149
Market research 93
Marketing 84–8
Maslow, A. 89
Mass culture 158
Masquerade 46
McDonaldisation 123
Meaning systems 3
Media
  alternative 106–17, 159
  literacy 2, 32, 136
  management 104
  organisations 79–80
  see also audiences, hypermedia, multi-
    media, texts
Mediasation 79
Memory, human 90, 153
Metaphor 35, 149
Metonymy 35
Micons 144
Mimesis 32
Mind, unconscious 44, 68
Miniaturisation 36, 56
Mirror stage 45
Mise en abime 36
Mise en scène 14, 16–17, 34, 46, 86
Mission statement 83
Mobile framing 11
Modality 32, 37, 46, 53
Modernism 48–9
Monomodal constructions 52
Montage 9, 14, 48
Moral panics 69, 159
Morphing 35
Motifs and styles, visual 17
Multimedia 140, 172
Multimodal constructions 52
Multi-step flow theory 158
Mystification 73
Myths 31, 44, 52

Narrative 7–16
  codes 14, 31
  film 108
  grand 48–9
  structure of 12
Narratology 12
Narrator 10, 54
Narrowcast 99, 156

Navigation 140, 148–50
Needs, human 89
Negotiated reading 6
New Audience Research 121, 168, 174–5
News
  alternative 110–17
  reporting 74
  television 26, 50–1
  texts 6, 14, 50
Nominalisations 73
Non-diagetic sounds 12, 85
Novelty 80

Object 28
Oedipus complex 45
Ofcom 136
On-screen space 10–11
Open stories 7
Open text 6
Oppositional reading 6
Organisations, media 79–80
Orientalism 57
Orientation 149
Oslo Challenge 134
Overlexicalisation 74

Paradigmatic analysis 13, 38
Parallelism 36
Parapraxis 44
Parent-child relationship 5
Parody 46, 49
Participatory action research 169–74
Passivisations 73
Pastiche 49
Personification 36, 57
Phallocentrism 45
Picons 144
Pierce, C.S. 29
Plot 7
Poetics 34–6
Point of view 8, 54
Polysemic texts 6, 31
Postmodernism 48–51, 127
Poststructuralism 47
Preferred meaning 6, 172
Presentations 144
Press Complaints Commission (PCC) 129–32
Privatisation 26
Promotion 84–8
Pronunciation, received 50
Propp, V. 12–13
Psychoanalytic approaches 43–7, 62, 68
Public interest 131
Public service broadcasting (PSB) 26, 91
Publicists 104
Publicity 103–5
Pun, visual 35
Purposive sampling 167

Queer identity 46
Questionnaires 165–8
Quota sampling 167

Racism 57, 68
Radical view 80
Random sampling 161, 167
Ratings 96
Realism 33, 54
Reality 109
Reception analysis 168
Reference material 145, 164
Referent 28
Referential code 14
Regulation 126, 128–39
Reification 73
Relativism 138
Relay function 31, 35
Relexicalisation 73–4
Repetition 36, 46
Representations 52–63
   systems of 52
   visual 75
Re-regulation 129
Research, survey 165–6
Rhetoric 32
RISC AmericanScan Programme 90–1

Sample 97, 161, 167
Saussure, F. de 28–9
Scheduling 98
Scopophilia 43
Script 8
Self-regulation 129
Semantic code 14
Semiotic analysis 37–42, 52
Semiotics 27–33, 84
   social 28, 31
   structuralist 28, 42
Sexuality 44–5, 47, 57–8
Share 96
Shots, film 11, 60
Signified 1, 3, 28
Signifier 1, 3, 28, 31, 37, 100
Signs 1, 4, 14, 27–33, 45
Simile, visual 35
Simulation 145
Social categories 94
Sound 12
Spectatorship 43, 45, 62, 76, 155
Spin doctors 160
Staging 34
Stars 59, 100–1
Status, celebrity 102
Steadycam 9, 11
Stereotyping 18, 57, 65, 68
Stories 7, 44
   features of 7
   functions of 12
   reasons for 15
Stratified sampling 161, 167
Structuralist method 12–13
Subjectivity 43, 47

Surrealism 35, 44, 110
Survey research 165–6
Symbol 30, 39, 45
Symbolic code 14
Symbolic exchange 31
Synaesthesia 36, 153
Synchronicity 44
Synecdoche 35
Synergy 80, 101, 126
Syntagmatic analysis 13, 38
Systematic sampling 161

Target audience 89–92
Television
   commercial 91–2
   documentaries 53–5
   global 125–7
   news 26, 50–1
   public service 26, 91
   reality 55, 105
Texts, media 2
   active uses 3
   deconstructing 3–4
   identifying 37
   passive uses 3
   reading 6
Textual function 32
Thematics 21–2
Toolbox, navigational 149
Tordorov, T. 13–14
Tracks and trails 149
Transformations 73
Transitivity 33, 73, 108
Transparency 109
Triangulation, cultural 119
Trope 35, 38
Two-step flow theory 158

Unconscious mind 44, 68
Undecidability 47
Undercurrents 110–17
Uses and gratifications 164

Video diary approach 11, 55
Videogames 39–40
Violence
   aesthetics of 17, 171
   screen 159, 170–1
Voyeurism 11, 43, 55, 59

Web-casting 137
Websites 22–4, 50
Westerns 20
Womanliness 46, 57–8
World wide web 71, 124, 141 see also
   internet

Zines 109–10